THE SKEPTICAL BELIEVER
TELLING STORIES TO YOUR INNER ATHEIST

THE SKEPTICAL BELIEVER

TELLING STORIES TO YOUR INNER ATHEIST

DANIEL TAYLOR

 BOG WALK PRESS

Published by BOG WALK PRESS
1605 Lake Johanna Blvd.
Saint Paul, MN 55112
651.631.9235

Daniel Taylor can be found online at www.WordTaylor.com.

Cover and book design by Taylor Design Works

A number of the unsourced epigraphs from contemporary writers come from a series of essays in the literary and arts journal IMAGE (Number 55, Fall 2007).

Bible translations are by the author.

ISBN: 978-0-9706511-5-0

For the ones who persevere to the end.

"Not all those who wander are lost."

J.R.R. TOLKIEN

CONTENTS

3. THE STORY NATURE OF FAITH

4. OBJECTIONS TO FAITH

5. ARGUMENTS FOR FAITH—ALL OF THEM RESISTABLE

6. THE FAITHFUL SKEPTIC: LIVING THE STORY

7. MY STORY WITHIN GOD'S STORY

8. CONCLUSION: JOY, RISK, ADVENTURE,
AND LOVE—JUST THE RIGHT KIND OF STORY

THE SKEPTICAL BELIEVER

TELLING STORIES TO YOUR INNER ATHEIST

There is an island there is no going
to but in a small boat the way
the saints went... .

Am I too late?
Were they too late also, those
first pilgrims? He is such a fast
God, always before us and
leaving as we arrive.

Was the pilgrimage
I made to come to my own
self, to learn that in times
like these and for one like me
God will never be plain and
out there, but dark rather and
inexplicable, as though he were in here?

R.S. THOMAS, "PILGRIMAGES"

Does the one who argues with the Almighty wish to correct him?
Let God's accuser give the answer.
...Brace yourself like a man. *I* am going to ask the questions,
and you must answer them.

JOB 40:2, 7

1. DEFINITIONS AND DIAGNOSES

THE SKEPTICAL BELIEVER — DON'T LET THE SMOKE GET IN YOUR EYES

Those who believe that they believe in God, but without any passion in their heart, without anguish of mind, without uncertainty, without doubt, without an element of despair even in their consolation, believe only in the idea of God, not in God Himself.

MIGUEL D'UNAMUNO

Tell your children about it, and let your children tell their children, and their children from generation to generation.

JOEL 1:3

The Skeptical Believer. No, it's not a contradiction in terms. It's a simple, everyday reality for many people of faith. And it's a way of believing that is acceptable to God. (*Acceptable to God? How do* you *know what is and isn't acceptable to God?*)

Skepticism is both a technical term in philosophy and, as used here, a more loosely defined word that suggests a certain attitude toward life. (*When did God give you a list of things he finds acceptable and unaccept- able? And in what sense is God a "he," anyway?*) My informal definition of skepticism is as follows: *a habitual resistance to accepting truth claims*.

Each term is important. A truth claim is most any assertion about most anything—any claim that something is the case, whether objective or subjective. ("It's going to rain." "Everest is the tallest mountain." "The Yankees stink this year." "God is just.") The skeptic questions many particular truth claims (whereas the cynic disparages even the possibility of genuine truth), the more significant the claim, the more the questioning. And the skeptic does so reflexively—it is a habit, a first response (not always conscious), the default mode when confronted with a claim, especially a confident and contestable one.

A more street-level definition of skepticism could be as follows: *the suspicion that anyone who claims to know most anything with certainty is Blowing Smoke.* And the less testable the claim, the more the skeptic smells Smoke. (*For that matter, how do you know there is a God at all—he, she, it or none of the above?*)

Smoke Blowing is a favorite human pastime. It is not simply affirming a belief that something is true. (*And even if there is something bigger than us that you could call God, why the Christian version rather than anyone else's?*) It is a *manner* of assertion that combines high confidence with low verification. Here are some telltale signs of Smoke Blowing:

- making claims with a confidence (often smugness) in excess of what is supported by either reason or experience
- substituting strength of conviction for evidence (*And what about how awful Christians have been? Does the word "crusades" mean anything to you? How about burning witches? Or calling people "fags"?*)
- speaking as though anyone who sees things otherwise is stupid or ignorant or evil or all three
- making excessive claims simply because there is no one else in the room equipped or given the opportunity to say otherwise—all talking and no listening (*I'm still waiting for a good answer to the old question: Why is there so much suffering in a world supposedly created by a good God? And please don't tell me it's our fault. We'll both just end up mad.*)
- treating dissenting voices as enemies to be defeated rather than as fellow seekers from whom to learn
- using the tools of the mind and the heart manipulatively, for the purpose of winning an argument, not for finding truths that help us live (*Admit it, doesn't all this God, heaven, happy-ending stuff strike you as more than a little implausible?*)

There's a lot of Smoke in the world. Always has been. People of faith often Blow Smoke. Scorners of faith are often big time Smoke Blowers too. Smoke, Smoke, everywhere Smoke. How can you help but be a skeptic with all this Smoke?

And then there is the "believer" part of "Skeptical Believer." What is a believer? In the general sense, *a believer is someone who accepts something as true or real or worthy of affirmation.* ("I believe all people are of equal value." "I believe in God the Father, maker of heaven and earth." "I believe democracy is a better form of government than absolute monarchy.") There are certain characteristics I tend to associate with the word "believer" (religious or otherwise):

- *Risk-taking.* A believer is someone who buys stock in a promising company, realizing that it could go bust. ("And Abraham set out, not knowing where he was going.")
- *Hunger for meaning.* Believers' hunger for meaning is stronger than their fear of being wrong. ("'Lord, if it is you,' Peter replied, 'tell me to come join you on the water.'")
- *Openness.* Openness to the spiritual, the unverifiable, the mysterious, the intuited, the imagined ("And after the earthquake a fire, but the Lord was not in the fire—and after the fire a soft whisper.")
- *Love of companions.* To the believer a shared belief isn't joining the herd, it's multiplied pleasure and shared risk. ("The apostles gathered around Jesus and reported to him all that they had done and taught.") There's something deeply satisfying about hanging out with kindred spirits. (*There's no delusion like a mass delusion.*) We both believe today; if I can't believe tomorrow, you believe for me—and I'll do the same for you.
- *Action.* A believer is someone who does not simply affirm with the intellect an abstract conviction; rather, a believer is someone who acts on that belief, who allows that belief to shape choices and repeated, daily actions. ("Let us go too, so that we may die with him.")

Belief can be in anything. When it is in something religious, we tend to call it faith—though all understandings of reality require faith, including secular ones. (I will not use terms in this book with a philosopher's rigor. Sometimes by "belief" I will mean simply acceptance of or assent to something. Other times I will use it to refer to religious belief and use it as a synonym for faith or commitment. Context will clarify.)

Skepticism and belief tend to have different goals. As James Beilby pointed out to me, the skeptic aims to believe as few falsehoods as possible; the believer aims to believe as many truths as possible. The first goal results, in my view, in a constricted life. (*Right. That's your view—and nothing more.*) The second increases the possibility of believing untrue things, but greatly multiplies the possibilities for richness and meaning in life.

There are millions of skeptics in the world. And billions of believers. But how many Skeptical Believers (or faithful skeptics)? The word "skeptical" isn't often linked with the word "believer." Skeptics are skeptical. And believers, well, aren't.

Unless they are.

The two concepts can, and often do, go together because we live in a fallen world where knowledge of the truth is always partial and often distorted. Skepticism is a form of protection against believing too much. Belief or faith is a protection against believing too little. Skepticism keeps us from believing lies. Belief keeps us from failing to embrace truths. If I have no skepticism at all, I will be a sucker for anything. If I have no belief at all, I will be an even bigger sucker for skipping the possibility for meaning, because meaning, in the most significant cases, requires believing things beyond what can be proven.

So, is it good to be a Skeptical Believer?

Not necessarily. It is simply one way of believing, and one way of being skeptical. It is not the best way to believe, there being no single best way. It is, in fact, a rather precarious way. Skeptical Believers often have their skepticism overpower their belief. They are prone to dark periods when belief, if possible at all, hangs on a thread. They often are plagued by an incessant grinding of the mind that leaves them weary and paralyzed. Their faith is prone to being theoretical and attenuated rather than practical and robust. Encouraging spiritual highs are followed by new rounds of analysis and doubt-filled lows.

I don't think I would choose to be a Skeptical Believer if I had the choice. I would rather be the Peter who walks on the water than the Peter who almost drowns beneath the waves. But I take some comfort that the water walker and the doubter and the denier and the apostle and the martyr are all the same person. Peter was both skeptic and saint—a combination that holds out hope for me.

And I must admit that Skeptical Believers are among my favorite Christians. They are the Pascals and Flannery O'Connors and Apostle Thomases of the faith. They do not take kindly to Smoke Blowers. They ask uncomfortable questions when everyone else is smiling vacantly. They take clichés—intellectual and spiritual—as personal affronts. They tend to be more honest even if they are often wrong and at times more prickly. Skeptical Believers sometimes make lousy members of church committees, but they can be first-rate spiritual warriors. As long as they are allowed to say their piece before battle.

We didn't much use the term "skeptic" in the churches I grew up in. We called such people doubters. Sometimes backsliders or carnal or lost, but mostly doubters. I didn't know exactly what a doubter was, but I knew pretty early that I was one. And I knew enough to keep it to myself. Sometimes I even kept it *from* myself. Nevertheless, even though I write the occasional book about it, I'm not a champion for doubt. I'm willing to argue, however, that there's room for us doubters—us skeptics, if you will—in this story we call the Christian faith.

Skeptical belief—is this a problem, a challenge, a contradiction, a blessing, or simply a description? (*You really like word lists, don't you?*) I'm not sure, perhaps it's all of the above. I am sure that it more or less describes me— not the entire, complex (and charming) me, but at least one part of who I have been and still am. And so when I speak of the Skeptical Believer, I am talking about and to myself. (*Talking to yourself—not a good sign.*) And here are some things I tell myself that make it more possible for me, a skeptic by nature, to emphasize that I am even more truly a believer:

First, I remind myself that I have been invited not into an argument but into a story.

Second, I recall that this story gives me not just something to believe but something to do.

Third, I propose to myself that the real test of any story is what it asks me to love and what kind of life it requires me to live.

This book will explore all three—and a lot of other things as well. It will argue that a reasonable person knows when not to depend entirely on reason. It will suggest that faith is more like a marriage (sometimes a rocky marriage) than a science experiment. It will affirm that the beauty of the story of faith is just as legitimate an argument for embracing it as its truthfulness, maybe more so. It will say a good word for mystery, suggest that God will never be plain, and admonish people like me to quit whining so much and put our shoulders to the wheel. As a bonus, the book will solve the problem of evil in just a few pages.

What this book will not do is prove anything. (*You can say that again!*) It will *defend* some things here and there (the meaning of "apologetics"), but will *prove* nothing. The closer one gets to things that really matter in life, the further one gets from any easy notion of proof. The book will proceed not by close argument and logical proofs but by reflection and rumination (chewing) and storytelling. No one will want to read this book who believes that the things of faith are certain (in the sense of "no possibility of being wrong"), that true Christians have a watertight answer for every objection to faith, that God gave us absolutes so that we could sleep better, or that nonbelievers are all foolish, ignorant, or unusually evil (okay, some are, but look down the pew and tell me what you see). If you believe those things, this book will just make you mad (which, perhaps, you enjoy).

You will not, after reading, have more irresistible evidence for the existence of God or unassailable arguments for why you ought to be a Christian (or even a theist). All evidence is resistible. All arguments are assailable. Significantly, the same is true for arguments against faith. All arguments, all attempts to make meaning out of human experience, leak. Anyone who tells you differently is Blowing Smoke. If that depresses you, get over it. It's actually good news.

I do wish this book to be an encouragement, something that makes faith more possible, not less, but in the long run I don't think we are encouraged or made more faithful by Blowing Smoke. Life is hard. God both pursues and hides from us. Maybe—let's just say it—God isn't there at all. I find it strangely freeing to say so. Maybe he's not. (*There's that "he" again.*) But I'm betting my life (like Pascal and so many of my favorite kindred spirits) that he is and that he is who he says he is. I'll try to explain why—to you and to my Inner Atheist and to myself. And maybe I'm also explaining myself to God, the one who is telling me my story.

(*Yada yada. Just get on with it.*)

DOUBT, YES. CYNICISM, NO.
SKEPTICISM, SOMETIMES

I believe I have no prejudices whatsoever. All I need to know is that a man is a member of the human race. That's bad enough for me.

MARK TWAIN

there is safety in derision.

W.B. YEATS, "THE APPARITIONS"

It's useful to have words mean whatever you want them to mean, especially when arguing (with yourself or others). The person who controls the definitions wins the argument. (*Unless the other person has a gun.*) And since I hope to win this argument with myself fairly (*You'll never win, because I'll make sure the contest is never over*), I will try throughout to be clear about my definition of key terms without falling into the philosopher's quagmire of endless torturing of terms and definitions without progression—like polishing and polishing a car but never driving it anywhere.

This is a book, in part, about doubt. Its focus is the doubt of a believer, one who is living or has lived in a religious (in our case, Christian) context. It does not directly address the convinced nonbeliever, nor the former believer no longer interested in matters of faith. I am more attracted to internal apologetics (how we defend faith to ourselves) than in external apologetics (doing battle with the infidel—an abusive but useful word meaning "one who is not faithful" and used historically by Christians, Muslims, and Jews to describe each other).

Actually, as the years pass I am less interested in doubt as an abstract phenomenon that can be poked, pinched, and philosophized about. I am much more interested in living a useful life of faith while, it may be, doubting, wondering, head scratching, and even complaining a bit. ("I don't know if I believe in God anymore." "That's fine," the rabbi replied, "but you're still praying, right?")

Still, whether talking theoretically or practically, definitions are important. I will start with a definition of doubt.

Doubt is *misgivings about truth claims.*

Religious doubt is *misgivings about the claims made by faith* (any religious faith).

Christian doubt is *misgivings about the claims made in the Christian Bible and in subsequent church history about God, Christ, and the human experience.*

I choose the word "misgivings" carefully because it can include both the emotions and the intellect (each of which is relevant to doubt)—and because "misgivings" does not necessitate either disbelief on the one hand or unquestioning belief on the other. It is a word that suggests uncertainty without closing off any options. It says, "Let's chew on this a little longer" (which, for the Skeptical Believer, can be a lifetime).

Doubt can lean either toward belief or away from it. Sometimes we doubt something we fervently hope is true (that God and goodness exist, for instance). Sometimes we doubt something that we fervently hope is not true (a diagnosis of a terminal disease). In one, we want to be convinced and have our doubts dissipated. In the other, we want our doubts to be confirmed. But in either case, our doubting is not conclusive—it is a *misgiving* about a claim, not a settled conviction. (*Well, I have some "settled convictions," and one of them is that no reasonable person believes this junk. Doubting everything is the only way to keep from being fooled.*)

Like tolerance, doubt is not in itself automatically a good or bad thing. It is neither a virtue to doubt nor a virtue never to doubt. As usual, context is crucial. One must ask what is being doubted and in what spirit and with what result. There is healthy doubt and less healthy doubt. One feature of healthy doubt is a refusal to settle for lousy answers to good questions (the Blowing Smoke phenomenon). One symptom of unhealthy doubt is paralysis. When doubt leaves you unable to commit or act in life, then you have a diseased, disabling form of doubt, not a healthy questioning. (*So now you're a doctor, huh?*)

When doubt becomes a habit of life, like smoking or reading the newspaper, it verges into skepticism. Hence my definition of skepticism as *a habitual resistance to accepting truth claims.*

The key word is "habitual." Everyone, I have said, doubts something every day of life. But when doubting becomes the instinctive response to every assertion, one has become a skeptic, someone constitutionally wired to object (out loud or in one's own mind) to most every claim that happens down the road.

In philosophy and the sciences, skepticism can be a powerful methodology (with a long history) for verifying sound thinking. In day-to-day life, it is often a defense mechanism against uncomfortable claims on one's life and, unlike misgivings, often comes with a bias toward disbelief. Household skeptics tend to think significant truth claims are groundless unless they can be demonstrated by proof. If there is the opportunity to disbelieve something, especially if that something would be aggravating if true ("God wants your life," for instance), the skeptic tends to capitalize on the opportunity for disbelief.

There is a strong psychological as well as logical component to skepticism. The single greatest fear of a skeptic is to be taken in. More precisely, it is to be *seen* to be taken in, to be fooled and therefore a fool. (The ancient Greek skeptical philosophers—*Skeptikoi*—exercised great caution so as not to assert anything that might possibly be shown to be false.) (*Good for them.*)

Just as with the word "misgivings," I choose the word "questioning" carefully. The recurring response of the skeptic to any claim is a question: "How do you know that's true?" It's often a good question, which is why skepticism is often healthy, but it can also be a way of deflecting what is true. ("Know" and "true," two other words that cry for definition—and that's a problem. Every definition calls—Hydra-like—for many others. It's exponential, like rabbits.)

Skeptics tend to be risk averse. If there is a chance a claim may be false, they find it safer to maintain a distance from the claim (even though this kind of safety can actually be quite dangerous).

And then there is skepticism on steroids—cynicism. Cynicism is radicalized and cosmic skepticism. Cynicism is *the radical insistence that all truth and value claims are unprovable and therefore likely false, and that they arise from selfish motivations.*

Garden-variety cynicism (which has very little connection with the ancient Greek philosophy of the same name) suffers from all kinds of problems, not least that it is self-refuting. Its own claims are truth claims and, by its own logic, unprovable, likely false and selfish, and therefore not to be trusted. More important, it's impossible to construct a healthy life around cynicism. That does not keep it from being a popular position, especially when used ad hoc to cast contempt on outlooks and assertions one finds unappetizing.

The carefully chosen word in this definition is "insistence." (*My, my, aren't we the subtle thinker?*) Cynics take their own suspicions and absolutize them, demanding that their own inability to arrive at something they can affirm as good and true must, of necessity, be the case for every thinking person. It is, essentially, the position of an intellectual adolescent: "If I'm not having fun at this party, I'll make sure no one is having fun!"

Many of the "power" arguments in contemporary social debate are based in cynicism. Everyone and every organization (*pace* Nietzsche) are seen as seeking power over others. Truth claims are a grab for power, and justice therefore requires exposing truth claims as essentially selfish. (Never mind, again, that such a view is a truth claim and therefore a power grab and, from a cynical point of view, not to be trusted.)

Cynicism is the "bah humbug" approach to life of a philosophical Scrooge. Ironically, cynics are often former idealists, people whose high hopes for life have been crushed by their personal experience. Disappointed in life themselves, they project their disappointment on everyone around them. (*Very good, Dr. Freud.*)

An excess of any of these three conditions in life—doubt, skepticism, cynicism—can have life-constricting results. Too much doubting produces anxiety, too much skepticism tends toward paralysis, and even a moderate amount of cynicism promotes rot (if there even is such a thing as degrees of cynicism). None are pleasant things to live with, but for each of them there is hope. (*So now you are the great giver of hope?*)

These three positions do not exhaust the spectrum of reactions to the claims of faith. If I had to fill in some others, I would tentatively suggest a continuum something like the following:

Fideism—Certitude—Belief—Doubt—Skepticism—Indifference—Cynicism

All of these terms will come up in later discussions. I mention them now to get some things on the table. Note that contiguous terms can co-exist—fideism and certitude, belief and doubt, indifference and cynicism. Skepticism can lean toward belief and doubt or, with much different consequences, toward indifference and cynicism. With all of them, what matters most is the choices you make and the life that you live.

So what about the title of this rumination ("Doubt, Yes. Cynicism, No. Skepticism, Sometimes")? I am going to argue that doubt is entirely compatible with faith. In fact, it is required. If you doubt nothing, you are not exercising faith at all, because you think you have certainty (more later). Doubt is an inescapable consequence of being a finite creature in a broken world. It goes hand in hand with all kinds of necessary risks, including the risk of belief. Therefore I say "yes" to doubts, which is handy because I have quite a few of them, and allowing them allows me to stay in the story of faith. (*Convenient how you always work things so they come out justifying what you already believe.*)

To cynicism I say "no." Doesn't work. Doesn't make sense. And makes life thoroughly unpleasant for you and those around you. It's easy to say no to cynicism—and so I do.

To skepticism, I say "sometimes, but with reservations." (*Very bold of you.*) Skepticism, as we will see, has led to a lot of progress in some areas of the human experience and can be a great Smoke detector. But it can also be a blindfold. So I say "sometimes" with this reservation: be as skeptical about skepticism as skepticism is about everything else. Skepticism should have to answer its own question about itself: "How do you know this is true?"

I'm calling myself a Skeptical Believer and am writing this book for others who may be kindred spirits. I want the believer part to dominate, but I also have a skeptical bent (sometimes expressing itself in the voice of my Inner Atheist) (*How kind of you to acknowledge me*) and so, to avoid Blowing Smoke, I will keep the terms together. It's the only way I can make it work, and I'm counting on God's grace that it does.

THE BELIEVER PART OF THE SKEPTICAL BELIEVER

I draw my conclusions not from the philosophical works I've read but from the life stories I hear in prison.

ALEXANDER SOLZHENITSYN, *IN THE FIRST CIRCLE*

We must all assimilate other lives in order to live.

W.H. AUDEN

It's easier to define the terms "skeptical" and "believer" separately than it is to describe what you have when you put them together. When combined the two terms shape each other in not fully predictable ways. The skepticism of a skeptic who believes is not the same as the skepticism of one who doesn't, and the belief of a believer who tends toward skepticism is not the same as the belief of one who doesn't.

The Skeptical Believer does not have a generic "belief," salted with a dose of "skepticism." Nor a generic "skepticism," leavened with belief. The skepticism is part of the belief (just as the Inner Atheist is part of you) (*How kind of you to say so*), and the belief is part of the skepticism. Perhaps it would help to run the words together—"skepticalbeliever"—to better show how the two are more like a chemical compound than a simple mixture of two separate things. I prefer the term "Skeptical Believer" to the reverse—"believing skeptic"—because I think belief is the essential and, ultimately, defining term and skepticism is the modifier, not the other way around. (Like a seasoned steak—belief is the steak, skepticism the seasoning that modifies the taste.)

Skepticism modifies belief as any other mental, spiritual, or personality trait might modify belief. One might speak of the emotional believer, or the passionate believer, or the courageous believer, or the quiet, conventional, credulous, unreflective, rational, suffering, confident, pompous (and so on) believer. Being a Skeptical Believer is another of the endless ways of being a believer—and of being a skeptic.

So what do I mean by "believer"? (I'll keep circling back to this question.) I have proposed putting two different things together (skepticism and belief) to create a third thing: the Skeptical Believer. If skepticism is the habit of reflexively questioning truth claims, then what is belief? Distilling a thousand definitions and with apologies to ten thousand learned thinkers, I will define belief simply as *assent to a claim*—or, perhaps less ambiguously, as *acceptance of a claim* (intellectually at least, and sometimes emotionally as well). It's a place to start a discussion. (*I'll give you my definition of a believer: someone who wishes the world were different than it actually is and pretends it is so.*)

But I'm not particularly interested in *discussing* belief—I'm interested in living it. So I will make a distinction between abstract belief and engaged belief (otherwise describable as lived, embodied, or storied belief). I would define the latter kind of belief as *life-shaping acceptance of a claim*. At the risk of being a little too cute, one might call this be-life—the wedding of belief with living to create an actual, tangible human life shaped by commitments to less tangible (but even more important) realities. Theoretical belief is less important than be-life. Our creeds call us to be-live something, not simply believe something. (Be-life requires beliefs, of course, but it gives beliefs substance and credibility by showing that they "work" in actual living.)

Engaged belief is assent or acceptance that flows out of the mind into the spirit and body. It passes through and helps shape your will and desire and decision making. It flows into the heart and into the vocal cords and out to the feet and fingertips and from there into the physical and spiritual space in which you live. It shapes who you are and how you choose and the contours of each day and therefore becomes a force in the life of everyone you meet and every activity you engage in. The influence of your individual engaged belief goes quickly beyond you and is multiplied by the communities of which you are a part and extends through time and space and eternity in ways known only to God.

As the wings of a single flapping butterfly set in motion, we are told, incalculable consequences, so do the potentially eternal consequences of engaged belief. I am going to call such belief "storied belief," because I think "story" offers us the single best paradigm for making sense of the human experience and discovering how to live meaningfully within it.

To give biblical examples, storied belief is that of Abraham, Rahab, Elijah, Mary Magdalene, and Paul. From the slices of history I know come Augustine, Julian of Norwich, More, Pascal, the Wesleys (including Susanna), Sojourner Truth, Hudson Taylor, Bonhoeffer, Weil, King, and Graham. Then the there are the writers and artists: Donne, Milton, Bunyan, Dostoevsky, Eliot, O'Connor. To these I must add the examples from my own family history: Nick and Maureen, Lucille, Max, Sam and Peggy, Darrell, Nita. And then my teachers: Mr. Jenkins, Miss Owens, Drs. Ericson and Lynip and Evans. And then there's the storied belief of friends, and coworkers, and Sunday school teachers, and the people I worship with in church. (I had forgotten how many butterflies have had their effect on me.)

But I'm still being too abstract. Let me tell you the story of one such person—briefly, and mostly as it affected me—which actually requires me to tell the story of three people. On the day I was born in the hills east of San Diego, Alexander Solzhenitsyn was living in Moscow in the first circle of hell—imprisoned by Stalin but with much worse awaiting him. He had not yet written a word of the books that would make him famous (infamous to those who can't abide his moral vision). Eddie Ericson was eight years old and living on the north side of Chicago (though a Sox fan), a year away from contracting polio—and he hadn't heard of either me or Solzhenitsyn.

Eddie Ericson grew up, went to Hope College in Michigan, then to the University of Arkansas, and eventually found his way to Santa Barbara, California, and teaching at a small college called Westmont. I went up the coast from San Diego to Ventura to four places in Texas to Azusa, back to Ventura, and then to Santa Barbara and eventually to Westmont myself.

Meanwhile Solzhenitsyn went from his Moscow imprisonment to much harsher camps in Siberia to internal exile to completely unpredictable fame and then to years of external exile before returning to a post-Communist Russia as improbable as his own life.

While in prison, Solzhenitsyn became a believer—not abstractly, but in a storied way. He began to evaluate his own life and those around him by new criteria. He even got on his knees and thanked God for allowing him to be sent to prison. He found his actions and values reshaped (sometimes rediscovered)—old things passed away, and, behold, all things became new. Based on his experience, he created poems and stories in his head while in prison, writing them down afterward. His writing was discovered by others (like gold in a stream bed, after much sifting), and he was persecuted again for letting his beliefs continue to flow into his life.

When his first novel, almost miraculously, was appearing in print, I was a Los Angeles fourteen-year-old, starting to notice (from a fearful distance) girls. Ed Ericson was getting his PhD in literature in Arkansas. Six years or so later, now Dr. Ericson was teaching me that novel at Westmont College, along with Mikhail Bulgakov's *The Master and Margarita* and not a few others. It resulted in what physicists once called "action at a distance"—the influence of one object on another, distant object with no known intermediate agents.

Of course there were intermediate agents. There was the novel itself, words distilled from a life and arranged by an imagination on a page to create a story that can be shared. And then there was Dr. Ericson, almost as unlikely to become a literature professor, given his working-class Chicago roots, as prisoner Щ-854 was of becoming a Nobel Prize winner. If Solzhenitsyn's storied belief had not moved Dr. Ericson, it would not have reached me. Story calls to story which calls to story.

And to multiply improbabilities (exponentially perhaps), Solzhenitsyn, who was then living in seclusion in America, read something sent to him by a small-college professor, something he found more insightful than most things the prestigious scholars had produced. Dr. Ericson was also bold and insightful enough to suggest that Solzhenitsyn's great, multivolume account of life in the concentration camps, *The Gulag Archipelago*, would find more readers in America if reduced to a more accessible size. He offered to help and the great writer accepted. The Chicago north side meets the labor camp in Ekibastuz, Kazakhstan.

Meanwhile, with more than a nudge from Dr. Ericson, I became a teacher of literature in my own right. And, not accidently, I included Solzhenitsyn in the literature I taught. And one young woman, maybe twenty years ago now, created, unbidden, a work of art in clay for me that had on it the words "One word of truth... ," a fragment from the end of Solzhenitsyn's Nobel Prize acceptance speech (a sentence which concludes, "outweighs the world"). And now, as I write, these words hang behind my desk, interrogating my own words as I type them.

Last year, Dr. Ericson e-mailed me that Solzhenitsyn's son, Ignat, would be speaking in my town. And so I went to hear him and now, next to my silk screen of Solzhenitsyn's head (a gift from my great friend John) and my photo of Ed and Alexander standing together, is a photo of Ignat and me, he almost smiling (which Ed tells me is a compliment, given the Russian taste for stern looks in photographs).

The idea of "action at a distance" was important in physics in developing the concept of fields—a condition of space in which an energy is present that will affect an object that enters that area or field (think gravity). I see myself as living in the energy field of Alexander Solzhenitsyn and of Ed Ericson (and every other person—historical and familial—listed above). Their storied beliefs impinged on my own storied beliefs, not creating a passive satellite, but altering my own course through time and space.

My point is not that people are influenced by books. My point is that belief does not become significant until it becomes storied—in your life and in mine. It would mean little for me to know that Solzhenitsyn believed similar things to what I believe. (We have similar lists? So what?) It means much more that he tried, not always successfully, to have those beliefs inform his life. Beliefs changed his life. His life changed his beliefs. His life and writing changed Ed Ericson's life, and therefore mine. A writer's storied life, taking the shape it did because of storied belief, was transformed by the imagination into a written story and offered to others, including me, whose own beliefs and story were, at the time, up for grabs. And I have passed it on.

This is the only kind of belief that interests me. It interests me more than my skepticism does. I have come to terms with my skepticism. It will have to come to terms with my belief.

LEARNING TO LIVE WITH YOUR INNER ATHEIST

Ourself behind ourself, concealed—Should startle most—
EMILY DICKINSON

There's someone in my head, but it's not me.
PINK FLOYD

Atheism is wasted on the non-believer.
RICHARD RODRIGUEZ

The first time I can remember doubting God was when I first heard about sex. I was seven, and it sounded so disgusting that I shouted to the kid who told me about it as he walked away, "God would never let that happen!" But inside a little voice (*That was me*) wondered if God had, in fact, let that happen, and, if so, it asked, "Can God be as good as you have been led to believe?" (*Still a good question in my book.*)

I've been hearing that little voice ever since, and probably before. It is the voice of what Richard Rodriguez calls my "Inner Atheist." (*Thanks for the capitals. I like it.*)

Atheists come in two varieties—external and internal. External atheists are a dime a dozen. I want to speak respectfully of them—they are trying to figure all this stuff out, just like the rest of us—but it is difficult. The ones in print and on cable television often sound too much like their Christian fundamentalist alter egos (in fact, both are fundamentalists). Lots of braying, bluster, and bravado. Like most culture warriors, they speak much too confidently on things they know much too little about.

I read the books and hear the talks of professional atheists and respond, "Methinks thou protests too much." These people claim not to believe in God, but in truth they are obsessed with God. Few religious people I know have as much God-hunger as public atheists. They feed that hunger by talking about God endlessly, but it only makes them more ravenous. Strangely, they organize their lives around something they don't believe exists. It's like spending your life guarding the world against a Martian invasion and believing you are being successful. If there's no God, then relax, folks and find something to make yourself useful. (*I'm sure they think themselves quite useful, protecting the world from the likes of you!*)

But the real reason I feel public atheists are mostly wasting both their time and mine is that they are redundant. I have an in-house atheist all my own—and so do many others. No external voice of disbelief holds a candle to the disbelief I carry in my own head. (*I'm flattered.*) Disbelief is the background noise of my belief. It is that static on a radio station when the signal gets weak. It is the irritating bass thumping through the walls from my neighbor's stereo.

Robert Frost was speaking of something similar (perhaps only a psychological insight rather than a theological one) when he wrote the following:

> They cannot scare me with their empty spaces
> Between stars—on stars where no human race is.
> I have it in me so much nearer home
> To scare myself with my own desert places.

Yes, desert places. I know of such things, though I'm often too torpid to be as scared as I should be.

This Inner Atheist knows me well because he *is* me. (I disagree with Pink Floyd on this point.) He is only a part of me, to be sure, but he is not a part that can be isolated from the rest of me and surgically cut out. He is fully integrated, a member of the family, often annoying but undeniably a blood relation. (*Annoying? Moi?*)

My Inner Atheist is always with me. I am tempted to compare him to an inoperable brain tumor or a cancer cell, but I can't bring myself to do it. That's so unfriendly. He isn't really an invader, something alien. He's me. He's me when I'm tired, when I'm a bit discouraged or feeling cynical, or maybe when I've been feeling a little too smart and educated for my own good.

Yes, he's me, but for a long time I wanted to kill him.

I am capable of murder. There, I've confessed it. (*Nothing I didn't know.*)

There was a time in my life that I was a proofmonger. I bought into the idea that if God was real, we should be able to prove it, or at the very least offer a case that was much stronger than that for any other way of understanding the world. I repeated the mantra, hoping to believe it, that faith could not be simply subjective. It had to be based on facts, on careful reasoning, on proofs or near-proofs. Subjectivity was for the emotionally and intellectually weak. Worse yet, the next step down the slippery slope from subjectivity was—*gasp*—relativism!

But somewhere along the way it occurred to me that I was, for better or worse, a subject. I certainly wasn't an object, so if subject and object were my only two choices, then I was and am a subject. And anything I believe, know, think, feel, intuit, imagine, suffer, enjoy, laugh or wonder about is going to be as a subject and will therefore be—dare I say it?—subjective.

Does that mean everything is merely subjective ("merely" being the all-purpose put-down word in these contexts)? No. All these things I know, feel, and so on can be genuine responses to things that have genuine objective existence—can be true, if you will. (I subjectively feel pain in my toe, and, yes, there objectively is a rock that I stubbed it against.) But my experience of them can never be anything but a subjective experience, because I am a finite, limited, fallen, time-bound, culturally conditioned hunk of subjectivity.

And my Inner Atheist will never let me forget that. (*Damn right!*)

Okay, my belief is subjective. So what? Everyone's belief about everything is subjective. There is no fact in the world, however brute, that does not require interpretation. That does not have to be cleaned off, inspected, spruced up, taught its manners, dressed up, and introduced politely at the grand ball of whatever system of thought of which it is to be a part. (Does electrical activity in a certain part of the brain increase when one has strong emotions, including spiritual ones? All right, that looks like a fact.

But when you try fitting that fact into an *explanation*, especially one about human nature or the human experience, you have become subjective.)

This kind of talk drives rationalists crazy—including rationalistic apologists for faith. How can we be certain about something if it's *merely* (that dismissive word again) subjective? (We can't.) That opens the door to every loony idea and ideology imaginable! (Including the notion, loony to some, that there is a God.) It is irrational to believe something without evidence! (It is also irrational to think that reason alone can decide what counts as evidence—or can weigh it unfailingly.)

Somewhere around the time I made peace with subjectivity, I also made peace with my Inner Atheist. (*It's a truce at best, fella. I'm reloading.*) I started by cutting back his rations. I learned from experience that he gets fat off hostility and oppression. My attempts to kill him with definitive answers are his meat and potatoes. (*Yum, yum!*) "You want to play the questions-and-answers game?" he says. "I invented the questions-and-answers game. My questions have questions. I thought of my tenth question while you were still fumbling with your first answer. I have more questions than the ocean has drops of water. I am the $E = mc^2$ of questions. I was asking you questions before you could even talk. When you have given your last answer with your last dying breath, the last words you will hear from me as the lights go out will be another question. And none of your answers, in case you're wondering, will satisfy me in the least. Not one." (*I sometimes get on a roll.*)

See how mean-spirited this guy can be if you feed him? (*I'm not mean, just persistent.*)

But if you don't feed him, he's not so bad. If I decide to hear him out rather than drown him out, he kind of deflates down to a manageable size. He's a bit of a Wizard of Oz figure: "I am Skepticism, the Great and Powerful!" But in fact, he's just a little man behind a curtain playing with knobs. Having looked behind his curtain, I sort of like him. My Inner Atheist still talks trash now and again, but once you see through him, he's almost entertaining. (*Hey,* I'm *the guy who sees through things. You're talking awfully confidently here. I've seen that before. It will fade.*)

I've also noticed that he gets quiet during stories. I think, in fact, that my Resident Atheist may *like* stories. He doesn't complain nearly so much during a story as when I feed him propositions and facts. He tends to sit in the corner and listen, not affirming but not protesting much either. Sometimes he'll say, "That's just a story," hoping the word "just" will frighten or irritate me. Or he'll grouse, "Well, other people have their stories too," (*Well, they do*) as though stories cancel each other out. But he really doesn't know what to do with stories, and so he mostly shuts up.

So, here's the deal we've struck. I let my Inner Atheist have his say. I let him ask his question, express his doubts, roll his eyes, vent his spleen, pass a little cynical gas—whatever he feels the need to do. I even compliment him occasionally when he makes a good point. (He hates that.) (*I do hate that—the self-satisfied bastard.*)

Then I go on believing. I go on trying to live my part in the story.

I've thought about this a lot. I don't think this is stubborn belief despite the facts or glorying in irrationality (what some would call fideism). I think it actually quite a rational response to the limitations of reason and the rewards of belief. The upside of believing, of being part of the story, is enormous. The only downside is the possibility of being wrong. I can live with that—maybe forever.

WORDS FOR MAKING SENSE OF IT ALL

The realities of human life are messier than is dreamed of either by dogmatic rationalists, or in the manichean rigidities of embattled orthodoxy.
CHARLES TAYLOR, *A SECULAR AGE*

We use what we call reason to preclude thought.
MARILYNNE ROBINSON

Go not to the Elves for counsel, for they will say both no and yes.
J.R.R. TOLKIEN, *THE LORD OF THE RINGS*

We have more words for thinking than Eskimos have for snow—and they have dozens. All of our thinking words are attempts to get at some aspect of the ceaseless human process of making sense of things. The following are all words related to some part of the process, and this is the short list: intellect, logic, reason, intuition, judgment, curiosity, experience, evaluation, measurement, calculation, comprehension, creativity, discernment, cognition, weighing, memory, prudence, perception, inference, deduction, induction, explanation, discrimination, understanding, and imagination.

Also part of the process—irritating to some—are emotions, personality, desires, hopes, aspirations, experiences, fears, will, prejudices, commitments, character, and guesses.

All of these concepts and activities, and many more, contribute to the ultimate purpose of all thought: to help us survive and thrive in a sometimes perilous world. What we are trying to do, in a phrase, is make sense of it all.

Making sense is messy. It is also at one time or another difficult, wearisome, scary, contradictory, and impossible. At the same time, it can be satisfying, comforting, encouraging, confirming, and thrilling. Some people pretend to give up on making sense of things, but no one ever really does. No day passes in anyone's life in which they don't engage in some sense-making activity. For the reflective person, the day is filled with moments of trying to figure it all out. (*And I'm always here to help!*)

You are probably such a person, or you wouldn't be reading this. (*Or perhaps somebody is trying hard to "help" you by shoving books down your throat.*) Think over your own life: how often do you read a book or an article or listen to someone in hopes of better understanding some part of yourself or the world or the human experience? How often do you find yourself turning over ideas in your mind or probing and questioning something that others believe without question? How often do you try to put two and two together or tie yourself up in mental and psychological knots with the hope that a little more reflection will untie them? (*How often do you write tediously long sentences?*)

The messiness of sense-making has certain implications for any thought-filled person, including the Skeptical Believer. They include the following.

Humility and Sympathy. Because the sense-making process has more potholes than a Minnesota road in springtime, arrogance about what one believes is a form of foolishness. I respect every person of goodwill who is trying to understand the world, live justly, and treat others well. I sympathize with anyone trying as hard as I am to make sense of things. I not only respect them, I want to learn something from them. That doesn't mean I want to trade my understanding of the world for theirs, but it does mean I am open to the possibility that they have learned something I need to learn. Humility will lessen the chances of my becoming a Smoke Blower.

Risk and Commitment. Commitment is not, as some would have you believe, incompatible with intellectual humility. Humility (and uncertainty) does not necessitate relativity. It is, in fact, the very messiness and imprecision of sense-making that makes commitment crucial. If all it took were intelligence and reason to arrive at the meaning of life and a knowledge of how to live, then all intelligent and reasonable people would arrive at the same position and no great commitment would be necessary.

Simple observation teaches us that this is not the case. Equally intelligent people equally committed to being reasonable arrive at wildly different conclusions about almost everything. (*Exactly!*) Reason itself tells me that a lifetime of floating without ever committing to anything important (because it's too risky) is a form of irrationality and not conducive to happiness, meaning, or usefulness. Given that the sense-making process cannot rightfully promise certainty, it is sensible to make commitments, including to risky belief, rather than waiting for a no-risk final answer that neither reason nor anything else can ever produce. (*Come again?*)

Community and Listening. No one can make sense of things all alone. Like it or not, we are in this sense-making adventure together. Personally, I like it this way. I have never had a completely new thought, and I never will. I owe someone else for everything I think, even if my own exact configuration is unique. Countless people before me spent their lives trying to do what I am trying, and they left an endless variety of records of their efforts: stories, music, paintings (some in caves), dances, weavings, letters, sermons, songs, systems, books, buildings, machines, logical arguments, theories, theorems, experiments, poems, prayers, protests, manifestos, benedictions, and on and on. All of them have something to teach me, a few by negative example.

Diversity. Because there are so many ways of making sense of things and none of them is adequate alone, it is sensible to expose oneself to many ways of understanding. People who limit themselves to reason are not being reasonable. People who limit themselves to the scientific method are not being scientific. (Ought not one's experiments in life go beyond the lab or the equation or the numerical calculation?) Similarly, people who limit themselves to imagined worlds will miss exciting things in this tangible one.

Perseverance. Because sense and meaning do not come easily, we do well to cultivate the virtue of perseverance. Neither life nor God yields readily to human understanding. At age ten, having learned to read and having already endured years of school and Sunday school, I thought I knew the important questions and the important answers. At age fifteen I still thought I knew most of the questions, but I knew I didn't know all the answers. By age twenty-two I knew I would never even know all the questions, much less all the answers—and it bothered me. The main difference now? It doesn't bother me much anymore.

Which isn't to say I've given up. I'm not a Pilate, who asks, "What is truth?" with a bit of a sneer. (*How do you know he sneered? Maybe he really wanted to know.*) I am as hungry for an answer to that question as when I was twenty-two—and as willing to listen. It's just that I believe now that the question is likely to be answered in many different ways, that the answer is less likely to be one enormous assertion and more likely to be a mosaic of many little answers, each hard-won, each subject to revision, many contributed from unlooked-for places. I can, of course, formulate big assertions—about God and humanity, about time and eternity, about good and evil—but the truth of those assertions will only be meaningful in the living of them, in the unimpressive details of my life and yours. I need, like Paul, to learn to run the race, even when I am tired, even when it looks like I'm losing, even when it looks like there is still a long way to go. When making sense of things, I need perseverance.

Trying to make sense of things goes on in the darkest places.

A story.

Like many people, I have gone to Auschwitz. After the gas chambers no longer poisoned their thousands per day, of course. After the satanically ironic words over the gate—"Arbeit Macht Frei" (Work Makes You Free)—were no longer a death sentence. Auschwitz is a black hole that almost obliterates (I first wrote "obliviates," and that works too) sense and sense-making, and no one should pretend otherwise. Nevertheless, it is also a place where, for evil and for good, people continued to be human.

Within Auschwitz is a wall between two buildings where many were executed by firing squad. In one of those buildings, prisoners were held for interrogation, torture, and eventual execution. In this building Father Maximilian Kolbe and others were starved to death. I have looked in the room they died in, and I can say I was unable to take it in. I lacked, perhaps fortunately, the imagination.

But in a nearby room I saw something more tangible that speaks to what I am trying to say here. It is a rough etching in the wall of the head and torso of Christ. A figure, presumably the image's creator, clings to Christ around the waist. That etching floats there in the semi-darkness, a testament to one person's final effort to make sense of it all. I do not focus on the fact that it is Christ—though that was essential for the one who etched it. It could have been, as it was elsewhere, a Star of David or a flower or that person's own face.

I bring it up here because I see it as an emblem of that sense-making hunger in all of us. I know nothing of this person's life or convictions. All I know is that at his end, awaiting execution in a place of evil and nullity, he continued trying to make sense. He found meaning—and hope—in the story of someone who had been humiliated and executed two thousand years before. By etching that image in the dark cell, he showed a commitment to a community of others who had also taken that story as their own. He did not, it seems, give himself to despair or bitterness. He persevered—to the end. And now his story, or at least this sliver of it, is part of my story. And now part of yours.

The influence on me of this visit to Auschwitz is not primarily rational or pragmatic. Scraping marks on the wall did not save him, nor will it me. But it helps us both make sense of things.

BELIEF AND STORY—A WHOLE-PERSON, WHOLE-LIFE EXPERIENCE

The responsible man… tries to make his whole life an answer to the question and call of God.
Where are these responsible people?
DIETRICH BONHOEFFER

Are passions, then, the pagans of the soul?
Reason alone baptized?
EDWARD YOUNG (CITED BY SØREN KIERKEGAARD)

No one believes anything important with the intellect alone. Believing is a whole-person, whole-life experience. If it isn't, it is not belief in any significant sense; it's simply an idea.

Believing enlists all the various aspects of the mind (including intellect, analysis, intuition, memory, curiosity, imagination), and of the emotions (including desires, affections, fears), and of the will (including intention, purpose, resolve, motivation, perseverance). What and how we believe is also influenced by personality, temperament, and character. (*You left out the stomach.*)

And, of course, all the things above are deeply influenced by life experience. Our beliefs about God, personal ethics, the future, and about endless issues like poverty, abortion, terrorism, race, illegal immigration, the role of women, homosexuality, and so on cannot be separated from thousands of life experiences—conscious and unconscious, subtle and overt.

How obtuse, then, to think that we arrive, or even should arrive, at our important beliefs through any single faculty—including leaky reason.

Reason is a powerful tool, but it is a tool that will serve any master, including the most odious. (Tell reason where you want to go, and it will get you there, even if it has to run a few red lights.) We do well to reason as clearly as we can, but we are foolish to pretend that reason—or any other mental function—can alone tell us what is true, what is important, what to believe, or how to live.

"What is true?" The very existence of truth is highly contested in our time, above all for the Skeptical Believer. The traditional metaphors we have used for our desire for truth include hunger and thirst and pursuit. They convey how foundational that desire has been, how central the notion of truth has been to any conception of the good life. I, myself, believe in truth—that it is real, essential, and, to a limited but significant extent, knowable. But I also believe there is something we desire more than truth, something we use truth as a stepping-stone to achieve. And that something is meaning or significance.

Humans are not necessarily truth-seeking creatures. (*You can say that again.*) Many people go about life focusing almost exclusively on the daily, practical matters in front of their noses. If they are asked about truth, not to mention Truth, they may show some interest for a few moments but are likely soon to shrug their shoulders, offer some version of "Who's to say what's true?" and go back, in Pascal's phrase, to "licking the earth."

But even the person who has long given up on finding truth is likely still in hot pursuit of significance. We may not know or even care what life is all about, but we want very much that our own lives should count. Even the least reflective person needs the feeling that his or her life (and human life generally) is not trivial. When we no longer have that feeling, we fall into boredom, grimness, cynicism, and even despair. I can go on under the worst circumstances if I believe there is purpose in my going on. If I don't, I will have a hard time even getting out of bed.

If reason alone will not lead us to meaning and significance, what will? My answer is story. (*That's your answer to everything. Give it a rest.*)

Story provides the most fundamental and most fertile way we have of making sense of human experience. Whenever, as human beings, we have had to explain something important to ourselves, we have told a story. And we should do the same when we need to explain our own lives.

This is not a metaphor. Life is not *like* a story. Life *is* a story. Your life is not like a novel. Novels are like your life—and that's why we read them. Novels are exercises in imagined lives. Our own lives are embodied stories. The challenge of living is to discover (some would say create) a story that is worth living and then to live it well.

The human brain, in fact, is an organ whose primary function, while at the same time regulating breathing and blood flow and the like, is to find a story line in all the myriads of sense data that flow constantly into it. Our brains are constructed to process reality narratively, as a story, and without that ability to find a plotline in the chaos of sense impressions, we could not exist.

Why is story more effective than reason in helping us understand and live in the world? That is a question this book will attempt to answer, and it will use stories in doing so. Suffice it here to say that story is more effective than reason alone because story engages us as whole persons. Stories light up our minds, play across our emotions, and call us to action with our bodies. They may be read or heard in stillness, but good stories will not leave us alone until we change ourselves and the world.

We do well to remember the story-shaped nature of human experience when we think about belief. My contention is that the single best way to think of faith is as a story, a story that you have been invited to join as a character with a role to play. If lived honestly, with commitment and hope and perseverance and grace, it is a story that will fill your life with meaning and significance in a way that no competing story can match.

But is the story true? The best test for that is found in the living of it.

DOUBT, CERTAINTY, AND FAITH— WHICH TWO GO TOGETHER?

Doubt is not a pleasant condition, but certainty is absurd.

VOLTAIRE

A person's faith can collapse almost overnight if she has failed over the years to listen patiently to her own doubts, which should only be discarded after long reflection.

TIM KELLER, *THE REASON FOR GOD*

Everyone is a doubter. I have defined doubt as misgivings about truth claims, and all of us doubt many of the things we hear asserted around us every day. If we didn't, we'd have to believe a thousand contradictory things before breakfast—some of them dangerous (from "You should vote for me" to "Taking this pill will help you"). Doubting things is a needed mechanism for survival—intellectual, spiritual, and physical.

Doubt has historically had a bad name in any circle that has an orthodoxy, including religion. It's sort like having a cold sore on your lip on prom night. You can try to cover it up, but it's definitely bad news. In my childhood churches, if you found yourself having doubts, the idea was to get rid of them as soon as possible. Sort of like sloughing the queen of spades in the card game Hearts (or the Old Maid in the childhood card game). It's okay for a doubt to pass through your hand now and then, but don't get caught holding it too long.

Doubt is, however, actually a neutral term. It can signal misgivings about either a positive or a negative formulation of a claim. You can doubt the claim that God exists, and equally you can doubt the claim that God does not exist. So even the most ardent believer is doubting like a trooper every minute of his or her life.

The desirability of doubt in any specific case hinges on the truthfulness or usefulness of the thing doubted. If the claim is true ("This vaccine will protect your child against polio"), then doubting is potentially harmful. If the claim is false ("Anyone who answers this ad will become a millionaire"), then doubting is a form of protection. And when the claim is a mixture of falsehood and truth ("You can be whatever you want to be"), doubting can help you sift the wheat from the chaff.

So what does this say to the Skeptical Believer weighing the claims of faith, given that Skeptical Believers are generally big on doubt?

First, it says that doubt is not the opposite of belief or of faith. The opposite of belief is disbelief. The opposite of faith is absence of faith (almost always involving faith in something else). Doubt involves misgivings—sometimes resulting in hesitancy to commit, sometimes not. Doubt is also not the same thing as questioning, skepticism, cynicism, fear, or grouchiness—though it can be combined with all these things.

Doubt includes questioning, but not all questioning originates in doubt. Some questioning springs from curiosity ("Why do you think God gave us free will?") or desire for knowledge ("What does Paul say about marriage?").

If the opposite of doubt is not faith, what is?

The opposite of doubt is certainty. By "certainty" I mean *no possibility of being wrong*. Doubt hinges on the possibility of a claim being false; certainty refuses to consider that possibility—or considers it and rejects it. If doubt is as common to the Skeptical Believer as death and taxes, then certainty is equally as common to the fundamentalist (secular or religious).

One should distinguish, however, between certainty and certitude. Certainty is philosophical state regarding knowledge, while certitude is a psychological state regarding feeling. Certainty involves near universal agreement that something is true ("The earth is round"). Certitude is a psychological state grounded in the firmness with which one holds to something, whether it is true or not ("I am certain that this lottery ticket I am buying is going to be the winner!").

Lots of people feel certain about what they believe in many areas of life, but much of it is only certitude. They feel certain and that's a good feeling, and if you go messing with that feeling (by expressing your doubts, for instance), then maybe we need an Inquisitor or a People's Court or a meeting of the board to help you get over your doubts.

So which is more compatible with faith—doubt or certainty? I'm going to vote for doubt. I believe doubt and faith need each other, whereas certainty does not need faith at all. If I am certain of something—no possibility of being wrong—then why do I need faith? And even if I only have certitude—the psychological feeling of certainty—that feeling is going to greatly diminish any sense of risk that is inherently part of the concept of faith. I may speak of "my faith in God," but if I require it to be certain, then I am really speaking more of my certitude about God than of either certainty or faith.

If I doubt and yet still commit, *then* I have faith. My definition of faith (in the generic sense) is as follows: *faith is believing and committing to something despite uncertainty.* Christian faith is believing and committing to (living out) the core claims of Christianity despite uncertainty. (And I am arguing in this book that those are largely story or narrative claims.)

It is not irrational to commit to something about which one is uncertain. It *is* irrational to commit only to things in life which *are* certain, since those things are just a small slice of life and do not include that which is most important.

It requires no faith for me to believe that two plus two equals four (being tautological in a base-ten system), nor that I want my favorite football team to win. I know that for certain. But if I say, "I believe it is possible for there to be peace in the world," that requires faith, because I am not at all sure that such peace is possible. Nonetheless, such peace is so desirable that I believe I should work for it, even though it may not in fact be realistic or attainable.

Similarly with the things of God. As with my desire for world peace, I find the biblical description of a world based on grace and created for shalom so attractive that I am willing to take the chance of living by it, even while aware that it may prove unreal. My assessment is that the preponderance of evidence and the weighing of alternatives make my faith rational—even though they do not make it certain. And the desirability and reward of the Christian description of reality are so strong for me that I do not demand that faith be certain before I will believe and commit.

That's a slice of my propositional defense of doubt as it relates to faith. It strikes even me as a bit tedious. It may hold water logically; it may not. Most likely some will say it does; some will say it doesn't; some will say it partly does and partly doesn't. That's how it goes with logical argument. But if the thesis of this book is correct, the more powerful argument will be my life. I am telling you bits and pieces of that story all along. More important than the telling, I'm trying to live it as a follower of Christ each day. I often mess it up—more usually through sins of omission rather than commission. But the reality of messing up is accounted for in the story. It is a story *for* people who mess up.

We Skeptical Believers advocate for doubt. We insist on its legitimacy, as I have here, and may even take a little pride in it, thinking it makes us just a little smarter than those with few or no doubts. Like most skeptics (and all cynics), we are deathly afraid of being fooled.

I say this to you as I say it to myself: be neither boastful nor apologetic about your doubts, especially when it comes to matters of faith. Do not be boastful (you may be doubting something true and good); do not be apologetic (you may be doubting something false or illusory). Instead, in the midst of your doubts, test the claims. Test them in your mind, in your heart, in your commitments, in your relationships, in your life. Which is to say, put them to the story test. Does the truth of these claims bear itself out in the story of my life? That test, of course, requires me to live as healthy and committed a version of the story of faith as is available. Otherwise, it's not really a test at all.

FACTS, TRUTH, AND STORY IN A POSTMODERN WORLD

The world is full of interpreters; it is impossible to live in it without repeated…
acts of interpretation.

FRANK KERMODE, *THE GENESIS OF SECRECY*

Everyone writes history within some understanding of the human condition.

CHARLES TAYLOR, *A SECULAR AGE*

Postmodernist thought hasn't given us a lot that is useful (or new), but it has rightly emphasized that most everything is part of a story. This is not news to God, but it is a bulletin that many skeptics and rationalists seem not to have received. (*You've missed a few bulletins yourself, buddy boy. Like the one about religion being consigned to the junk heap of history.*)

It is generally agreed by those who think about such things that all truth claims, all worldviews, all systems of thought and fragments of systems, all "I believe" (and "I don't believe") credos, all assertions of all kinds are claims made within a story of some kind. Included in this are all political, economic, social, and ethical systems, all art and all science. Also included are all personal and private understandings, convictions, beliefs, opinions, desires, and hopes—including yours and mine. No exceptions, actually.

One thing this suggests, among many, is that truths of all kinds are not independent little pebbles of facts lying on the beach, waiting to be picked up by passersby, transferrable to anyone's home to sit in a rock collection, looking the same in one collection as in another. Truths are more like notes of music on the score, waiting to be played—well or badly—by this instrument or that, in this composition or that, finding their places—perhaps for the first time—beside other notes, played together in varied tempos and with greatly different effect. A C note is just a C note until it joins with other notes to become *The Messiah*—or a commercial jingle.

Facts are not truths until they are placed in a story. Or, to keep the metaphor going, in a musical score. And truths are not true until they are played. That is, abstract truths do not operate as truth until they are put to work within a larger story. They are potential truths, as musical notations on paper are only potential music.

Applying this metaphor (which has the advantages and disadvantages of all metaphors), there are many seemingly independent facts in the universe, but they do not become truths until we see how they work together in a particular story or score. Misused, a fact can be made to serve a larger falsehood. Truth can die in our hands (or in our hearts) if we do not treat it with respect and humility—and give it good companions.

Every child, for instance, should be loved. Because that statement is a value judgment, it is not a brute fact, but one could buttress it with observed facts about child development. It operates as a general but unlocalized truth—or at least has the potential to be a truth. If you place that truth into a specific life story, however, and two parents use it as a reason for not disciplining their daughter (because it gives her pain to be disciplined and giving pain is unloving), then that general truth is put in service of a falsehood. You could say it is still true—every child should be loved—but it is not operating as truth in this particular story context because it has been misapplied.

That pushes us, of course, to consider what is meant by "loved" and what are legitimate and illegitimate uses of pain. This gets complicated quickly, and all of our responses will be conditioned by our own stories—personal and public. Even those who claim their responses are purely rational and scientific will do so because their own stories advocate rationality alone (or the appearance thereof) and a commitment to the story of science to resolve such questions.

Consider a parallel theological example. God is love. My story tells me this is a foundational truth about the universe (*Paid much attention to the condition of the universe lately?*)—and I accept it as so. (It does not bother me that science cannot verify this as a fact.) If, however, one agrees that this is true but then argues that therefore a loving God does not judge anyone, then one has used a truth to promote a falsehood.

Likewise, God is just. If one uses this truth to argue that God's dominant stance toward sinners is wrathful, then one has used a truth in service of a falsehood (perhaps to justify one's one wrath).

I realize I am not using terms—fact, truth, story, and the like—with the exhaustive precision a philosopher would like. If I tried, you and I would both soon lose interest (and the philosopher still would not be satisfied). Let me attempt, however, to be a little clearer about the word "story" and why I say so much of life is story-shaped and story-dependent.

When I suggest that truth is like music, I am using a metaphor. (*Simile, actually—got you there!*) I am comparing the status of truths to the status of musical notes in hope of saying something useful about truth. There are some ways in which truth is like music, and many more ways in which they are not alike at all.

On the other hand, when I say our lives are stories, I do not believe I am using metaphor. I am saying our lives are most accurately described by the words and concepts we associate with story, just as the physical body is most accurately described by the concepts of chemistry and biology (at least that's the story the West has accepted about the body for the last few centuries).

Some of the terminology and concepts of story are character, plot, theme, motivation, time, narrator, protagonist, antagonist, climax, anticlimax, and the like. It is not the case, in my view, that these terms belong to the novel and other forms of storytelling and can be borrowed and applied, metaphorically, to our lives. Rather, these are understandings we have always had about our lives (apart from any specific terminology), and we learned to apply these understandings to imagined stories like novels. As I said earlier, our lives are not like novels; novels are like our lives.

And because, as I have already claimed, story involves us as whole beings—not only as reasoning or emoting or desiring creatures—all our responses to the world will be affected by our entire story, not just by one part, especially not by the calculating part alone. So when I claim that God exists (or does not exist), or that capitalism works for the better good of all than socialism (or vice versa), or that Faulkner is a better writer than Hemingway, or even that global warming is caused by human activity, I am operating out of many contributing stories that together form the larger story that is my life and our lives together.

These stories will have come to me primarily from family, from education, from place of worship, from popular culture, and from my own individual experience. The exact configuration of these stories in my story will be absolutely unique (hence the need for each of us to tell our own stories). In responding to the questions life presents, I may use a lot of seemingly objective data—a lot of facts—but I will orchestrate them (another music metaphor) in a way that is entirely, and appropriately, subjective. I will use the facts I need to tell the story that I think I need to tell. (And if that story fails me, I will likely change stories.)

You may find this way of talking attractive or threatening (*Or tedious— yawn*), especially if you are a person of faith. It seems to offer a kind of freedom ("My faith doesn't have to be exactly like everyone else's"), while at the same time potentially eroding stability and security ("If there's no one version of the story, then maybe there's not really a story at all"). I feel both of these things myself.

Emphasizing the story nature of all truth claims can both undermine and support the claims made by faith, including by Christians. It undermines the assumptions made when the essentially religious view of the world was the only story in town. At that time, now long past, it was easier to see faith as transparently true, the only logical guide for life. Reason and emotion both approved the faith story, and there was no serious grounds to doubt its truth, even if one found it difficult to actually live. But if faith is just my story talking, and not the irrefutable nature of things, then how can I be confident in my faith, or in anything else?

Crucially, however, the same cultural and intellectual forces that have undermined one traditional way of conceiving and defending religious faith have also undermined all of the great enemies of faith in the last three hundred years. They greatly weaken three centuries of claims that the Christian story has been shown, even proven, to be false by the so-called discoveries of science (Darwin, Einstein), or history (Marx), or the social sciences (Freud, Weber, Skinner, et al), or any other developments in intellectual or artistic history. (*Finally, some people you can respect.*)

A largely unforeseen consequence of postmodernism (now itself largely passé) and other assaults on old verities is a leveling of the playing field such that no general truth claims have an automatic advantage over any other. Neither scientism (the unreflective and absolute faith in science and the scientific method), naturalistic materialism (the faith that all reality is matter), hedonism, humanitarianism (the parasite of religion that elevates doing good things to the highest value), nor any other of the endless and often amorphous visions of reality have any more, or any less, starting claim in our current cultural climate than does religious faith. All are subject to withering critique, and likewise all have a chance to convert any thinking, feeling person to their cause. All are, if you will, just stories. (I will contest the "just" part throughout this book.)

This is bad news if you are pining for the days when faith was culturally easy and uncontested and certain. It is good news if you have a hunger for God but have gotten the impression that such a hunger was stupid, ignorant, sentimental, or evil. We now live in the age of story wars. In these wars, people appear to throw "fact stones" at each other from their rock collections, but most conflicts in the world are actually story collisions. My story of the world collides with your story of the world, and each of us wonders why the other can't see the facts for what they are.

In many ways we are in the same position as the early Christians spread throughout the Roman Empire. We have had no direct, physical experience with Jesus. We didn't hear him speak or watch him heal. We have stories handed down to us from people who did. (*If you believe them.*) These stories call us to an absolutely radical reorientation of our lives. And yet we live in a culture that overwhelmingly believes other things and other stories. (*Thank goodness. If there is a "goodness," that is.*) We have relatively little temporal power qua believers (though we make an occasional awkward splash in politics), and the idea that we can remake culture in God's image seems increasingly strained. We can certainly do culture some good, but perhaps more by modeling an alternative way of living, as did the early Christians, than by successfully exercising temporal power.

This alternate way of living is described in the New Testament as the Kingdom of God ("kingdom" now seen in some circles as an offense to our superficial egalitarianism), and its defining characteristic is shalom: all things doing what they were created to do and thereby flourishing. Our story tells us that our task in life, as voluntary members of this community, is to repair and extend shalom, for shalom is always falling apart and it's always being repaired and extended.

None of this is possible in our own power, but only through the power of God in the Spirit. None of this is coerced—our participation in this kingdom and community is perhaps initiated by God, but it is accepted by each of us. In both Roman and current times, we are not coerced into belief by culture or by the reigning intellectual orthodoxies (quite the opposite). If we feel coerced by family or our social context, that fades with adulthood. We are free to choose this story or not.

This is an ancient story. (*There are older ones.*) It has been conceived of and lived out in many different ways and has often been marred by human failure, but its essence is described in the New Testament, building on the Old, and it forms the basis of the Christian understanding of the narrative that defines the human experience.

It once seemed the only story in town. Then it was widely considered a story no thinking person could embrace. (*Amen!*) Now, as two thousand years ago, it is offered to anyone who hears it, no more or less provable than the competing stories that surround it, but therefore available to anyone who feels its call.

WATER, WATER EVERYWHERE: WHY ALL EXPLANATIONS LEAK

We find it hardest to think about what we have
most completely taken for granted.

FRANK KERMODE, *THE GENESIS OF SECRECY*

Can it be that even the greatest Philosopher ever arrived
at his goal without putting aside numerous objections[?]

JOHN KEATS

For what a man had rather were true he more readily believes.

FRANCIS BACON, *NOVUM ORGANUM*

I want to start by declaring what I am not going to say, because, being a skeptic, I know all too well the human eagerness to misunderstand and misrepresent. (*Feeling a bit paranoid, are we?*) I have not said, will not say, and do not believe that human reason is incompetent, weak, or useless. (I would say that of some people in high places who claim to be reasonable, but not of reason itself.) I also am not saying, and do not believe, that reason is the enemy of faith, that it has no role in matters of faith, or that people of faith should glory in irrationality. What I am saying, and do believe, is that all explanations leak, including those claiming to be based on reason. And we are better for recognizing that fact in the larger meaning-making process.

If I believed that competing, equally far-reaching explanations of the world were greatly more approved by reason than the Christian story, it would bother me—mildly. Or if I thought that the Christian understanding of reality was uniquely risky, I might lose a night or two of sleep. But I believe neither is the case, because all (and I do mean all) explanations of reality leak. The only way to diminish leaking is to diminish the significance of the claims, until one reaches the point where one can be close to certain, but what one is certain about is of little importance. (*I myself am certain that most of what you're saying is far too dry or convoluted for the majority of your readers, which is why I am not bothering to contest it much. You're too boring to be convincing. I'm going for a snack.*)

All explanations of the world leak, including the Christian one, because human understanding leaks. (God doesn't leak, but we do.) Even the supposedly most watertight aspect of human understanding—vaunted reason—leaks like a rusty bucket, especially when it comes to addressing the "big questions." Let me suggest three reasons why.

Human understanding leaks at the level of *presuppositions*. A presupposition is something one assumes to be true, and wishes his or her audience to assume, without having to prove or demonstrate it. Presuppositions can be conscious but are often unconscious, or were once conscious but now are assumed without having to think about them again. Most scientific arguments, for instance, presuppose a regularity and order to the universe. If there is not such an order, then the thing I have proved with this experiment might not still be the case when the experiment is repeated, which would be the end of science.

We are all awash in presuppositions, many of which cannot actually be proved even if we stopped to try. (Most who believe in God do so without having gone through an extended analysis of the evidence. The same is true for most who do not believe in God.) Many presuppositions are trivial, but others are foundational to how we see the world.

If we are wrong at the level of presuppositions, our reasoning will not only leak, it will likely not hold any water at all. If all my reasoning about the claims of the Bible, for instance, is based on presuppositions about the Bible that are not true, then I am like the man who built his house upon the sand. ("And the house on the sand went splat," as we sang in Sunday school.) If I presuppose that the exotic metaphors and images of the book of Daniel and elsewhere give me the data to calculate the date of the end of the world and I am wrong, then all my calculations, no matter how good my math, come to naught (and you can bet someone, somewhere, is doing that calculation at this very moment).

Likewise, if one reads all prophecy and miracle accounts in the Bible with the presupposition that such things are not possible in our naturalistic, materialistic, rationalistic universe, then that reading will be of little worth if the presupposition is false.

If my analysis of evidence is based on faulty presuppositions, then I will not only misread the evidence, I won't even consider much evidence that might be relevant to my conclusions (not seriously considering the evidence of the Resurrection, for instance, because "everybody knows" that such things don't happen).

I have used examples from the world of faith, but the same is true across the board. (Think about the presuppositions people make in the abortion debate.) Reason leaks when presuppositions leak, and they often do.

A second reason why our explanations often leak comes at the level of *logical reasoning*. There are many connection joints in the pipeline of reasoning that moves from premises to conclusions, and at each joint there is the potential for leakage. The list of classical logical fallacies is long—ad hominem, circular reasoning, begging the question, appeal to authority, false dichotomy (either-or), post hoc, slippery slope, straw man, and so on. Any of these mistakes, at any point in the pipeline, will cause your explanation to leak, and even the most careful thinkers are not immune, especially when they are thinking about the most important things.

Consider the common argument that since there are so many religions in the world, it is unreasonable (worse yet, intolerant) to claim that only one of them is true. The weakness of this argument (which I will expand on later) is many-fold, but among others things it fails logically. The fact that there are many religions and different explanations of the world (and that is a fact) does not lead logically to the conclusion that no single one of them is true. There were once many different explanations of the physical structure of the world (flat and riding on the back of a turtle were two), but the variety of explanations has not prevented us from reasonably claiming now that the world is more or less round. (And if you think you've detected a flaw in my reasoning, that just supports my overall point about explanations leaking.)

It is possible, of course, to avoid (or seem to avoid) logical fallacies. But that would plug just one source of leakage, not all. And I am not claiming, as might a nihilist, that all higher-level claims are false, only that all are contestable—the bigger the claim, the more contestable. No claim that rises to the level of a general explanation of reality (be it religious or secular) can be stated or argued in such a way that reasonable, well-meaning people cannot find objections to it. You may be satisfied with the watertightness of your claims, but somebody else just as smart or smarter will not be. (*Allow me to say clearly, I am not satisfied with yours—or with any of this—and if you give me a moment, I'll figure out why.*)

A third source of leakage, and to me the most important and inescapable, comes in *the assessing and weighting of evidence.* When we assess evidence for use in our reasoning and explanations, we not only try to discover what is true (the facts), we must also assess how significant those facts are to the issue at hand, and how much influence to allow them in our final conclusions. We can unanimously agree on what the facts are in a case, reason without any logical fallacies or false presuppositions, and yet still come to radically different conclusions on what should be done in light of those facts, based on our different weighting of their significance and on the different prior commitments we have made.

Should our country, for instance, intervene in the affairs of another, even to the point of using military force? We might agree that the other country is hostile to us, that it is developing weapons of mass destruction, that it has a history of attacking other countries, and that it is terribly abusive of its own citizens. But we won't agree on what to do about it, because our equally reasonable weighting of factors will lead us to different conclusions. (I may be most moved by the need to stop the slaughter of their own people; you may be moved by the need to prevent the loss of life that comes with war.) You can call this a leak in our reasoning or simply diversity of views, but either way we discover that reason alone is not a sure guide.

And how does one weight the evidence for and against God? How much weight to the testimony of others? To your own experience? To the historical record? To philosophical claims and counterclaims? To your doubts and questions? To your hopes and desires? To the attractiveness or credibility of alternative stories? What if you believe God has spoken to you?

What if you think God hasn't spoken to anyone? How much does it matter that a lot of smart people don't believe this? How much that a lot of smart people do? How much weight do you give to your own limited ability to understand the rational arguments for and against? To your emotions and intuitions? To what your mother said—or the contradictory thing said by your father or teacher?

In short, equally rational and well-meaning people will assess and weight evidence differently and therefore come to very different conclusions. I see this as a leak in the ability of reason to be decisive in many matters of great importance, including faith. You can call it something else (perhaps just finitude), but my point is the same. People who say these things should be decided by reason (especially if you agree to reason as they do) do not understand much about reason. They are Blowing Smoke—often into their own eyes.

These do not exhaust the leaks in our attempts to reason ourselves to truth and a good life. There are others, such as language, for instance, about which I will eventually say more. We simply do not mean exactly the same things even when we use exactly the same words—making it hard to know at times if we are really agreeing even when we seem to agree. How many possible shades of meaning and varying concepts are in words like freedom, justice, rights, truth, fairness, reason, evidence, assent, good, useful, and health, without even mentioning the G-word (*Granola?*)—God.

And then there are all the leaks possible because of human nature—shortsightedness, stubbornness, laziness, anger, naïveté, irresponsibility, and the like. (*And they say I'm a downer. Any more wet blankets in your closet?*) You get the idea.

None of this, I say again, is an argument for eliminating reasons and reasoning from our choices in life. I am reasoning like crazy (*And some of us think not too well*) in giving my reasons why I don't think reason alone can settle these issues. If I didn't think reason valuable, I wouldn't bother. I simply want reason to know its proper place and show a little humility. And I want you and me to get beyond this idea that we cannot commit to anything unless reason can prove it irrefutably true. If that's your standard, you will never commit to anything important, and you will live an unnecessarily stunted life.

SKEPTICISM OF THE EMOTIONS

We are in fact all acting, thinking, and feeling out of backgrounds and frameworks which we do not fully understand.

CHARLES TAYLOR, *A SECULAR AGE*

"Enjoy yourself."
"I am," said Pooh.
"Some can," said Eeyore.

A.A. MILNE, *WINNIE-THE-POOH*

Human beings are not nearly the thinkers we think we are. We like to believe we come to our views and values and act as we do after a careful process of evidence gathering, evaluation, and analysis. That's pure Smoke. More often we see and value and act as we do because of shaping forces that extend far beyond reason, all the while using the whole sense-making process (including reason) to shore up and defend the place we have arrived at by other means. (*So who's the cynic now?*) We claim (to ourselves) to have arrived at the station on the train of logic, but in fact we hitchhiked on back roads almost the entire way.

So I want to talk about a different source of skepticism. I am defining skepticism as the habit of reflexively questioning truth claims. The common tendency, and a common emphasis of this book, is to see these questionings as originating in the rational processes of the mind. Reason, logic, analysis, and the like produce objections to claims about how the world is or what one ought to do in it, including the claims of faith. (And I do believe that Skeptical Believers tend toward the rationalistic—no smarter than anyone else, but more inclined to appeal to this complex of faculties we vaguely label "reason.") There is a powerful kind of skepticism, however, that is rooted not in reason per se, but in the human emotions.

If anything, this skepticism of the emotions is harder to deal with—even within one's self—than rationalistic skepticism because it is ghost-like, never quite materializing into a tangible form or even into a clear objection. This kind of skepticism is more haunting than attacking, an in-the-bones feeling that keeps the things of faith at a distance or powerless, feeling to varying degrees unreal or irrelevant.

Emotional skepticism can range from a mild indifference or weariness to a full-blown "dark night of the soul" (see St. John of the Cross). The milder versions may be more threatening to healthy belief than a full-blown crisis of faith, because the latter is by definition acute (a crisis), insisting on a resolution and often being a necessary step toward a deeper and richer faith. A floating detachment, on the other hand, can last a lifetime, keeping one just beyond commitment but short of disbelief—in spiritual limbo.

I know about spiritual limbo—not heaven, not hell. "Limbo" means "edge" or "boundary," and that partially describes the emotional feeling as well—being on the edge of something, not quite in, not quite out. Something is drawing you in, something is pushing you away. You stay in orbit, like a satellite, circling around something but keeping enough distance to allow you to orbit without either joining in or vectoring away. I was orbiting spiritually for much of my twenties—or at least it seems so looking back. I sometimes return even now. I do not consciously choose it, it is not the result of an intellectual calculation, it is simply where I wake up one morning and find myself (the result of many small decisions I have made). And I can stay there for a long time if I do not do the things I know to do in order to return from limbo.

One cause of this emotional skepticism is the practice of keeping faith an idea rather than a life. Ideas detached from daily living can become bloodless, ephemeral, interesting perhaps but not engaging, not shaping this moment or this choice. So why would a person, confronted with the most exciting possible idea—that a personal God who made the universe wants to be known by you—neither reject it nor embrace it but keep it at a safe distance?

Maybe the word "safe" provides one key—for understanding skepticism of all kinds. Skeptics (and cynics—industrial-strength skeptics) are often wounded idealists. At some point in their lives—likely in youth—they thought the world was a wonderful place. Life experience taught them differently—a painful lesson—and skepticism gives them a form of protection against that painful disappointment happening again. If I don't commit, I won't be hurt. It happens in love; it happens in faith.

Sometimes this emotional skepticism around matters of belief springs less from a desire for safety than from anger at the abuses and misuses of faith—of religion, if you will. I'm not thinking so much of the historical failures of the church—inquisitions, crusades, burning people at the stake, and the like—as of personal experiences with hypocrisy, legalism, intolerance, and other besetting sins within the body of believers. It can be difficult to give yourself fully to a story that includes so many people you otherwise would not want to hang out with. (Even if one might be willing to admit, as many skeptics do not, that you are yourself no great prize and subject to the same shortcomings.)

A third source of emotional skepticism is simply the clutter of everyday life. I was about to call it "busyness," but clutter is an even better word for it. Clutter is the impeding accumulation of stuff—physical stuff and mental stuff and "stuff to do"—that may be of no great value in itself but that distracts us from more important things. A less important thing that blocks us from a more important thing becomes, by default, the most important thing of that moment. If it is the thing we most attend to, it becomes the thing we treat, experientially, as the most important.

The great deception of a cluttered life is that it presents itself to us as inevitable. These are things I *have* to have or *have* to do—"I have no choice." But of course we do. We could choose quite differently. But that would require living a different life, and as much as we complain, we prefer the cluttered life we know to the life we don't know (see Flannery O'Connor regarding preferring the devil you know to the devil you don't). The most likely place for God in a cluttered life is somewhere on a shelf, along with other knickknacks and odd bits. Too valuable to throw away ("might need this someday") but not so valuable so as to throw away instead many of the other things and make God central.

There is simply a numbing quality to the everyday ordinary—the chug, chug, chug of day after day, task after task, routine after routine. Spiritual highs happen along from time to time, but they quickly disappear into that bottomless pit we call the past. One of the problems with great worship experiences and other encounters with God is that you don't die right after they're over. You have to go to the parking lot. Many people find it difficult to reconcile deep spirituality with everydayness, and emotional skepticism can be the result.

No matter what its source, emotional skepticism makes the things of faith feel less real than other things in your life—childcare, school or job, relationship demands. And "feel" is, I think, the right word, because this is an affective and not a cognitive issue. "I believe in God. I acknowledge the value of faith, the church (maybe), morality, and all that. But," as the slang expression goes, "I'm just not feeling it. It bounces around in my head but doesn't reach my heart, much less my bones." You're not against God at all; God just doesn't visit very often in your neighborhood. You've got other things to attend to.

So what's the cure for this—assuming you're even interested in a cure? (Ironically, one of the signs of spiritual torpor—acedia—is an inability even to desire a cure.) You aren't going to like my answer. You didn't like it from your mother, and you won't like it from me. The cure is the dreaded "job jar." "You bored, kiddo? You got nothin' to do? Then let me get the job jar, and you can pick out a ticket with a chore written on it and get to work." Ah, thanks, but I think I'd rather be bored.

Helmut Thielicke wrote soon after World War II that the cynicism that was spreading throughout Europe, especially among intellectuals, was the result of taking a spectator stance toward the devastation that surrounded everyone—intellectual, spiritual, and physical. One could observe it carefully, make beautiful worded and sensitive comments on it, or one could try to help in the rebuilding. (I discuss this in *The Myth of Certainty*). There is something wonderfully (maybe even irrationally) healing about doing a small, needed task, Thielicke argued, rather than simply reflecting on how bleak and meaningless life has become.

Engagement itself—as an act of commitment—becomes the cure for the malaise that infects you. It isn't that the doing erases the situation, certainly not instantly, nor changes a rational analysis of it. But the doing changes how you feel about the situation and, eventually, will usually also change how you think about it. For we are, after all, thinking-feeling creatures, not just one or the other.

I am calling here for engaging in the story of faith, but I am not calling for more busyness. I'm not saying to add the practices of faith to your to-do list. For some people, beginning to take belief seriously will mean a cessation of doing (even of good things) and a season of sitting still.

But, as I will argue later, faith *is* a kind of performance. There are things you are called to do as a character in this story. You need to perform them, whether the feeling is there or not. The answer to safe or angry or harried emotional skepticism is risky engagement. You need to fall out of orbit (and into love), to leave the border regions, to cross the boundary into the story. Engagement does not erase all skepticism, but it gives skepticism less opportunity to be the defining quality of your life.

STORY AND THE UNIQUENESS OF BELIEF AND OF DOUBT

People are generally better persuaded by the reasons that they have
themselves discovered than by those that have come into the minds of others.
BLAISE PASCAL

The ways in which you believe and doubt are as uniquely your own as your
DNA. I enjoy reciting creeds and traditional prayers together with others
because it reminds me that I am part of something larger and much older
than myself. But I also find myself scanning ahead at the next sentence
to ask myself whether it proclaims something I actually believe myself
and am willing to say out loud. And even as I say something I do believe
without reservation—"I believe in God, the Father, maker of heaven and
earth"—I know that I don't believe exactly the same things about God or
in the same way or with the same result as even my wife standing next to
me, much less the African or Asian believer who may be saying these same
words today half a world away. Not to mention how we all might differ regarding gender language (Father), the Trinity, and all sorts of other issues
embedded in what seems like a simple declaration. (*Excellent points! And
you don't even yourself understand the same thing from the same words from
one day to next. A beautiful muddle!*)

All belief—of any kind—happens within the context of a specific life and life story. It is influenced by forces both external and internal. The exact contours of that belief—and how it works itself out in living—is absolutely unique. No two people have ever believed or disbelieved in exactly the same way and to the same ends.

So it is not the case that Skeptical Believers are united in one class and all other believers are together in another. Each believer is in a class of one, even though each believer understands and works out his or her belief as part of a larger community.

I am a believer, skeptical or otherwise, for many reasons, each of which would require many stories and many explanations to unfold. I believe for rational reasons, for emotional reasons, for volitional reasons, for world and personal history reasons, for intuitive and imaginative reasons (some of which will come out as this book unfolds), and so on.

My doubts spring from all those same categories.

No one believes in the same way I do. I am not, for instance, drawn to the idea of Jesus as my friend or the healer of my wounds, a way of thinking about God that is very powerful for millions. I am also, as this book makes clear, not drawn to proofs or to rationalistic arguments for God, an approach that also is central for millions. I am not very mystical and don't much feel God in nature or sense him directing each of my steps. I believe for a thousand little reasons and for a handful of bigger ones, not least because I love the idea and the reality of mercy and grace and justice and haven't discovered any foundation big enough for them other than God. The best way to say it briefly is that I believe because I have yet to find a better story. And it's not for lack of looking. (*I keep offering you better stories, but you're stubborn and out of date.*)

Whatever the configuration of my faith, it is a configuration unique to me. Given that God made each of us one at a time and that no two people live the same life, it could not be otherwise.

I also doubt and disbelieve in my own ways. I do not find the existence of evil or pain particularly threatening to my faith, problems that devastate the faith of others. God's seeming absence or distance or silence isn't a great obstacle for me. (Like the Israelites at Mount Sinai, I'd just as soon he speak directly to others, not to me.) Nor are God's supposed offenses to reason or to tolerance or to gender or to modern sensibilities a great personal concern. I doubt, as I believe, for a thousand little reasons and for a handful of bigger ones, not least because on some days the story of faith seems far too optimistic. I'm postmodern enough to be suspicious of happy endings, and God tending to and finally redeeming his creation seems at times impossibly happy.

Whatever the configuration of my doubts, it is a configuration unique to me.

So what? "Everyone is unique. Everyone is special." We've heard that since *Sesame Street*. What practical value does it have to say we believe and doubt uniquely?

Maybe none, but here's a shot.

I think it's helpful to know that not every argument for belief is meant for me. When I hear someone patiently and enthusiastically laying out the "argument from design" for the existence of God, knowing they have devoted to it longs hours, perhaps long years, of thought and research, I tip my hat to them and wish them well, despite its having little force for me. Someone out there needs to hear that argument and will respond to it gratefully.

When I hear someone testify that their life was a wasteland of addiction and brokenness and that Jesus healed them and changed everything, I share their joy and rejoice at the wonder of a life transformed. But I do not find that their experience of rescue answers the questions in my own heart.

Many years ago I wrote a book called *The Myth of Certainty*, which focused on issues of faith and doubt. One reviewer thought the book a waste of time for anyone with doubts, suggesting that all such a person needed was a good book of traditional apologetics to answer their questions. I think for many believers he was right. The book was literally meaningless for certain kinds of believers. (*I didn't think much of it myself.*) On the other hand, I have a thick file of letters from others who over the years have told me the book saved their life—or at least their faith, or at the very least kept alive for them the possibility of faith. The reviewer wasn't wrong about the value of a good book of apologetics; he just made the mistake of thinking everyone believes and doubts as he does.

Story is a form of understanding and communicating that embodies and honors our uniqueness better than any other, including the uniqueness of belief and doubt. Story—as a form, as a means of organizing data—accommodates specificity, complexity, flexibility, changes of direction, paradox, competing truths, and mystery better than any other form. Proposition and logic are, by comparison, heavy-handed, lead-footed, and simplistic.

Stories can take their time. They can pile up details—of setting, character, history, plot. They need not rush to judgment. They can show not just both sides of an issue or circumstance, but all sides—present and past, inner and outer, real and imagined. They can embody contradiction—within the same character—and nuance. And they can do so in a way that is at the same time unique and universal. There is no other character like Ahab and no other story like his obsessive hunt for the white whale in *Moby Dick*. Ahab is unique. And yet there is something in his story that finds echoes in the stories of Saul and Othello and Ben Linus. And it also finds echoes within me.

My story, likewise, is simultaneously unique and a replaying in a different key of other stories. Because I believe and disbelieve uniquely, and because no one else has the exact mix of experiences and abilities and sensibilities, I have a role to play in the story of faith that no one else can play. I am not a generic marker filling the generic slot labeled "believer." I am Daniel William Taylor, born not long after World War II in the hills behind San Diego, middle child of flawed but God-loving parents, reared up and down the southern California coast and on the plains of Texas, gifted with a certain amount of intelligence and stamina, blessed with an education at Westmont College and Emory University, shaped by boyhood friendships with Jon and Larry and Chuck and Ben and Bruce, further blessed by marriage to Jayne and by four children, and on and on.

And therefore, I had something to do in Ukraine, a small sliver of something larger, but something that no one else could or was supposed to do. In the mid 1990s I twice went to Ukraine with a group of Minnesota Christians to encourage and learn from Ukrainian Christians in a small town named Zolotonosha. Each person had an expertise in something, or, if not, a simple willingness to serve. Because I was a university professor, I was assigned to speak to teachers and to lecture at the university in the nearby city of Cherkassy.

One earnest young woman heard me speak to the teachers. Afterward she asked if I was speaking anywhere else. I told her I was giving a series of talks during the week at the university, starting the next day.

That next afternoon I was being driven to the university for the first of the talks, and I happened to look over as we passed one of the trolley buses that provide the only transportation for many people in the city. These buses are incredibly overcrowded. A Westerner sees the door open at a stop, with the passengers packed nose to ear, and assumes there is no room for a single additional person. The locals simply ram their way into the pack, and the bus that was more than full before is now fuller still.

As we passed one of these buses, I noticed the woman who had been at the teacher's conference, pressed against one of the windows. I caught her eye and waved at her, and she smiled and waved back. A few minutes later she appeared at the lecture.

Nothing in my teaching experience prepared me for teaching in Ukraine. After one talk (something about American literature, I think), a young woman stood when I invited questions and asked, in perfect English and with Slavic seriousness, "What do you think is the main thing in life?" You have to understand that the kinds of questions I'm used to from American students are along the lines of "Will this stuff be on the quiz?" But in Ukraine I was speaking to young, inquisitive minds in a society whose basic explanation of reality had just officially collapsed. They were interested in bigger things.

The afternoon lectures to which the woman in the bus came were about living as a character within a story, about the qualities of a healthy life story, and about why I thought faith was one of those qualities. I have no idea what sacrifices were necessary for her to attend those afternoon lectures—nothing is done easily in Ukraine. But she was at each of the talks during the week, and when the last was over, she came up to me and said through my interpreter, "I want you to know that your being here has changed *my* story forever." All I could do was look into her very blue eyes and say, "Thank you."

That woman was letting me know that I had made a difference in her story. By doing so, she was giving meaning to my own. I don't believe I was prepared for that opportunity because I believed a certain set of propositions. The propositions I believe are not unique. What *is* unique is the working out in my life of the truth that those propositions are trying to capture. That intersection of her story and my story took place in the way it did because God had uniquely prepared each of us. I was the only person who at that time could say what I had to say to have that effect on that woman—whose life has since been lived in ways known only to God. The uniqueness of my story, and my way of believing and living, met the uniqueness of her story at that moment, and both of our stories are different for it.

Do not be surprised if your reasons for belief are not the same as someone else's. Do not be surprised if you cannot defend them well to others. Do not be surprised that you cannot always defend them even to yourself. But do be concerned if there is a wide gap between what you believe and how you live. It is the living of faith—being a character in the story—that is important. The living—not the defending—will prove or disprove the story for you.

God knows you are unique. God knows what you need to be part of the story. God knows what makes the story hard for you. What you need will come to you, like bread upon the waters. Perhaps in the form of this book. Perhaps in the form of a friend. Perhaps in the form of a song. Or of something painful. But in whatever form, it will reveal itself uniquely as part of your story.

I believe uniquely because my story is unique. I believe like others because our stories are rooted in God's story. I doubt uniquely because my story is unique. I doubt like others because there are recurring patterns in the human condition that cause us to question whether life is meaningful or good. To this point in my life, my belief outweighs my doubt, not least because it gives me a better story to live. It lets me go to Ukraine and be a blessing to, and be blessed by, a woman who rides the trolleys.

ALL VALUE CLAIMS ARE FAITH CLAIMS

For a state of affairs in which everything hangs together, we accept a measure of private intermittency in our interpretations.

FRANK KERMODE, *THE GENESIS OF SECRECY*

Anyone who has ever claimed that one thing is better than another is a person of faith. Whether it is an important claim—truth is better than falsehood, justice than oppression, love than hate, life than death—or a trivial claim—dogs are better than cats, baseball than football, apple pie than cherry—if there is an implied value or ought in the claim, then there is an implied faith that cannot be entirely confirmed by reason, facts, or any operation of the intellect. As a Skeptical Believer, I find this both reassuring and a sinful pleasure.

The sinful pleasure is the delight it gives me when I hear anyone talking about how rational and logical they and their values are (Smoke). It's the pleasure of watching the pompous man slip on the banana peel—inflated self-importance instantly made human, like the rest of us. A difference, of course, is that the people who think of themselves and their values as models of reason and logic neither see the banana peel nor feel the fall. They make their pronouncements and are quite happy about things. But I find myself smiling at them and feeling as superior to them as they might feel to me, which is of course a sin on my part. God forgive me. (*Sounds like a fake confession.*)

The reassuring part of understanding that all value claims are faith claims is realizing that my faith is no riskier and my value claims no shakier than anyone else's. It is not the case that people of faith have to cross their fingers and hope their antique ways of seeing and valuing might somehow, despite all evidence, turn out to be true—while modern, secular people, standing on the solid ground of reason and the scientific method and the inevitable tide of progress, believe and value only what the mind approves. We are in the same boat. We are both making commitments beyond the brute facts. We are both creating and living in a story.

Let me explain a little more fully why I say that all value claims are faith claims. They are so because the methods by which we commonly claim something to be certainly true ("certain" meaning no possibility of error) are not methods that deal conclusively (or even usefully, for the most part) with *oughts*. Oughts—as in, "you ought to do this," or "we ought to do that," or "society ought to structured in this way," or "you ought to vote for that politician," or "I ought to treat these people is this way," ad infinitum. Human beings are inescapably and at every moment "ought" creatures (for example, the claim that we ought to decide things rationally), and to get to any ought, we have to take at least a little leap beyond the provable facts, and often quite a large one.

Consider the person who claims that racism or sexism or homophobia is wrong. Those are oughts, each of which I agree with. But none of those oughts can be derived from a purely materialistic view of the world common to many secularists. If all of life has no higher beginning or goal than the collision, combination, and recombination of atoms, then there is no basis for any claim of ought. The material world concerns itself only with *is*, not with *ought*. Ought becomes merely opinion and preference for the materialist. You can argue for the usefulness of your opinion, and you can band together with others to punish those who do not go along with your opinion, but you cannot establish an unimpeachable logical ground for your opinion that derives from your materialist assumptions about reality.

Put another way, the moral imperatives of materialistic secularists are built on clouds. You say to the racist or the abuser, "You ought not to treat others that way." They ask, "Why not?" And the answer to that "why not?" can never get past "because it hurts people" or "it's harmful to the community" or, if desperate, "it slows down evolution" (an argument only an academic could love). And those answers are a problem because there is nothing further to say when the response is, "I don't care about any of that" or, more subtly, "I think my views and actions are good, and everyone has a right to their own opinion."

Even the environmental ought that we need to protect the planet in order to protect life is based on the earlier ought that a person should care about any life beyond their own—or even care about their own life, for that matter. All you can do when people reject your oughts (whether with an "I don't care" or a counter-ought) is make rules and use collective force to punish those who don't go along. Or shrug your shoulders. In a purely material world, we are making morality up as we go based on perceived self-interest, and there is no ground—other than force—to compel others to see their interests as you do.

I want quickly to say that I am not claiming that the person of faith is, in terms of certainty, on much safer ground. (*Took the words right out of my mouth.*) We are more logically consistent with our oughts because we claim that they are derived from the character of the Creator and are built, like gravity and the speed of light, into the very nature of the world—that they are, in fact, natural. But that won't help us much in an argument because we will quickly be asked to prove that such is the case, and while we can offer evidence, we cannot offer proof. (*I thought not.*)

So I am inclined to say that the ought claims of secularists are illogical, based on their professed view of basic reality, while the ought claims of people of faith are logical but not provable. Put another way, if the presuppositions and arguments of radical secularists about basic reality are correct, their moral imperatives are illogical; if the presuppositions and arguments of Christians about basic reality are correct, their moral imperatives are both logical and natural. (I'm sure you'll let me know if I'm being illogical about this.) (*Okay, I don't see the flaw in your thinking at the moment, but I'm sure somebody has. I'll work on this.*)

So this is not the usual screed against relativism in favor of believers basking in the warm sun of certainty and absolutes. I do believe in absolutes, but I also believe our knowledge of them is partial and flawed and therefore, in that limited sense, relative—or at least subjective. There is a warm sun, but it is often behind the clouds or even, during the night, not visible to us at all. This sun is too bright to look at directly, so we see it reflected in a glass darkly.

I find the faith-based nature of all value claims—secular and religious—reassuring, then, because it frees me from the nagging feeling that I'm taking a bigger risk than necessary. These other people are as moral as me—look at all the good things they are for—and yet they don't have to believe in creations or incarnations or empty tombs or coming agains or even in messy things like sin and forgiveness and salvation and you name it. They are good without God; why do I have to carry all this extra baggage?

Because they aren't good (neither am I) and because it isn't extra. They have no logical right to the words "good" and "ought." They have had to make claims about goodness and oughts that their prior claims about reality do not support ("You can't get there from here"). I also cannot prove my "oughts," but they at least follow logically from my claims about God as Creator. The things of faith are not extra baggage; they are the truths about reality that make goodness real and the leap worth taking. Those are some of my value claims, that is my faith, and this is my story.

THE NATURE OF ANSWERS

Never give an answer to a question that doesn't satisfy you in the first place.
ALISTER MCGRATH, *MERE APOLOGETICS*

Defenders of atheism… treat the ultimate mystery
as if it were a high-school debate topic.
SYDNEY LEA

"He's Winnie-ther-Pooh. Don't you know what *'ther'* means?"
"Ah, yes, now I do," I said quickly; and I hope you [the reader] do too,
because it is all the explanation you are going to get.
A.A. MILNE, *WINNIE-THE-POOH*

Every question has an answer, and every answer has a question. Sometimes they're just not matched up usefully. It is important to understand that different questions call not just for different answers, but for different *kinds* of answers. If your answer to every "How do you make… ?" question is "hammer," then there are a lot of things you won't be able to make.

Our culture's most widely accepted form of answer is the

scientific—hypothesis, experiment, proof. Great where it's useful. Unfortunately for many of our most important questions, it's not particularly useful (and not always useful even in science). In many areas, we get clues, testimonies, speculations, arguments, and best guesses rather than proofs (including most areas dealing with human beings beyond the purely physical). The matters of faith and the spirit are certainly one of these areas.

I find this understanding helpful when I am asking questions about most things human and all things spiritual. It keeps my expectations realistic. Here are five categories or kinds of answers and examples of the kinds of questions for which those answers are appropriate (*Listing things makes you feel in control, doesn't it?*):

A. Definitive answers: These settle things and do not invite rebuttal. (At what temperature does water boil? What does the Bible say about who created the universe?)

B. Persuasive answers: These are not proofs but are widely convincing. (How important is the role of education in a flourishing society? What is the biblical view of the poor?)

C. Direction-pointing or reflective answers: These do not offer proof and will not persuade everyone, but these answers give you something to think about, a direction your thinking might go. (What is a just society—and is ours one? What makes a work of art great? Can God be good if there is evil and suffering in the world God created?)

   (One can address the problem of evil in a talk, but almost no one, including the speaker, will go away saying, "Well, now that's no longer a problem." But many might well go away saying, "That was something I hadn't considered before; I'll have to think about it some more.")

D. Speculative answers: These are in the spirit of "Well, I don't really know, but perhaps... " The most attended to speculative answers come from people who at least are knowledgeable about the area out of which the question arises, but even experts should be humble when speculating. (Where's the economy likely to be in two years? What will heaven be like?)

E. Evasive or question-begging answers—aka Blowing Smoke: These answers take many forms: refusing to recognize the question as needing an answer, dismissing the questioner in hopes the question will go away, offering an answer to a different question than the one asked, offering a glib or superficial or humorous answer and hoping everyone will be satisfied, quoting an irrelevant Bible verse, claiming there's no time now for an adequate answer—and snorting, harrumphing, or changing the subject.

When it comes to serious questions about faith and its legitimacy, only a few questions can be given definitive answers, more can be given persuasive answers, though of course what persuades one will not necessarily persuade another (and some people decide in advance they will not allow anything contrary to their present views to persuade them). Further, for all questions of faith that I know of, there are reflective answers and directions that can be pointed. And speculation can at least be interesting.

Some questions are big (or complex) enough that more than one category of answer comes into play. For instance, what can we do to make ours a more just society? A great number of people have weighed in on this question, both believers and unbelievers. For people of faith, it is not hard to find individual, definitive statements in the Bible about God's concern for the poor and oppressed. It is also not hard to build a persuasive overview of how a just, shalom-based, God-fearing society should treat the poor. It is more difficult to translate that into specific laws, policies, and institutions, but most people of goodwill are eager to hear thoughtful reflections on this task and to have directions pointed. Some of this will verge into speculation—"If we did this, then we would get that"—but even this speculation (and counter speculation) could be in a spirit of goodwill and a common goal. But, of course, in any question this complex and important, you will also get great billows of Smoke Blowing.

So how is any of this helpful to the Skeptical Believer? It helps, I think, because it keeps us realistic (and a bit humble). We can ask any question we want, but we ought to expect a category of answer that is appropriate for the question. If we ask a speculative question, for instance, we should not expect a definitive answer, nor be discouraged or upset if we don't get one. The same applies when we try to answer questions—our own or otherwise.

Of course, some people think they have the definitive answer for every question. They believe that the more confidently (even aggressively) they answer the question, the more true their answer is. These people tend to confuse certitude with certainty, and they tend to give Skeptical Believers hives.

There are, broadly, two different explanatory and apologetic approaches to making sense of reality. One centers on words such as argument, evidence, facts, assertions, logic, premises, experiment, proof, and the like. The other deals in words such as clues, pointers, testimonies, stories, intuitions. They are not mutually exclusive, though one set will be more effective with one kind of problem or question and the other with another kind. When it comes to ultimate things, neither will be effective with someone who does not *want* to find a way to God.

I spent too much of my life looking for definitive answers to questions that I should have recognized could only be answered persuasively or reflectively. It would have helped if I had recognized earlier that God was offering me not an argument but a story. (*Yeah, whenever I have you on the run with an argument, you hide behind a tall tale. Coward!*) It is a story that has facts and assertions and history and even argument in it, but it is not a story that is asking me to prove something, but to live something. (*Why live it when it might be bogus?*)

There are no new questions, certainly no new spiritual questions (though occasionally there is a new context or application). People of wisdom and commitment and honesty and intelligence have thought about these questions since Job and before. I am not going to ask a single question that has not been asked already, but that doesn't mean I shouldn't ask it. After all, I wasn't around the first time it was raised. I can profit, however, from hearing what others have to say, knowing that, nonetheless, I have to work out my own faith (in the company of others) with fear and trembling.

ANOTHER WAY TO FALL OFF THIS HORSE: THE POSTMODERN TAR BABY

The overcoming of all prejudices… [is] the global demand of the Enlightenment. [This goal] will itself prove to be a prejudice.

HANS-GEORG GADAMER

326. Have beliefs, but don't believe.
228. Live without a big picture.
181. Hemorrhage paradigms.
298. Negotiate truth.
210. Never arrive.

ANDREW BOYD, *LIFE'S LITTLE DECONSTRUCTION BOOK*

After World War I, the French built the Maginot Line. It was designed as an elaborate, technologically advanced but static defense against attack from the northeast (Germany comes to mind) and was incredibly effective—except it wasn't. It was effective in dissuading the Germans from fighting the Second World War as everyone had fought the first—mostly in trenches. But it simply forced the Germans to invent another strategy—the Blitzkrieg, Lightning War based on tanks and mobility.

Christian apologists of the last few generations have built a sort of Maginot Line against secular attacks, largely rationalistic and materialistic, arising from the eighteenth-century Enlightenment and its descendants. These apologists have been quite effective in blunting and sometimes refuting what were once thought quite impregnable arguments in the name of Reason and Science and History against traditional religious faith. We owe them a debt.

Those kinds of attacks on religion are still around, and still sell books, but they have the feel of week-old pizza—still chewable, but not much sizzle. More powerful now are those who seek to kill religion with kindness, more like a Tar Baby than a Blitzkrieg. After fooling around with hard-core relativism for a while (which collapses rather easily, such that no respected thinker admits to being a true relativist anymore), the underminers of traditional faith today prefer a kind of soft-relativism, all acceptance and smiles, but perhaps more devastating to any particular faith than anything that has come before.

This Tar Baby strategy goes something like this. Of course there is truth, and of course the spiritual is one way to truth, but every culture and every person has his or her own understanding of it. Every culture and every person has, if you will, his or her own story. We've seen many stories rise and fade over the long course of human history—political, social, economic, intellectual, and, of course, religious. We now see, as people could not see so easily before, how foolish it would be to think that any *one* story is *the* story. Instead, we should embrace the many truths found in many stories, emphasizing especially those that help us to be kinder, more generous, more accepting, more affirming. (*Couldn't have said it better myself.*) Anyone who thinks the truth of his or her story is more true than someone else's is simply intolerant. And intolerance is the sin than which no greater sin can be conceived. (Pardon the phrasing borrowed from a famous medieval proof for God's existence.) (*Yes, medieval indeed!*)

I call this the Tar Baby approach because it seems so benign and positive that to resist it is to be tarred with words like "intolerant" and "fundamentalist." Who doesn't want a world where people get along, respect differences, affirm peace, and acknowledge their own limitations? And who doesn't see how many different stories there are out there, so that affirming one over the others appears, at the least, impolite? Punch against this argument, and you are up to your elbow in tar. It is so pliable that it absorbs all blows. Punch again with your other hand, and you are now stuck entirely. (And don't even think of a head butt.) In the end, you are covered in tar and the Tar Baby is still smiling—soft, compliant, all sweetness and light. Or so it seems.

I'm going to argue at greater length against this view later on, but I want here to make two points. First, it sounds disconcertingly like what I have been and will be saying myself. (*Glad you see that.*) Story. Uniqueness of belief. Humility. Protean nature of truth. All things I seem to be commending.

But since it is *not* what I am saying or what I believe, I want to say concisely what I think is the enormous difference. *I believe faith is best thought of, defended, and lived out in terms of story, but I also believe that the Christian story, stated in its biblical and creedal simplicity, is God's story (therefore reality's story) and that all deviations from that story are (with God being the judge, not me or you), to the extent that they deviate, distortions of the truth.* I am willing to capitalize that last word if you wish. (*Egads! Boringly orthodox after all. No fun!*) Though I am not willing to claim that I know fully what is True, I do believe I have been given enough understanding to build a life on.

I accept that this renders me intolerant in the eyes of many. But I don't think they actually understand what tolerance means. (See my *Is God Intolerant?* if you want to know what *I* think it means.)

Which gets me to my second point. The skepticism of many Skeptical Believers is rooted less in undue rationalism and more in an uncritical acceptance of postmodernist soft-relativism and a terror of being intolerant (actually or in the perception of others). I find this especially strong among the young, the *Sesame Street* generation that has been taught that sharing the paint and the paper is the only way for everyone to make their own picture. (*So you hope to influence the young by insulting them? Nicely done.*) To them I want to say that there is nothing intolerant about believing the gospel, even if it means not believing significant parts of other stories. Not all news, after all, is good news.

And the postmodern Tar Baby is actually no more tolerant than the person, like me, who thinks the orthodox Christian story (empty tomb, Christ for all) best describes reality. Because the "affirm everyone" approach is itself an orthodoxy. It is itself *one* story, not the acceptance of many stories. In fact, it rejects key elements (often the defining elements) of every story that it pretends to affirm. And it demands that you bow to its orthodoxy or it will call you nasty names.

More on all this in due time, but I want to get this on the table early. I do not wish to be part of building a Maginot Line. Neither do I want to fall off the other side of the horse in embracing the smiling intolerance of postmodern tolerance. I want to stay on the horse and ride it as far as it wants to take me. (*Mixed metaphors for sale!*)

2. A PROFILE OF THE SKEPTICAL BELIEVER

A SIDE ORDER OF SPIRITUALITY: FAITH AS OPTIONAL

To be a modern believer is to recognize that in the deepest personal sense, belief is optional.

ROGER LUNDIN, *BELIEVING AGAIN*

I think that religion stops people from thinking. I think it justifies crazies. I think flying planes into a building was a faith-based initiative. I think religion is a neurological disorder.

BILL MAHER

The Skeptical Believer is keenly aware that religious faith in the modern, Western world is a choice, not a given. (Belief and faith in *something* is not optional, because everyone believes things they cannot prove, but *religious* faith is.) Furthermore, it is not a popular choice in the circles in which Skeptical Believers often find themselves. If you are drawn to the worlds of books, ideas, film, the arts, academics, or left-of-center politics— to name a few such circles—choosing faith is choosing a road less traveled. (*Thank God for progress. I mean, thank Progress for progress.*) It can even be a disqualifying choice.

Wallace Stevens saw this shift in our cultural assumptions decades ago when he wrote ("Of Modern Poetry"):

The poem of the mind in the act of finding
What will suffice. It has not always had
To find: the scene was set; it repeated what
Was in the script.
Then the theatre was changed
To something else. Its past was a souvenir.

At one time, religious faith was natural in our part of the world (as it still is in many others). "Natural" in the sense of being a given—the automatic, culturally reinforced way of explaining reality. It required no deep reflection, no wrestling, no internal conflict, no particular choosing. There were always people who rejected it, but they were a small and not particularly influential minority.

No longer—and not for quite a long time now.

The situation at the moment is more as it is with marriage. At one time, marriages were often arranged. Someone else decided who would be good for you (or for them). You were presented with a spouse, as you were presented with a religion. And you rejected either at your peril. Our views of marriage evolved to the point that each person was expected to fall in love and pick his or her own partner. They are currently evolving further, to the point where marriage is seen as an option, and it is culturally acceptable simply to live with someone for as long as is satisfying and then move on. (*Very reasonable.*)

Something similar is true of religious faith. Once your religion was decided largely by forces outside yourself. Later it was possible to choose a religion. Now you can choose to "be religious" or not. ("I'll have ethics medium-rare, with a side order of spirituality—hold the religion.") You can pick from a wide assortment of established choices or mix and match to create one of your own, for as long as it pleases you. But it certainly isn't required, nor is passionate commitment, and it might not even be advisable, depending on which circles you run in.

I think the optional nature of faith is mostly a good thing. God is not honored by coerced faith, whether the coercion is with a sword or with social pressures. Coerced faith is, in fact, not faith at all. It is simply conformity.

But this situation also creates anxiety. Since belief in God, and, more important, commitment to living out that belief, is optional, the individual must come to a decision about a matter in which there is powerful and conflicting evidence. And we are not talking about deciding which shoes to buy; we are talking about a choice that defines a life and perhaps an eternity. So much is at stake—and so much argues against whichever choice you make.

As we have seen, how we think and feel our way through this decision varies greatly from person to person. For some the decision does seem easy. The claims of faith are obviously true and match their experience, or they are obviously false and do not match their experience. But for Skeptical Believers, the choice is not easy at all. Even when they make it, they often continue to wonder whether they have chosen rightly. (For this is one of those decisions that can be reversed endlessly from moment to moment until the end of life.)

Reason, as we have seen, will support the choice either for faith or against it. It's just a matter of how you evaluate the evidence. Through much of Western history, reason seemed largely on the side of belief. (*We know a lot more now, thank you.*) For the last three hundred years, professional reasoners have more often weighed in on the side of skepticism or disbelief. At present, as Tim Keller has put it, faith is "rationally avoidable."

But if belief is "rationally avoidable," so is disbelief. Secularists often argue as though disbelief is the natural given and that belief must make an ironclad case for itself if it is to be taken seriously. You can just as easily argue the opposite—historically, religious faith is so common across so many cultures that it can more easily be called natural than can disbelief. Therefore, given the many benefits of belief (which current social science has enumerated), the burden should be on disbelief to offer ironclad arguments for why it should be embraced.

I tend to favor neutrality on where the burden of proof lies. (*How balanced of you.*) Religious faith can be culturally coerced; so can secularism (see the history of both totalitarianism and the academy for examples). I accept that faith is now optional and am comfortable with that. It creates a certain amount of anxiety in my life—knowing that I have to choose and that the choice is enormously consequential—but it also gives significance to my choice. I have chosen faith, God, and the Christian story. I can defend the choice, though I cannot prove it.

In the Old Testament, God is often shown to be disgusted with culturally coerced religion. When Israel performs the religious rituals but lacks the right heart, the result is said to be a stench in God's nostrils. All religion, apparently, is a stench in Bill Maher's nostrils. I'm more worried about the former than the latter. I don't think the Skeptical Believer should lament that faith cannot be proved, nor that our culture does not support it, nor that therefore they feel the anxiety of choice in their lives. It is the price of freedom, and it makes the choice meaningful. And God would not have it any other way.

LOOKING EVERYWHERE FOR GOD—HOUND OR HIDDEN?

To experience the absence of something or someone is not just very different from, but incompatible with, treating that something or someone as nonexistent.

ALASDAIR MACINTYRE, *EDITH STEIN*

At least to pray is left, is left.
O Jesus! in the air
I know not which thy chamber is,—
I'm knocking everywhere.

EMILY DICKINSON

The question "Does God exist?" can be addressed at many levels—from the highest, most abstract and abstruse philosophical argumentation to the hollowness in the pit of your stomach. And every place between.

It's an important question, no doubt, but it is not the question that many people, including most Skeptical Believers, are actually asking. The more pointed question is, "Can God be found—be known?" More pointed still, "Can I trust God?" Or, with a touch of complaint verging on accusation, "Why does God seem far away?"

Poets and poet-songwriters have long been looking for God. Sometimes successfully, sometimes not. Emily Dickinson says, "I'm knocking everywhere." Bob Dylan, a century later, uses the same metaphor—"Knock, knock, knockin' on heaven's door." (At least he seems to know which door to knock on, but in another song he worries that heaven's door may close before he gets in.)

Deus absconditus—God as hidden, secret, cryptic, even absent—is Luther's term (building on Aquinas). God both reveals and conceals himself. Now he's here, now he's not. Theologians debate it, many people live it. Even those who accompanied Jesus and felt his power were sometimes confused as to who, exactly, he was.

Evangelicals don't much like this notion of a hidden God. Not cheery enough, perhaps. Better to emphasize God's availability. Always present, ready to help and to speak, if only we have ears to hear. ("What a friend we have in Jesus," says the hymn.)

And then there is this other truth about God. He's also a bloodhound. So says the late Victorian poet Francis Thompson in "The Hound of Heaven." In that poem, it's you and I who are doing the hiding, and God is a bloodhound always pursuing:

I fled Him, down the nights and down the days;
I fled Him, down the arches of the years;
I fled Him, down the labyrinthine ways
Of my own mind; and in the mist of tears
I hid from Him...

And Gerard Manley Hopkins, in his lighter moods, finds God absolutely everywhere—in the kestrel flying overhead, in the dappled things of nature, in the colors of the dragonfly, in the sunrise ("ah! bright wings"), in his laboring neighbor's face. In fact, he declares that "Christ plays in ten thousand places." How can one *not* see God?—he's crying out from every nook and cranny!

So which is it? Is God hiding, not there, not listening (or, even more maddeningly, listening but not answering), absent, on vacation (you know how easy it is for God to lose track of time—millennia can pass while he attends to an itch), playing hard to get, mysterious? Or is he always hanging around, always waving his hand (hoping we'll notice), always speaking (hoping we'll listen), always available (hoping we'll make ourselves available too), always, as the hymn says, wanting to be our friend?

You know what I'm going to say. (*Yes, you're nothing if not predicable.*) I'm going to say both. Both/and, not either/or.

God reveals. God conceals. God is in his creation and wishes a relationship with it. God is beyond and altogether different from his creation. God draws near to those who seek him. God is not a dog who comes when you whistle. God is intimate and loving. God is fearful and strange.

I believe everyone is born with a God-hunger. We are made, as Augustine and others have said, to be always restless until we find our rest in the one who made us. That hunger can be misdirected to other things, and often is. Even when it is directed toward God, that hunger is not always satisfied.

Many times we wish it were different. We would like God to be as dependable as the morning paper—always there, to be picked up or not as we desire, waiting patiently for us to work up sufficient interest.

Or, when we do seek God, we want him on call, like a loyal butler, standing in the wings waiting for the bell to ring. But he's not that way. Sometimes we ring and ring and God never comes, or so it seems. (Paul Moses argues that God is more likely to show himself to those who are seeking a relationship and less likely to those who are merely seeking information.)

I'm not being entirely fair to us. Our motives can be sincere and our attitudes appropriate and still there can seem to be nobody home. (Consider the long, dark night of the soul of Mother Teresa.)

This is the human condition, and I, for one, have accepted it. (*You have a choice?*) Even the Hopkins who found Christ in ten thousand places also knew profound darkness. He declares, "No worst, there is none. Pitched past pitch of grief... Comforter, where, where is your comforting?" And in another poem, he proclaims, "My lament / Is cries countless, cries like dead letters sent / To dearest him that lives alas! away."

In feeling God sometimes close, sometimes far away, I am experiencing what people of faith have always experienced—throughout the Bible (think Psalms) and since. Even God knows the feeling. The same Jesus who says, "I and the father are one," asks on the cross why the Father has abandoned him.

What none of the biblical people of faith did was stop looking. I can understand why anyone might be an atheist. The evidence for God is not irrefutable, and humans are very good at refuting whatever does not appeal to them. What I understand less well is why anyone would stop looking.

How can you decide at fifteen or twenty-five or sixty-five that there is no God and then not at least keep the question open for the rest of your life—hungry for further information? Is there really a bigger question? Does anything change our understanding of and acting in the world more than the answer to this question?

Which means, to be fair, that I have to allow the possibility that the answer to the question is, "No, there is no God." (*That's what I've been trying to tell you, egghead.*) I have to be open to the evidence too. Maybe that God-hunger is just wishing. Maybe we are, after all, just accidental creatures on a smallish planet revolving around a minor star in one of countless galaxies, waiting for extinction—personal and planetary. That this is a grim view doesn't make it untrue. And one can gloss it over with more positive spins, as many do. (*As if you aren't spinning yourself.*)

But it's not my view. It's not a view that logic or the evidence compels me to adopt, so I do not adopt it. I believe I am offered, and have accepted, a place in a better story. My story has both dark nights of the soul and mountaintop experiences. It has a God who died to be known and yet can never be fully known. It has a God who hides and one who plays in ten thousand places. With the poets and songwriters, I plan to keep knock, knock, knocking on every door. Nothing else seems to me reasonable.

LUKEWARM: THE FEAR OF BEING SPEWED

Master, what is this which now I hear?
What people is this, which seem so overcome with pain?
And he to me: 'This miserable manner
The melancholy souls maintain of those
Who lived without disgrace or praise.
Mingled are they with that cowardly choir
Of angels, who were neither rebels
Nor were faithful to God, but were for themselves.

DANTE, *THE INFERNO* (CANTO III)

Lord, not you, it is I who am absent.

DENISE LEVERTOV, "ABSENT"

When I was a kid, I worried a fair amount about being spewed. The preacher or Sunday school teacher would cite Revelation 3:16 and then, I was quite sure, look straight at me: "Because you are lukewarm, and neither hot nor cold, I will spew you out of my mouth." Some translations have "spit" and others "vomit" (cue Wayne and Garth), but any way you put it, it's a serious declaration that ought to cause serious reflection by more than just young boys in church.

I think it's an especially disturbing verse for Skeptical Believers—and should be. Neither hot nor cold is an apt description of the person paralyzed by too much thinking and too little committing, who neither abandons faith nor fully commits to it. And Dante has an especially large place in hell for those, along with some of the fallen angels, who had neither rebelled nor committed but "were for themselves." (*Dante? Angels? Hell? Have you checked the calendar lately?*)

We Skeptical Believers would like to think we are not "for self" so much as we are "for truth." (*Ahh, truth. Now there's something I like to talk about!*) We only want to believe and live what is true, and it doesn't seem selfish to ask for that. And it isn't selfish, as long as we don't use our desire for *truth* as an excuse for never committing to anything that can't fully satisfy our desire for *certainty*.

Desiring truth is not selfish; requiring certainty is. It is insisting that God and life provide you with a level of proof about ultimate things that will make your own commitments risk-free. "I will commit as soon as all my questions have been answered to my satisfaction and I am convinced there is no possibility of this commitment not working out in the way I would like." (Try that with a job offer or marriage proposal.)

It is important to make distinctions here:

You don't get spewed for having questions, even serious doubts and objections.

You don't get spewed for not feeling close to God at times, maybe most of the time.

You don't get spewed for feeling angry with God.

You don't get spewed for being upset with other Christians and the church.

You don't get spewed for being a sinner or broken or just messing up.

You don't get spewed for being often wrong in your theology.

You don't even get spewed for not believing in God. This frightening biblical spewing prophecy is spoken to a lackadaisical New Testament church. It is aimed at lazy, indifferent believers, not nonbelievers—which is why Skeptical Believers need to pay attention.

When and why, then, *do* you get spewed? (*Spewed? How intolerant. How messy!*) These are my guesses:

You risk getting spewed for downplaying what is at stake.

You risk getting spewed for prolonged indifference.

You risk getting spewed for putting off commitment interminably.

You risk getting spewed for being a professional doubter rather than a reluctant one.

You risk getting spewed for playing games—intellectual and otherwise.

You risk getting spewed for blaming life and others for you own spiritual sloth.

You risk getting spewed for not valuing properly things of ultimate value.

In summary, you risk getting spewed for refusing your place in the story that is offered you.

People in my boyhood subculture talked a lot about "losing your faith." When someone says, "I lost my faith," the sympathetic me wants to offer them comfort and conversation. The snarky me wants to ask, "Have you looked in your sock drawer?"

Losing your faith—in anything important—can be extremely painful, because a faith in something important is usually at the center of your life and its loss lessens your sense of purpose and meaning. It can feel like a betrayal, even if you're the one doing the leaving.

But I find that many don't lose faith or leave faith so much as stagnate in some feeble version of faith. Personally, the story is hardest for me to believe and live when I play my role in it weakly. I become like a bad actor in a play who condemns the play for not being very good. If I am a lousy Hamlet, it's probably not Shakespeare's fault.

I think the Inner Atheist is happier when you have feeble faith than if you abandon faith altogether. (*Please don't speculate about my happiness. Fact is, I'm never happy. It's too risky.*) If you clearly and irrevocably adopt some other story, then the Inner Atheist has less to do and a lot less fun. (Perhaps the Inner Atheists of the professional, book-writing atheists take long naps. Or maybe the atheists' version of the Inner Atheist is the Inner Believer, whispering to them that maybe there is a God after all.)

When I was a kid, I thought the only way to prove I wasn't lukewarm was to tell the guy on the bus next to me about Jesus, or to be a missionary to Africa (where I was certain I would die prematurely and violently). I didn't do either one, and I'm still here, pretty sure I haven't yet been spewed. So I think it's going to take more than that to get God to give up on me. Which, in fact, God never will. And—as a Skeptical Believer—that is my greatest reason for hope.

QUESTIONS DO NOT HURT GOD'S FEELINGS

"My God, my God, why have you abandoned me?"

MATTHEW 27:46

When I was a kid, I worried less about making God angry than I did about hurting Jesus' feelings. I had a keen sense that he had suffered a lot *for* me (before I even existed), and I didn't want him to suffer any more *on account of* me now. So I tried to be the best kid I could be—for hours at a time. I still think it was an honorable impulse, and I'm probably the worse for not feeling it as strongly as an adult. (*Save yourself the guilt trips. No God, no guilt. It's easy.*)

But I no longer believe what some of my Sunday school teachers suggested: that questions and doubts put you in trouble with God. I don't think God is that easily upset. God has heard it all. You have never had a fresh doubt or question. This is not to be dismissive of your questionings; it is intended as an encouragement to get them on the table. God knows your heart and mind anyway, so you may as well be open with him.

God even asks himself searing questions. You have nothing to say to God that is as pointed and painful as the question Jesus asked on the cross: "My God, my God, why have you abandoned me?" If one believes, as I do, in the doctrine of the Trinity, then this is a question God is asking himself. If there is, as I believe, an eternally intimate, inseparable, monotheistic fellowshipping among the three aspects of the Godhead (I'm sure this description is not adequate), then this is an internal question of ultimate significance expressing indescribable pain. There is endless theological richness and mystery in that short question, including putting the lie to any view of God as an impassive Unmoved Mover or detached Watchmaker (see the Greek and Enlightenment philosophers and too many contemporary Christians).

If God asks himself such questions, why hesitate to ask yours? Why assume God will be shocked, angry, hurt, or uninterested? Make a list of all the difficult questions asked in the Bible—including many which express doubt about God and his goodness (start with the book of Job, one of the oldest stories in the Bible, then move to the Psalms and the Gospels). It's a long list. And, of course, those questions aren't always answered, at least not in ways that make the questions disappear.

The best advice I have heard about what to do with your feelings about God (from Ben Patterson's fine book on praying the Psalms—*God's Prayer Book*) is to "talk to God about how you feel about God." This includes your doubts that God is even there to hear you.

Or you can do what we often do when we have a problem with someone—we talk to other people about the person and about the problem. Rick has done something that bothers me. (*Yes, he really let you down. You have every right to feel offended.*) I talk to other people about Rick—what he has done and how I feel about it and what's fair. I talk about Rick to myself in my own head. I construct imagined conversations with Rick—some of which turn out well (Rick admits he's wrong) and some of which don't (Rick punches me in the nose). I perhaps read articles or books that offer advice on dealing with conflict or on the issue I have with Rick.

We Skeptical Believers often do this with God. We have issues. We talk to other people about God and our issues with God. We conduct endless interrogations and analyses and ruminations in our head concerning God. We read articles and books (like this one) and the writings of past believers who have struggled with similar issues. It's like studying for a test that we never take or researching a book that we never write. We need just a little more information, a little more thought about this God stuff.

At some point, I need to talk to Rick. At some point, I need to talk to God.

Talking *with* someone rather than *about* someone makes that person more real. Rick is no longer an abstraction, a mental construct, an issue. Rick is the fellow sitting across from me and responding to what I have to say. Rick listens to my story and has a story of his own. Together we try to find a story we both can live in peacefully.

Similarly with God. The best way to move God from being an abstract issue in your life is to talk to him (and if saying "her" instead helps make the conversation possible, then go ahead). Tell God your worries, your pain, your doubts, your questions—even your accusations. Ask why he feels so far away, why you lost the one you loved, why the world he created is so screwed up, why your fellow believers are so obtuse. Or even, if you must, ask him why he has abandoned you. But also listen.

Give God the benefit of the doubt. Literally. If you are unsure that God exists, or that God is good, or that God has treated you fairly, and yet you are also not sure of the opposite, then do yourself the favor of voting for God—with your life. Talk to him, with your mouth and with your hands and feet. Acting is way of talking to God. We can do the acts of faith when the words of faith seem inadequate. This is not hypocrisy. It is simply staying in the story.

WANTING WHAT YOU CAN'T HAVE: CERTAINTY AS METAPHYSICAL GLUTTONY

I've always courted a lover I could not have—certainty.

JOHN SUK, *NOT SURE*

Hobbits… liked to have books filled with things that they already knew, set out fair and square with no contradictions.

J.R.R. TOLKIEN, *THE LORD OF THE RINGS*

I've had my say about certainty in a previous book (*The Myth of Certainty*) and elsewhere within this one. But I'm a broken record on this subject, so I'm going to say some more.

I've argued that if you have certainty (actually certitude, a different thing) about matters of faith, I, for one, do not want to try persuading you otherwise. But I've also argued that if you don't have it, faith does not require it. And now I want to add that if you don't have it, you shouldn't even want it. Which, I realize, is like telling an American male he shouldn't want junk food during the Super Bowl.

We want certainty because certainty is tied to security, and the desire to be secure—safe—is one of the two or three most basic human desires. It feels safer when we know exactly how things are—with crossing the street and strange dogs, but also with God and the future and truth and the afterlife and so on. So any offer of certainty-security-safety is a very attractive offer. And in a contest between someone offering a sure thing and someone offering a maybe thing, who isn't going to take the sure thing?

My answer to that question is "me." I will take the maybe thing over the sure thing if I think it likely the person offering the sure thing is Blowing Smoke. When the magazine ad says, "Earn $10,000 a month from the comfort of your own home," I don't even read the next line. When the apologist—religious or secular—offers me a tidy, all-questions-answered theology or ideology, I smile wanly, make my polite excuses, and comment on the weather. ("You say there is/isn't a God and you can prove it? Hmm. Looks like rain, don't you think?")

I am not arguing that there are no answers to hard questions. (I wouldn't be using up my dwindling life writing this book if I thought that.) I'm arguing that most answers to ultimate questions should be "best shot" responses (as in "this is my best shot at responding to the question") rather than "the answer" answers that expect no rebuttals. I suppose that once again I am arguing for human humility when confronting the human condition, even while declaring "the hope that is within us."

Confidence is a good thing, but with matters of faith it is closer to *assurance* than it is to certainty. And that assurance is a ground of faith, based on God's character and the history of God's faithfulness (as recorded in the Bible, in subsequent history, and in your own life). Combine certainty with condescension and you get smugness, a common trait of culture warriors on all sides. Combine uncertainty with fear (unwillingness to risk) and you get paralysis, a common trait of skeptics and cynics.

Again, if you are certain in your explanations of "the ways of God to man" (Milton), more power to you. But if you are not, don't pine for certainty. Demanding certainty is metaphysical gluttony. You are insisting on a state of knowledge inconsistent with the human condition. It's like demanding to be eight feet tall so you can dominate at basketball without having to work at it (rather than accepting that you are five-foot-eleven and therefore need to work on your ball-handling skills). It's like demanding to be rich and making that the focus of your life, rather than simply desiring enough to meet your needs, with perhaps some seasons of abundance here and there.

In short, quit whining. (*Ooh, tough guy!*) (This is my drill sergeant side; I also have a sympathetic side.) You can't be sure? You have your doubts?

You'd rather know for certain? You're in pain? Welcome to the human condition. Welcome to the world of Abraham, Mary, Thomas, Paul, Augustine, Teresa, Thomas More, Pascal, Newman, Hopkins, Eliot, Weil, O'Connor, Solzhenitsyn, and Taylor. (*We've seen this list before. Be more creative!*) Yes, I put my name in the list. You should put yours in too, unless you think that, somehow, life should be easier for you.

When I say above that I will take the "maybe thing" over the "sure thing," I don't want to suggest that the best I can work up for faith is "a wishin' and a hopin'" (Burt Bacharach via Dusty Springfield, 1960s). I can do a lot better than that. Even though I'm not much of a fan of certainty, I do, as I say, believe in assurance, which I define as *confidence based on trust earned by past performance*. (This could be a definition of faith as well.) When my friend says he will do something important, I feel confident—assured—that he will do it, because he has done what he said in the past. I am not, however, certain (no possibility of being wrong). Maybe this time he won't. But I feel a life-tested assurance that he will, and that frees me from anxiety or feeling the need to ask him to prove that he is going to do it.

Similarly with God and the things of God. I have enough evidence, enough records, enough witnesses, enough experience in my own life to give me assurance that God exists and that he rewards those who seek him. Certainty, no. Assurance, yes. Feelings, sometimes. Commitment, so far. What is needed to make it to the end of the race? Perseverance, grace, and the encouragement of a cloud of witnesses (past and present).

TIRED OUT TRYING TO BELIEVE: SINGING THE SOUL-WEARY BLUES

I got the Weary Blues
And I can't be satisfied.
Got the Weary Blues
And can't be satisfied—
I ain't happy no mo'
And I wish that I had died.

LANGSTON HUGHES, "THE WEARY BLUES"

I was much too far out all my life
And not waving but drowning.

STEVIE SMITH, "NOT WAVING BUT DROWNING"

Wars are always lost, and The War always goes on;
and it is no good growing faint.

J.R.R. TOLKIEN

Wrestling with God is exhausting. Ask Jacob. It's even harder to wrestle with nothingness. God at least holds on to you. Skeptical Believers tend to be wrestlers.

Struggling with ultimate questions is like a nineteenth-century boxing match with no predetermined number of rounds; you just fight until someone gets knocked out or gives up. How many rounds in a wrestling match over God? As many as you like. (*There's the bell. Come on, whatta ya say? Let's go another round!*) As many as there are questions: God or no God? If God, good or indifferent? Close or distant? Listening or busy elsewhere? Friend or tormentor? If no God, from where come values—real values, not opinions? From where comes meaning? Where are we going? Making it up as we go? What can we trust? Who can we trust? What lasts? What about suffering? (*What about other people's gods?*) Why am I not happy? Why do the happy people irritate me? What about science? What about reason? How do I avoid looking foolish? Does faith require hanging out with those people? (*Why not just be good on your own?*) Is there any such thing as good if I'm on my own? What's worth committing to? What's worth taking a chance on? How much risk is too much risk? (*How long do the odds have to be before it's foolish?*) What works? Why isn't it working for me? What does "works" mean? How can I know if I'm having a good life if I don't know what a good life is? (*Don't stop now. I can help you generate questions forever!*)

Add your own questions to that list, stir in long periods of pondering and brooding, fold in generous amounts of confusion and pain, add a big pinch of skepticism and disappointment, then bake at any temperature (low to high) for whatever time suits you (six months, six years, a lifetime). (*Answer C, Dan—"a lifetime."*) That's the recipe for the Uncertainty Soufflé. (*Oh, now it's food metaphors. Very homey.*)

If it were a song instead of a soufflé, we'd be talking the blues. Lots of pain, lots of struggle, lots of weariness—that is, lots of life. Not necessarily intense crisis-pain, oftentimes just long-haul, low-grade, worn-out weariness. To riff on Langston Hughes, "I got the soul-weary, wrestlin'-with-what-it's-all-about blues."

One reason it's exhausting is that the struggle is never simply a matter of trying to find an intellectual answer to an abstract question. Belief struggles are, as we've seen, whole-person, whole-life struggles. They involve our temperament, character, mental habits, relationships, history, education, health, cultural conditioning, spiritual condition, life experiences, and what we ate for breakfast. And anxiety about these things will unsettle not just our minds, but everything about and around us. If we are unsettled about ultimate things, it is difficult to be settled about everyday things.

We get the soul-weary blues in part because we realize, at some level, how much is at stake. We're not talking hem-lengths or car payments here. We're talking time and eternity and what does it all mean and why do I have a life anyway? Unlike so many questions we deal with, the answer to this one really matters. Matters most of all. The stakes are the highest possible, and therefore the level of anxiety is, in one sense, entirely justified.

If spiritual anxiety burned calories, spiritual wrestlers would look anorexic. Many fret more over belief than a strung-out junkie over the next fix. And it can leave you feeling exhausted. Going round and round—the grindstone of the mind—saps your energy, saps your joy, saps your will. (*I find it quite invigorating myself.*) It can make you unpleasant to be around, most of all to yourself.

We spiritual wrestlers are like some anorexics in another way—a part of us actually likes this thing that debilitates us. We like thinking of ourselves as a little smarter, a little tougher to fool, a little more demanding than the average person. In fact, one part of us actually loves the whole endless enterprise—our Inner Atheist. "Come on, let's go another round. Just for fun." (*I just said that. You're mocking me, right?*) "You and me and the meaning of life. Come on, give me your best shot. Let me put my sleeper hold on you just one more time."

So what do you do about all this? (*Nothing really. Just keep chewing. It's what you know best. Don't let this guy talk you out of being who you really are.*)

Well, first you name it. You call it what it is.

Okay, what is it?

Some people call it bad names (and call you bad names for showing signs of it). They call it disbelief or backsliding or wishy-washiness or weakness or being blown by every wind (see the epistle of James), or indecisiveness, or even the demon of intellectualism (I've had that one laid on me).

I mostly call it soul weariness. It's *the condition that results from being hyper-reflective about something of great value with no definitive way of coming to a certain conclusion and no requirement to do so.* You're sitting in your corner of the ring, having gone a thousand rounds, slumped on your stool, blood dripping from your nose, one eye swollen shut, and—clang— there goes the bell for another round. God or no God? If God, good or indifferent? Close or distant?...

Having named it (and you may very well name it differently), I think then you have a decision to make. Keep fighting or throw in the towel?

You aren't going to win this fight. Paul didn't win it. Augustine didn't win it. Emily Dickinson didn't win it. Melville didn't win it (of whom Hawthorne said, "He can neither believe nor be comfortable in his unbelief; and he is too honest not to try to do one or the other"), Camus (one of the better fighters I know of) didn't win it. I didn't win it. And neither will you. (*Come on. Don't let him discourage you. Let's just work this through once more. Give it more time.*)

My counsel is not to throw in the towel in the sense of giving up on the questions. It is to make a commitment in the midst of the questions. It is to choose a story to live by, letting the questions simmer in the background as you get on with the business of living as worthy a life as you can. If we lived forever in this world, we could afford to fight on endlessly without resolution. We don't, and so we can't. Or at least we shouldn't, if we want our lives to count for something.

If we do commit to a story—and I'm advocating for The Story—some of those questions that seemed so crucial will begin to seem less so. They won't have been answered so much as they will seem less important than the task of being the character you are called to be in the story whose call you have accepted. We may find ourselves saying, "I don't understand, but I do know what to do. I will do what people in this story have always done." This is not robotic obedience to something outside myself; this is a carefully considered judgment that *the story is wiser than I am.* I freely choose it because it best explains to me my own experience of the world. (*Wait, wait. You haven't heard all the other possible stories yet. Maybe there's a better one. Hold off on this!*)

I don't *know*—in the sense of "no possibility of being wrong"—that there is a God who made and loves and calls me. I will never, in this life, know that for certain. I do know that having committed myself to this story, I find the possibilities for meaning and love and purpose multiplied beyond anything I could reasonably hope for. I have found that to be enough—more than enough. More than I deserve. I call that grace.

The story of faith is a gracious gift to me. I accept it. My questions continue, but my soul-numbing wrestling days are over.

Somewhat paradoxically, perhaps (given that commitment sounds like effort), committing to this story can allow us to lighten up a bit. If we accept that risk and uncertainty are inherent in life (and part of what makes it interesting), then we can get over the idea that "If I just knew a little bit more, or if God would just make things a bit plainer, then I would know for sure and wouldn't have to struggle so much."

Accepting one's place in a story entails accepting the limitations on human knowledge, which can, in turn, free us from feeling obliged to figure everything out on our own. It includes living within our intellectual, emotional, and spiritual means. It's a step toward accepting what Jesus promises when he says, "I will give you rest."

RESISTING THE SPIRIT OF CALCULATION

The spirit of the Gospel is eminently that of the "open" type which gives, asking nothing in return, and spends itself for others. It is essentially hostile to the spirit of calculation, the spirit of worldly prudence and above all to the spirit of religious self-seeking and self-satisfaction.

CHRISTOPHER DAWSON, *THE DYNAMICS OF WORLD HISTORY*

After looking for what no reflection can ever bring about anyway, one breaks with the calculating wisdom of the world, the "wait and see" and the dallying with a decision.

PAUL HOLMER

My name is Dan, and I am a calculator. (*Hello, Dan.*)

Maybe that's why I am convicted (an interesting word—convicted—with its dual senses of moved by the Spirit and nailed for a crime) by Christopher Dawson's claim that the spirit of the gospel is "hostile to the spirit of calculation." It is an especially troublesome claim for a Skeptical Believer because we are, by nature and practice, masters of calculation. (*You're talking quantity, not quality—right?*)

How likely is it that there is a God? we ask. What are the odds? What evidence weighs for it; what evidence weighs against it? What would be the cost of being wrong about this? What's the minimum commitment necessary to be on the right side in case there is a God? If there is a God of love, wouldn't he (she? it?) probably let anyone off the hook for not believing anyway—especially if they were, ahem, a good person? (Am I genuinely a good person?) Is there a way of accepting all this without looking stupid or otherwise disrupting my life? (*Sure. Be spiritual without being religious. Keep it vague. That's enormously popular. It's what I've been advising all along.*)

And then there are the calculations of those who accept the call of the story of faith: What, exactly, does God require of me? How do I avoid being one of those lukewarm people who get spewed without becoming one of those annoying people who speak glibly of God speaking to them (as though they have "friended" God on Facebook)? How different do I have to be from those who don't believe any of this? Can I buy the same things, watch the same things, go to the same places, vote and speak and think the same way—or do I have to be queer (as in strange, weird, eccentric, odd, unusual)?

Why is all this calculating, according to Dawson, hostile to the spirit of the gospel? Consider the expression "looking a gift horse in the mouth." In horse-trading days, checking a horse's teeth was one way of assessing its health and therefore its value. To assess the value of a gift as one is accepting it (or worse, in order to decide whether to accept it) is a violation of the spirit of gift-giving and receiving. The gospel (the Good News of the Kingdom whose defining quality is shalom) is a gift in the form of an invitation. It is offered in a spirit of open-handed blessing. To constantly probe the gift, assessing its pros and cons, eyeing it suspiciously, calculating what's in it for me, is more than bad manners—it's a negation of the spirit of giving. (*What if one is being offered an illusion rather than a gift?*)

I once got a letter from a fellow who had left the church and faith because he was sick of Christians and of the burden of believing in God. He pronounced himself much happier among his new friends who didn't believe any of it. But he had a problem. He couldn't shake his belief that there was a God, and now he feared he was going to have to be a Christian again, and the thought made him sick. Could I help him? he asked. I wasn't feeling very tender and gracious that day. ("Sure, I can help. Turn around so I can kick you in the backside.") I told him not to do God any favors by dragging his own miserable self back to the church. If Jesus being crucified so he could be restored to a right relationship with God was inconvenient for him, then he should do everyone a favor and squash his lingering belief and concentrate on being a happy pagan. (Okay, so I'd be a lousy spiritual director.)

Does this mean we have to accept without evaluation everything that is offered to us (in the name of tolerance, perhaps)? Don't we warn children not to accept things from strangers? So why not an ongoing evaluation, calculation if you will, of the gospel story and our place in it?

Evaluation and testing—yes. Calculation and caution—not so much.

Compare it to marriage (or friendship). This person offers to share my life, to be with me in sickness and in health, in prosperity and in poverty, with the football game on and with the football game off. I do some necessary evaluation at the point that the relationship gets this serious, though I balance it against things that cannot be precisely calculated (such as love). But once I have committed myself to the relationship—to the marriage or to the friendship—I had better suspend much of the calculation.

If I continue as "relationship accountant," keeping neat columns of pros and cons, benefits and detriments, profits and losses, points won and points lost, I greatly increase the likelihood that this relationship will fail. My very method of evaluating the relationship becomes a central aspect (or characteristic) of the relationship, thereby weakening it and even contributing to its unraveling. By over-calculating, I change and damage the thing I am evaluating. (A danger whenever one reasons about anything to excess.) It's not a benign or neutral evaluation; it's an activity that alters for the worse the relationship it is evaluating.

It's something like that with the gospel and the whole story of faith. It's a gift freely offered. You are not required to accept it. You could not earn it if you tried (though many do try). It's the story of God's interaction with his creation. Maybe it's true. Maybe it's just a nice story (or terrifying, if you look at some of the details). You have to evaluate it at some level. It has to draw you, or there is no reason for you to accept it over any other story. But *you should also evaluate your evaluating process.* You should understand that there is a time for calculating and a time to cease from calculation.

Look that gift horse in the mouth if you must, but if you ever accept it (that's the "believer" part in "Skeptical Believer"), get on it and ride—and hold on tight.

SKEPTICAL ABOUT SKEPTICISM

If you tried to doubt everything you would not get as far as doubting anything.
The game of doubting itself presupposes certainty.

LUDWIG WITTGENSTEIN, *ON CERTAINTY*

Skepticism is an engine driving a great deal of intellectual progress over the last five hundred years. Questioning truth claims and not resting until one has improved on them (which therefore, of course, means never resting) has been a crucial component in advances in knowledge and practical life across the human spectrum, from pure science to engineering to the writing of history—perhaps including theology. (*The only good theology is atheology.*)

Skepticism is also one of the great roadblocks to human progress and happiness. In its determination not to be gullible, it often frightens itself away from meaning and significance, thereby making this life more sterile and insignificant than it need be. Doctrinaire skepticism says, "Don't take any chances," in a world where taking chances is the only way to a rich and meaning-filled life.

There are many kinds and degrees of skepticism. Formal, philosophical skepticism goes back 2,500 years and denies, to varying degrees, the possibility of knowing anything for certain. Some of the world's great thinkers have been skeptics or had a skeptical bent—Protagoras, Socrates, Hume, Descartes, Pascal, Oscar the Grouch. (*My kind of people, except for that French mathematician.*) These thinkers tried very hard to be logically rigorous and to fairly consider objections to their lines of thought. It's an honorable tradition. (*I'm sure Socrates is humbled by your approval.*) (Though being a world-class thinker doesn't keep you from being world-class wrong about many important things.)

On the other end of the spectrum is knee-jerk skepticism rooted in little or no grasp of logic, reason, history, or how human beings come to understanding and meaning in this world. This form of skepticism presents itself as the enemy of falsehood and delusion, but it is more often intellectual and emotional laziness. It hides behind a handful of tired clichés that are simply variations of "You can't prove that." Lazy skepticism often begets obstinacy, the stubborn refusal to seriously consider contrary evidence or other ways of making sense of the world (sometimes, as I will argue later, from a failure of the imagination). Not an honorable tradition, but one with many adherents, not a few of whom currently write books and make speeches.

Many Skeptical Believers are somewhere in between these two extremes. Neither great thinkers nor great naysayers, they bounce around like a bee in a bottle, buzzing wearily from side to side, hoping to get somewhere but forever flying into something they don't quite see. It can be an exhausting life. No observation passes by unchallenged. Every idle thought is barbecued on the grill of interrogation. (*Bees, bottles, barbecues. You are a fountain of invention—and mixed metaphors.*)

How does one get out of the bottle? A beginning, as I mentioned previously, is to turn your natural skepticism against itself. Not to eradicate it entirely (it is, after all, part of you), but to make it useful (for detecting Smoke) rather than paralyzing. When Wittgenstein says, "The game of doubting itself presupposes certainty," he is suggesting, I think, that skepticism assumes any number of unprovable things, including that truth, falsehood, doubt, proof, evidence, reason, logic, and so on are meaningful terms, that reality is knowable, and that there is value in distinguishing between true and false, real and illusory. If you really thought that reality is unknowable, it wouldn't be logical to say so, because that would mean that you know something for sure about reality, contrary to what you've just claimed. (*Medic! Aspirin! He's playing Philosopher again!*)

So even doubting operates by faith. Skepticism—the science of doubting—is based on leaps of faith. It ought—both logically and ethically—to be open, then, to leaps of faith in the spiritual realm, including the religious. If I am really a skeptic, my very skepticism should leave me open to the genuine possibility (not just a theoretic but minute possibility) that spiritual and religious claims are true and rooted in the very nature of things. Logically consistent skepticism will not prove the case for faith, but it will acknowledge that it cannot disprove it either. Each of us will make our decision on other grounds.

But is being skeptical about skepticism actually helpful to a Skeptical Believer? Does it relieve anything or move me anywhere? It might. It won't if it just gives me another thought to chew on. God knows I am a voracious chewer. It might if it gives me the courage to finally swallow. That is, if it removes an artificial obstacle to commitment and action. If it causes me to say, "I am not required by reason to think and be this way, therefore I purpose to think and be another way." Watch out for this—it might actually lead to doing something, which might reinforce believing something, which might even lead to change. It could even make you happy—sort of. It's been known to happen.

TOO SKEPTICAL—OR NOT SKEPTICAL ENOUGH?

A man who lives by his faith is necessarily isolated. At every hour of the day, he is in acute disagreement with his century.

JULIAN GREEN

Skeptics are used to being accused of being too skeptical, even cynical. Many actually hear the charge with a touch of satisfaction. ("No one's going to pull the wool over *my* eyes!"). But in my view we skeptics are often not skeptical enough.

Consider the age in which we live. (*Watch out. Sweeping generalizations ahead!*) It is generally thought an age not conducive to belief. Competing orthodoxies include many that are directly or indirectly hostile to traditional religious faith, from various "isms" (materialism, naturalism, feminism, rationalism, consumerism, postmodernism, defunct Marxism, and the like) to the simple "ism" of everyday living that looks for life purpose in toys, busyness, pleasure, and the pursuit of an elusive notion of success. (*Sounds good to me.*)

Once, it's suggested, it was easier to believe. ("The Sea of Faith / Was once, too, at the full" says the melancholic nineteenth-century agnostic poet Matthew Arnold.) Society and social institutions supported religion.

Even the great majority of intellectuals and artists supported religious faith in the West until well into the eighteenth century. Now, alas, it is not so. Hostility to religion is topped only by indifference, and that makes it hard for someone with a skeptical bent to be a believer. So they say.

I say baloney. If you are really a skeptic, resistance to religion should make it easier to believe. Your natural bent toward doubting truth claims ought to help you doubt the confused claims of our time that cast suspicion on faith at least as much as it causes you to doubt faith itself. I genuinely believe it is easier for me, personally, to be a Christian in a secular age than it would have been in any age I know of in the past.

As one who is skeptical at least around the edges, I am a natural contrarian. (Especially inside my head. Outwardly I love to get along.) Give me a fence, and I'll sit on it until I know what side you're on. Then I'll hop off on the other side. You think the poor are victims of oppression? I'll think the poor often make the bed they lie in. You think the poor are lazy? I'll counter that no one in the wide world works as hard as the poor. Same with politics, theology, sports, and snack foods.

So being a natural contrarian, my tendency in an age of faith would be to be skeptical of a faith that everyone supports without a second thought. Having been blessed by living in an age when faith is often disparaged or dismissed (especially in the academic world I have lived in), my contrarian skepticism often pushes me *toward* faith. You think religion the opiate of the masses? Then I think it's peachy. You think no reasonable person could possibly believe this stuff? (*Exactly.*) Then I think no reasonable person could possibly think that reason alone can settle what you should believe.

A very small example. I once contributed an essay on Christian humanism (of which I am a fan) to a volume honoring the memory of a much-loved professor. The last line of the essay used the word "One" in a not very subtle betrayal of my own faith in God. The academic fellow editing the book called me to ask whether I really wanted to capitalize that word. It clearly irritated him, and undoubtedly he thought it reflected badly on me as a scholar. He was giving me a chance not to embarrass myself.

Two things came immediately to my mind. The first was that the man we were honoring (who shared my faith) would not have been displeased, and maybe have been even a bit amused at my cheek. The second was, "I'm glad this reference to personal faith bugs this fellow. Maybe I should put something in there about being washed in the blood." I told him to keep it a capitalized "One." See—a contrarian (and not always cooperative).

Given that we live in a time that largely believes traditional faith passé or evil (at least among intellectuals), I'm glad I'm a skeptic. It helps me see through many of the confident secular pronouncements about what is reasonable, believable, acceptable, and relevant. If it also makes me a bit skeptical about some pronouncements coming out of parts of the church, that's okay. I need to discern the spirits there, as well.

If I sometimes need to be skeptical about external claims, I also sometimes need, as I argued earlier, to be skeptical about my own skepticism. I need to be skeptical about the many excuses, rationalizations, and self-justifications I use to deflect the call of faith on my life. When I hear myself saying, "Okay, I'm not that great a Christian, but I'm not trying for sainthood—and at least I'm not a hypocrite," I should be skeptical enough to see that for the feeble evasion that it is. The same holds if I trot out some clichéd objection to faith or the church and use that as a cover for my own flaccidity.

Can healthy skepticism be used to defuse unhealthy skepticism, or does skepticism about skepticism just lead to skepticism squared? In my own life, I think it has been more the former. When I have found myself piling up objections to faith in the past—and keeping it at arm's length— my own skepticism about my arguments and my motives have often led me back toward commitment rather than further away. The contrarian within me has addressed my Inner Atheist and said to him, "Given all your many objections to belief, I see that I need to either fish or cut bait." Then, after a pause for rhetorical affect (my Inner Atheist is a fan of rhetorical affect), I say, "I think I'll fish." (*And I'll say, "There are other boats to fish from besides this one."*)

So am I too skeptical? Maybe. But then, perhaps I'm not skeptical enough.

SKEPTICAL BELIEF—CON GAZ OR SIN GAZ

"Do you really believe that Jesus Christ was the son of God and that he came down to save the world?"

"Well, that's what I am choosing."

AN ACQUAINTANCE TO NOVELIST WALKER PERCY—AND HIS REPLY

Not all that impressive a response, is it? "Well, that's what I am choosing." Of course we don't know with what tone or energy he made that reply. Maybe it was an enthusiastic (*en-theos*, God-filled) choosing. But knowing Percy's writing, more likely it was a laconic, ambivalent, even resigned choosing—as in a choice made when no better choices were available, or when one wasn't at all certain it was the right choice. Maybe the questioner caught him at a low moment.

It brings to mind those previously considered biblical injunctions about lukewarmness and spewing. It also reminds me of my first encounter, in Europe, with the choice between "gaz" and "sin gaz" on bottles of water. "Gaz" indicated carbonation—fizz—and "sin gaz" indicated no carbonation—still water. The question is, "Can one be a believer without the fizz—or is that not belief at all?"

Skeptical Believers tend to disparage their own ability to commit. Some buy into the notion of many of their fellow believers that if there's no fizz, there's no faith. If you don't regularly feel the presence of God in your life, or love Jesus with all your heart, or know without question that all things work together for good (and so on), then you are at best "still water" and at worst no believer at all. Skeptical Believers often accept this either-or and find a place in the back pew—or fade away from faith altogether.

And why not? The Bible is death on all forms of fake faith (*Me too*): from wishy-washiness to legalism to power and status seeking to dead traditionalism to searching for thrills. Actually, Jesus is much harder on the professional and confident believers of his time than he is on the battered and doubtful ones. But let's not pretend that God desires you to be full of doubts and qualifications. I won't cite the passages that commend straightforward faith, but you and I both know they are there.

What I want to emphasize about Percy's response, however, is not the doubting (strongly implied in the "Well") but the choosing ("that's what I'm choosing"). I don't think the psychological or intellectual state in which one makes the choice is nearly as important as the fact of the choice. What I do think is important is that the choice is a living choice, not an abstract one.

It's a good thing if one has fizz accompanying his or her faith—energy, optimism, gratitude, wonder, a desire to share the Good News and shalom with others. I genuinely admire most people who have that. I do not instantly think they are naive or obtuse or less reflective than I am. (*How big of you.*) It is a gift and should be prized as such.

It *is* a gift, but I think a lot of it is given at birth, not at some later moment of conversion. We are created from the beginning with certain temperaments and personalities and ways of perceiving and expressing that will show themselves in our lives no matter what we choose to believe or how we choose to live. A Pooh will be a Pooh, and a Tigger a Tigger, and an Eeyore an Eeyore no matter what. So there will be Pooh, Tigger, and Eeyore believers, and that's just how it is. This is not shoulder-shrugging fatalism (a la Eeyore), just a recognition that God didn't make us using a cookie cutter.

So while I respect the high-octane believers, I also don't find myself wanting to be one. I don't envy what God is doing in their lives; I am grateful for whatever God is doing in mine. I think it crucial that I choose God and God's story for my life. I do not think it matters a lot in what outward style I live it. (*Same approach as with your wardrobe, huh?*)

But whether I have in fact chosen that story can only measured by what I do with my life—my everyday life. Life can only be lived day by day, not all at once in some big bang. So if faith is my choice, then it must show itself in a flow of smaller choices I make about what constitutes my life—day to day, week to week, year to year. (I'll talk about some of those choices elsewhere.)

I think it's significant that Percy used a verb tense that indicates an ongoing action ("am choosing"), not a completed one ("chose"). It suggests that he continued to choose every day—even on the gloomy days. He was repeatedly making an ongoing choice, a commitment. The Christian story was the story that he believed gave him the best shot—at truth, at meaning, at significance, at love.

I'm not sure about everything that Percy meant when he said, "Well, that's what I'm choosing." But here is what I mean when I say the same thing. "I choose to believe. That puts me as a character within this story. These are the things a believer in this story does. Since I have chosen belief—and this story—I will do these things. I have learned to trust the story. Sometimes, I even feel a little fizz."

BELIEVING AT THE BOUNDARIES

The existence of twilight is not an argument against the distinction between night and day.

SAMUEL JOHNSON

Skeptical Believers often live at the boundaries (in limbo, as we saw earlier). They are one thing, but almost another thing. (*And eventually they are no thing. Ha!*) And though the distance between those two things can seem quite small, the consequences may be all important, especially if the two things are skeptical belief and skeptical unbelief.

Personally, I believe in boundaries. I think they are real and necessary. My skin forms a boundary between the physical me and the rest of the universe. Without it, I spill out on the floor. The boundary between a universe conducive to life and one not is vanishingly small (see the anthropic principle). I also believe there are boundaries between meaningful belief and disbelief. One can cross over from one to the other—in both directions. We shouldn't pretend that boundaries don't matter or that they are necessarily artificial.

But even as a believer in boundaries, I am unsure exactly where many of them are. Some important ones have moved for me over the years, hopefully in healthier directions. (*Cue the "I was raised a fundamental-ist" stories.*) The challenge is to distinguish between God's boundaries (built into the very nature of reality) and humanly and institutionally created ones (that come and go). Sometimes they appear to match up; sometimes they don't.

I am not going to sing in praise of shifting boundaries; there's plenty of that available from the First Church of What's the Latest?, of which there are many members. But I will contend that a questioning of boundaries is an example of how the belief of a Skeptical Believer might differ from the belief of someone with a different caste of mind. If skepticism is the habit of questioning truth claims, and if I have a skeptical bent, then even *as* I believe, I am going to ask questions.

Why not? The Bible itself is filled with people asking tough questions. And many of those questions are addressed, directly or indirectly, to God—sometimes accusingly. In fact, I think there are few major biblical figure (from Adam in the Garden to St. John on the isle of Patmos) who didn't ask any tough questions or didn't ever go through a dark night of the soul. (Do you think Abraham was at peace when his son asked where the animal was that they were going to sacrifice?)

So I can fire away—and I do. But asking does not of necessity entail an-swering. Often the Bible does not answer the question or the questioner. (Jesus didn't get an answer to his most pain-filled question—at least it's not in the story.) Which suggests to me that I have a right to ask questions of God and the universe, and that both God and the universe have a right to remain silent. God is not an answer man at the beck and call of every chatterbox with a question—or a complaint.

I am not sure that the boundaries we identify are true boundaries. Per-haps the person we think is living on the edge (the ancient desert pole-sit-ters or Celtic anchorites) is actually in the center. Perhaps those in the satisfied middle are actually at the edge of disbelief, especially if engaged belief requires a radical life. If I really believe what I say I believe, could there genuinely be such little difference between how I live and how those live who claim not to believe in God at all? (I never read Jesus' comments about the sheep and the goats without thinking I may be one of the goats.)

Given all this, one of my comforts is that God is the God of the boundaries as well of the center. He loves the boundary people as much as he loves the saints, even when they screw up. He healed the child of the one who confessed his disbelief. He loved the disciples as much when they fled in terror as when they cast out demons and healed the sick. He loved Paul when Paul was killing believers and when Paul was being stoned for his belief.

This comforts me because I know well my own capacity for disbelief. Not merely intellectual disbelief ("There is no God"), but the more tangible disbelief of disobedience. As when my wife finds another person in need for us to help, and I start looking for cover. (When you're married to a rescuer, you can't avoid getting involved in the rescue. "Really," I find myself thinking, "you found an Ethiopian refugee in the parking ramp who needs us? Don't we have enough on our plate already with the single mother and her kids?")

My point is that living on the boundary is compatible with living a life of storied belief. And all my skeptical questions and complaints don't get me off the hook. If I am a Skeptical *Believer*, I have committed myself to everything that goes with engaged belief, skepticism or no. I insist on the belief part even as I defend the right (perhaps a self-granted right) to my skepticism. I have an Inner Atheist, but I also have an Inner Saint—or at least an Inner Disciple. I have consciously chosen to stay within the boundary of belief, as best as I can discern it, and I have therefore accepted my role in the story. I have not cut bait, and so I must fish.

Skeptical belief, then, need not be a synonym for tepid belief. As a skeptic, I can be as committed, even passionate, about belief as an explorer can be in the midst of a quest, even if he or she continually assesses whether this trail or that one is the best way forward. In fact, if one is skeptical, one may need more commitment than the confident believer, because one is more aware of the possibility of being wrong. It doesn't take much commitment to accept your lottery winnings, nor perhaps to accept heaven as your eternal fate if it never occurs to you that heaven might not be there. (*Which it isn't: Birth. Struggle. Death. Fini.*)

There are some common denominators in all genuine Christian belief. We can argue about what these are, but my own list includes an Emmanuel (God with Us), an empty tomb, a recognition of my own brokenness, a confession of need, an acceptance of forgiveness and grace, and a willingness to play my part in the larger story of faith.

If I have these things (and all the questions that go along with them), I do not think it matters much whether I tend toward skepticism or not.

Since I do tend toward skepticism, my form of belief will ask many questions, test the spirits, allow reason its voice, tolerate an Inner Atheist, be allergic to Blowing Smoke, and maybe humph and snort more often than others think helpful. All of that is compatible, I am confident, with a healthy version of belief.

If my skepticism begins to dominate or abuse my belief, however, then I may slide into paralysis, cynicism, naysaying, curmudgeonliness, emotional distance, and aversion to risk. I will have crossed a boundary, one that I probably did not see as I crossed it.

If so, I should consider crossing back.

3. THE STORY NATURE OF FAITH

FAITH AS STORY

Now that I am old and gray,
do not abandon me, my God,
until I proclaim your power to the next generation,
your strong arm to all who are to come.

PSALM 71:18

The Bible tells a story that is *the* story, the story of which our human life is
a part. It is not that stories are part of human life, but that human life is part
of a story.

LESSLIE NEWBIGIN, *THE OPEN SECRET*

"In the beginning, God..."

"There once was a man named Job who lived in the land of Uz."

"Now in those days a decree went out from Caesar Augustus..."

"There came a man sent from God, whose name was John."

"Jesus said, 'A man was traveling from Jerusalem to Jericho, and fell into
the hands of thieves...'"

God is telling the world a story. It begins in eternity past and stretches into eternity future. It climaxed two thousand years ago when God entered into his creation in a new way. It could reach its conclusion today—or in five thousand years. The theme of the story is shalom: all things in their created place, doing what they were created to do, in loving relationship with their Creator. And, miracle beyond miracle, it is a story into which God invites you and me as characters.

If faith were an idea, the intellect alone might be the instrument for addressing it. Since it is, instead, a life to be lived, we need story. It's no surprise, then, that the central record of faith in human history opens with an unmistakable story signature: "In the beginning... "

Why story?

Let me tell you one.

My earliest memories of movies were formed in drive-ins. Drive-ins were the product of excess land, America's love affair with the automobile, and our great desire to be entertained cheaply. Drive-ins were invented in the 1930s and reached their peak in the 1950s, just in time for a small, displaced Texas boy to learn about miracles. It was at a drive-in in Santa Barbara, California, out by the airport in Goleta, where the gardeners and maids lived, that I first witnessed the parting of the Red Sea.

Don't think you've seen the parting of the Red Sea until you've seen it on a huge outdoor screen, through your car windshield, holding a bucket of butter-wet popcorn. Charlton Heston stood up on that rock, with the weaselly Edward G. Robinson whining about the approaching Egyptian army, and he said something about the power of the Lord and raised his staff and—yowsers!—the waters boiled for a moment and then separated into towering walls on either side of a strip of dry land right through the middle of the sea. It was enough to make me stop chewing on the popcorn and start chewing on the idea that God was God and that, when he put his mind to it, he could do eye-popping things. (*Hey, it was just a movie. You know, props, make-up, fake pyramids.*)

Compare that experience with presenting a nine-year-old boy with the following proposition: God is powerful.

Certainly true. Nothing I would argue against, then or now. But also nothing that would make me stop chewing on my popcorn.

"Okay," you say. "But I'm not a nine-year-old boy, and Charlton Heston talks like a robot the whole movie, and besides, the special effects are primitive at best. The burning bush looks less believable than a

Saturday-morning cartoon. If you want to prove that God exists, you are going to have to do a lot better than that." (*Hear, hear.*)

Prove that God exists? I don't aim to prove that God exists. God exists or does not exist apart from anyone's proving or disproving. I want to tell you a story because I think it's more helpful. And I think that's all I can do, all the Bible does, and all that you and I need. Having a plot for your life is better than having a proof.

If that seems anti-intellectual, let me remind you that understanding stories involves the intellect; it simply involves more than the intellect. It is helpful to bring intelligence—at least story intelligence—to the story experience. But also bring your emotions and intuitions and imagination and, yes, your body. When I saw those waters part, I felt it in my stomach as well as in my brain. My breath caught and my pulse quickened. I was not just seeing something, much less just thinking something, I was experiencing something. I was, for those moments, in the middle of a story, standing with those frightened Jews, caught up in a miracle. (*So you liked the movie. Can you prove it ever happened?*)

It is now many years and a few educational degrees later. I can reason as carefully as the next fellow. I understand the value of propositions and evidence. And yet, if I had to choose, I prefer stories. (But I don't believe I have to choose—my story includes the appeals of reason.)

What is it about the nature of stories that makes them the single best vehicle for understanding one's experience and expressing one's faith? Most of the answers have something to do with creation—that is, with how we're made and the nature of the world.

We are intricate and integrated creatures, and, as I claimed earlier, stories are effective because they engage every part of us—intellect, emotion, will, body, and spirit. Anything that activates all of you is more powerful in the long run than something that activates only part of you. When we engage in an important story (hearing it or living it), less important things tend to fade away.

Human beings are biologically designed to be storytellers and story listeners. The brain is flooded with an endless barrage of data. It seeks to organize that data into clusters of related material that can be made use of and remembered. The best way the brain has found to do this is to make a story out of the data.

So the brain constantly searches for a narrative thread in the chaos of information coming its way. God made the brain this way. So it's no surprise that faith, in the Bible and in subsequent history, is presented to us in the form the brain likes best. We need to remember many things (including the things that God has done in the past), so God gave us stories.

We also are made for stories because we have been created as social creatures. We are made to be in relationship—with God, with the rest of creation, and with each other. The single most common and powerful way we relate to each other is by exchanging stories. We do it constantly, usually unaware that stories flow out of us like water out of a spring.

We tell many stories each day of our lives, even if we only tell them to ourselves. We constantly invite stories from each other: "How's it going?" "What have you been up to?" "Did you hear what happened?" "You aren't going to believe what I heard!" That ubiquitous question we ask when someone we know walks in the door—"How was your day?"—is a story prompt. And we don't want one-word answers: "Fine." We want to hear *stories* about the day, because then we can relive it with that person, as social creatures want to do. Stories give us the best chance of sharing the life of someone we care about, including God.

There are other qualities of story that make it the single best way to conceive of faith, some of which we will consider, but next I want to explore a specific story, a story of the Israelites crossing a large body of water, and it's not the one in the movie.

AND THEN GOD CREATED STORIES

In the beginning, God...
GENESIS 1:1A

Stories are God's idea. God is the one who created stories—the form of story—and us as story-shaped creatures. He has chosen story as the primary way to present himself to his creation. The Bible does not simply contain stories, it reflects God's choice of the story configuration as the primary means by which to tell us about himself and how to be in right relationship with him. It is also the form God has chosen to preserve that knowledge over many, many generations.

The Bible understands that stories are not only central to an individual's faith, they are also the natural carriers of faith from one generation to the next. The people in the Old Testament are constantly reminded of their master story—they are the people God rescued out of Egypt—and are admonished to shape their lives around that fact. Tell the stories to the children, read the newly rediscovered Scriptures by the wall of Jerusalem as you rebuild, hear from the prophets the stories of God's faithfulness in the past and the possibilities for the future. When God rescues you, tell the story (as Psalm 102 instructs):

Let this be written for a future generation,
that a people not yet born may praise the Lord.

Who is this future generation for whom the story has been recorded? It includes, among others, you and me. How is it we have the opportunity to know the God who created us? Because someone lived the story, and someone else told the story, and someone wrote down the story, and others chose to repeat the story, and many were willing to die for the story. And so, generation after generation after generation, the story of God's love for his creation has been told—and we are the beneficiaries.

Which prompts a question. Are we going to be the generation that does not pass on the story? (*I hope so, but I'm not as optimistic as I used to be.*) Stories are never more than a generation away from extinction. Our institutions for the elderly are filled with stories that are disappearing every day as those who lived them disappear from among us. So too will the story of faith, unless we tell it—in ways that draw people to make that story their own.

The Bible is many things, but among the most important, it is a big storybook devoted to memory. Not memories in the sentimental sense, but memory in the crucial sense of understanding where you come from and what you are to do. And the key to memory is story. The Bible is a book of stories in many different forms—poetry, biography, songs, history, letters, and more. It is a collection of stories that are chapters of the one great story: the story of God and his love for his creation. This is the meaning, says the Bible, of the story we call human history: God made us, God loves us, God calls us. That is the master plot of the greatest story ever told.

If you do not understand this story, you will never correctly understand who you are or why you are here. Americans have a great preoccupation with the self—self-analysis, self-help, self-fulfillment, and on and on. (*Don't forget "self-delusion."*) Do you want to understand yourself? Do you want to know the meaning of life? Or what you are to do? Let me tell you a story: "In the beginning God... " That is the opening line of the story of God's relationship with his creation. It is the story by which all other stories, including our individual stories, are to be understood.

The Bible offers a master story that we are invited to make our personal story. (Invited, not coerced.) We become characters in that story. If we join the story, we have both rights and responsibilities. One of those responsibilities is to remember what God has done and to tell it to the next generation.

Consider the story in the book of Joshua (chapters 3 and 4) of a second miraculous crossing of water in the Old Testament. It's not as famous as the crossing in Egypt that wowed me at the movies, but just as instructive. This is the crossing of the Jordan River into the Promised Land. Moses has died, and the nation of Israel is now under the leadership of Joshua (a leader, by the way, being primarily a steward of a story). They arrive at the river and find it at flood stage. How are they going to get across?

God tells Joshua to command the priests carrying the Ark of the Covenant to step into the river, and when they do so, the river stops flowing (skeptics may prefer the landslide upstream theory for a naturalistic explanation). They stand in the middle of the riverbed while the entire nation crosses. When everyone has crossed, God does an interesting thing. He tells Joshua to appoint one person from each tribe to go back into the riverbed where the priests are standing and pick up a stone.

They are to make a monument of these stones on the other side of the river "to serve as a sign among you. In the future, when your children ask you, 'What is the meaning of these stones?' tell them that the Jordan stopped flowing in the presence of the Ark of the Covenant of the Lord.... These stones are to be a memorial for the people of Israel forever."

This is a passage about the importance of memory, about the importance of telling stories. The nation of Israel had a problem with memory lapses. The prophets (who were primarily storytellers) were always urging them to remember the stories of the past because they were the key to the present and future. (Think of the prophet Joel, as we saw previously, commanding the people: "Tell your children about it, and let your children tell their children, and their children from generation to generation.")

When Israel remembered the stories that told them who they were, where they had come from, and who their God was, they prospered. When they quit telling the stories, they no longer understood who they were, and they invited disaster. And the same is true with us.

This is why Joshua ordered each of the tribes of Israel to contribute a rock to commemorate God's provision in leading them across the river Jordan. The rock monument in their midst is a story prompt. It will cause the children of the next generation to ask, "Why are these rocks here?" That question will prompt the story, and a new generation will understand the power of God.

This story in Joshua ends with these words: "He did this so that all the nations of the earth may know that the hand of the Lord is powerful, and so that you may always fear the Lord your God."

"The Lord is powerful." That is a proposition. A declaration of fact. A statement.

It is true. But by itself it doesn't have a lot of impact. It hangs suspended in the land of abstract assertion. To be meaningful to human beings, it must be given the body and blood of story—as it is in the two stories of crossings in the book of Joshua.

How do we know the Lord is powerful? Let me tell you a story.

What does it *mean* to say, "The Lord is powerful"? Let me tell you a story.

Let me tell you a story about the time the nation of Israel crossed the Jordan river into the Promised land... , a story about the time Gideon routed the enemies of Israel with a handful of men... , a story about the feeding of five thousand people... , *the* story about the empty tomb...

But what do all these stories mean to me, a Skeptical Believer trying to make sense of things in the twenty-first century—long, long after the events of which these old stories tell? The answer to that question is up to me. I can treat these stories as irrelevant for anything other than historical or literary interest, or as containing useful generalized insights like any story, or as stories that respond to life's most important questions and tell me how to live.

As a skeptic, I tend toward the second approach (generalized insights). As a believer, I accept the third (a response to all the big questions). As a Skeptical Believer, I wrestle with how to understand my own story in light of these ancient ones. What is their practical, everyday relevance to my life? Because the only truly important stories in our lives are those that affect our own stories now.

The people who built the stone marker at the river were testifying to something that happened that made their lives different. They wanted to remind themselves of it and wanted to be sure their future children and grandchildren knew about it. So they built a monument that would prompt stories.

Those stories still speak to me. They tell me how to live. They sometimes lead me to ask a girl to dance—as we will see next.

STORY ETHICS—ASKING THE LAME GIRL TO DANCE

The prophets... called Israel to live in light of its own story... They kept coming back to that story and asking once more what might be its implications.

JOHN GOLDINGAY, *KEY QUESTIONS*

What, practically, does it mean to say that faith is rooted in story? It means, among other things, that a story is much more likely to shape how I actually behave on a given day than propositions, rules, or analytic reason. Consider the following story from my own life.

I tell the story elsewhere (*Letters to My Children*) of being told when I was twelve that I should ask a girl to dance. Not just any girl, but a girl in our class who had had polio and therefore had a bad leg and a drawn-up arm. The boys lined up in those days and, one at a time, chose a girl sitting at her desk to be his partner for square-dancing lessons. Mary was always the last chosen.

Miss Owens, our student teacher, told me that wasn't right and that, as a Christian, it was my job to do something about it. "Next time we dance," she said, "I want you to choose Mary." It was an almost inconceivable idea, and I thought it pretty low of her to drag Jesus into it. I could handle Jesus in the Bible stories, but I hadn't much considered the idea of his being in mine (other than his answering my prayers to help the Dodgers win base-ball games).

I was fairly miserable from that moment until the day came for us to dance again, and it was even worse when I found I was first in line to do the choosing. Everyone watched to see who I would pick—everyone except Mary, who was looking down at her desk. Somehow I heard myself saying, "I choose Mary," and I was rewarded with a look of delight and surprise that I will never forget.

This story is an example of how ancient stories can shape our own. It has a number of implications for how I now conceive of faith.

First, I see that what motivated me to ask Mary to dance was a story motivation, flavored with a little fundamentalist guilt. Miss Owens was worried about two things at least: my own character and the well-being of a young girl. She knew that this have-it-all twelve-year-old boy needed to learn something about compassion. And she knew this beaten-down twelve-year-old girl needed a new way of seeing herself.

When Miss Owens said, "It's what a Christian should do," she was not appealing to a set of rules for Christians (nothing in the Bible about square dancing); she was reminding me of the Christian story. She was asking me to place that story next to my own story and to see what the juxtaposition of the two suggested.

And that's exactly what happened. I didn't think of any specific commandment—the Big Ten or otherwise; I thought of Bible stories. I thought, admittedly in a vague way, of Jesus' encounters with people in need. I couldn't have told most of the stories in detail, but I knew there were blind men and bleeding women and hungry families and crazy people—and I knew that in each case Jesus did something for them, sometimes pyrotechnically, sometimes quietly or in secret.

So even as a self-absorbed twelve-year-old boy, I was able to imagine what Jesus would likely do about a girl in his class with a bad leg when it came time to dance. And I knew it was something that I didn't want to do myself but that I should.

That's where the guilt comes in. Being raised as a good little fundamentalist, I was well-acquainted with guilt, and already growing impervious to it. But this felt different. If it was guilt, it was story-guilt, not rule-guilt. It said something like, "Here's the big story that you are part of. Here's what people in this story do. What are you going to do?"

My adolescent mind had limited capability for abstract moral calculations. But it was both wired and trained to understand story. Having imagined Jesus in my story—sitting in a portable classroom in a small coastal town in California, confronted with whether to choose Mary as a dance partner—I was unable to imagine him choosing anyone else. Not Linda. Not Shelley. Not even Doreen. My story gave me no other realistic option than to do the right thing. I couldn't have done anything else and still considered myself part of the story.

One reason the story was so powerful was that it addressed my emotions as well as my mind. I could perhaps have constructed reasoned arguments for why I didn't have to do it. I couldn't have convinced my emotions. I was very nervous when I said, "I choose Mary," because my spirit and emotions knew that more was at stake than my mind alone would allow. I don't credit myself with realizing how much might be at stake for Mary, but I did dimly know how much was at stake for me. If I played it safe and chose someone else, I would create this gap between my story as a churchgoing, Bible-reading kid and my actions in the real world. That would have been harder to live with than saying out loud, "I choose Mary."

I chose Mary. Why? My story made me do it.

LOVING OUR NEIGHBORS: PROPOSITIONS AND THE STORIES THAT GIVE THEM LIFE

Believing in [Jesus] is not the same as believing things about him… Instead, it is a matter of giving our hearts to him, of come hell or high water putting our money on him, the way a child believes in a mother or a father, the way a mother or a father believes in a child.

FREDERICK BUECHNER, *SECRETS IN THE DARK*

One way of interacting with the world is to ask, "What is true?" Another is to ask, "What is the best story?" They are not mutually exclusive or un-related questions, but they do indicate a leaning about how best to make sense of the world and live a good life. For many years, I tended to ask only the first question. I have found that God seems more often to answer in terms of the second. This sometimes leaves me frustrated and my Inner Atheist crying, "Foul!" (*Foul!*) But I'm learning to live with it (quite well, actually). I will try to explain a bit why.

Propositions are important: There is only one God. God is good. Jesus is the Son of God. Christ rose from the dead. (*Excellent! Let's argue about these.*)

But propositions depend on the stories out of which they arise for their meaning, power, and practical application. The story provides the existential foundation on which the proposition rests. If no larger story, then no significance for the proposition. And the story will tell us much more fully what the proposition actually means.

The Bible is loaded with propositions, assertions, and commands—everything from "God is love" to "Jesus is Lord" to "Feed my sheep." All of these make direct claims on the intellect and will. But almost all of the assertions of the Bible are embedded in stories. The stories serve to explain, illuminate, clarify, amplify, and give motivational power to the assertions. Separate the propositions and commands from the stories, and the propositions and commands dry up and lose their vitality. They become something to discuss rather than something to live. (*What? You afraid of discussion? Afraid you can't prove it?*)

Imagine having all the propositions of the Bible but none of the stories. No Genesis or Exodus, none of the historical books of the Old Testament, no Gospels, no Acts—only Romans, parts of the Epistles, and scattered assertions and commands from here and there. Those assertions and commands would still be true, but we would have very little idea of what to do with them.

Consider the Ten Commandments, perhaps the most famous assertions of all time. Many people see them as stand-alone rules that guide conduct and reveal moral truth—and they do. (*Your truth, maybe. Not Richard's or Ayn's truth.*) But why these ten? There are many more assertions in both the Old Testament and New that are just as important, some more important, that could easily have been included. (I once heard a Hasidic rabbi claim that there are 613 assertions of law in the Hebrew Bible and that he was trying to keep them all.)

One answer to "Why these ten?" is found in the particular story out of which the Ten Commandments arise. The giving of the commandments comes in the early stages of the story, stretching from Exodus to Joshua, of the rescue of the Jews out of Egypt, their forty years of wandering in the wilderness, and their eventual entrance into the Promised Land. They are surrounded by hostile nations and a panoply of gods. They are forced by circumstances to live a nomadic life together for a long time. No individual or family has the option of moving away if they can't get along, and if they can't get along with each other, they will die. They are, at one point, directly dependent on God for the very food they eat each day. (*Pshaw! Fairy-tales!*)

Why, then, these ten commandments? Perhaps because they are the ones most crucial to Israel's survival at this point in their story. They must learn something that is likely new to many of them—that there is only one God, and that to obey him, not the gods of the surrounding nations, is their only hope. They must learn to honor their parents because, unlike with us, their parents do not live in a condo or in Florida but in the same tent. They must learn not only not to steal from the tent next door, but not even to covet what their neighbor has, because such behavior breeds enmity in a people who must band together to survive. Nor can they speak falsely, whether through gossip or perjury, about their neighbor, because lies are poisonous and a threat to the community. And so on.

Each of these commandments is not only embedded in the story of the Exodus, each is also further clarified, expanded, applied, and empowered by other biblical stories. Throughout the Old Testament we have many stories about the consequences of following other gods (for one example, see the story of Elijah and Jezebel and the prophets of Baal). We understand better the admonition to honor parents in the story of Absalom and David. We learn, with story specificity, the consequences of coveting one's neighbor's wife in the story of David and Bathsheba.

What, in fact, is the entire Bible but a working out, story after story, of what it means to utter the proposition "God is love"? The propositional assertion is true, but the stories tell us much more of what it means—sometimes frighteningly—and what the implications are for my life and yours.

Propositions serve important functions. They are a sort of shorthand for the stories that allow us to talk about important things in a manageable space. Every time I want to talk about the implications of the truth that God is love, or that creation is both good and fallen, or that Christ forgives our sins, I cannot realistically tell all the stories that embody and convey to me these truths. And so I use the assertion, the proposition. But I do so knowing that the power of the assertion is rooted not in the abstraction but in the reality-revealing stories from which I learned this truth, including the stories from my own life. I do so understanding that if I only know and agree to the validity of these truths but do not let them shape my story, then they are of little value to me.

It is not a matter of choosing between propositions and stories. Stories and propositions need each other. Each provides a limit that the other must respect—a kind of mutual check. A story offers the richness and specificity and motivation necessary to keep the proposition from being merely abstract, inert, shallow, or legalistic. And the propositional truth acts as a check on how we interpret a story.

Bible interpreters often say that one should understand any given verse of the Bible in light of the entire Bible, as a guard against an idiosyncratic interpretation of a single verse or passage that flies in the face of the overwhelming teaching of the Bible elsewhere. I would argue similarly that any one story of the Bible is best understood in light of the other stories of the Bible. But it is necessary sometimes to distill those other stories, for a moment, into a proposition. A true proposition serves as a guide and corrective if we are faced with someone who interprets a story foolishly or cynically or maliciously.

Some contemporary Bible scholars, for instance, argue that the story of the Crucifixion, as traditionally understood, is a story of divine cruelty, even child abuse. It shows, they say, a wrathful, patriarchal god torturing his son to satisfy his wounded pride over human sin. One could combat that reading of the story by telling all the many stories that show that such is not the character of God. More practically, however, one can offer the proposition, derived from those many stories, that "God is love," and reject the malicious reading by appealing to that story-based truth. This is one practical use of propositions in dealing with matters of faith.

If propositions provide a check against misusing a story, stories provide a check against misunderstanding or misusing propositions. Consider the story of The Good Samaritan. Jesus is asked in the Gospel of Luke (chapter 10) what is necessary to inherit eternal life. He turns the question back on the speaker and asks what the Law says about this. The man responds with the two great commandments to love God and love neighbor, and Jesus says he has answered correctly. The man then asks, perhaps in order to make himself look good (and to show how clever he is), "Who is my neighbor?"

So far, everything in this scene is abstract and theoretical—and therefore safe. An abstract question elicits a responding abstract question that elicits a further abstract response that is followed by an abstract affirmation, eliciting yet one more abstract question. In the process, a number of true things are asserted or implied about God, love, eternal life, and human beings. We are told the man is a lawyer—an expert in religious law. This is the kind of game he is good at and enjoys. (*My kind of guy!*)

But Jesus breaks up the game with a story. "'Who is my neighbor?' Let me tell you a story. 'Once there was a man going from Jerusalem down to Jericho...'" Now we have entered another dimension of truth-telling—the story dimension. It has characters and plot and symbolism and meaning. It has the unexpected—the usual good guys (religious leaders) are the bad guys, and the good guy of the story is, for its audience, the usual bad guy (a Samaritan).

Most important for the context in which the story arises, it has implications for the primary hearer—the man asking all the questions. After telling the story, it is Jesus' turn to ask a question—a story-based question—"Who in the story acted as a neighbor?" The lawyer can't escape the story-based answer: "The one who showed mercy." Jesus then issues a story-based command: "Go and do likewise."

The story of The Good Samaritan does not simply "explain" the command to love your neighbor, like a nice illustration or as icing on the propositional cake. The story both precedes and lives on after the commands ("Love God and your neighbor") and the proposition ("God is love") out of which the command grows. The commands only have practical significance in terms of this story and many other stories. The stories clarify what the abstraction means, deepen our understanding of the abstraction by making it both specific and more complex, and motivate us to allow the story-truth to shape how we live ("Go and do likewise").

CHRISTIAN OR CHRIST-FOLLOWER?: MORE ON PROPOSITION AND STORY

The "doctrines" we get out of the true myth are of course less true: they are translations into our concepts and ideas of that which God has already expressed in a language more adequate, namely the actual incarnation, crucifixion, and resurrection.

C.S. LEWIS

The truth, in the sense in which Christ was the truth, is not a sum of sentences, not a definition of concepts, etc., but a life.

SØREN KIERKEGAARD

It is not a matter of choosing between proposition and story. It is a matter of recognizing which is foundational and which derivative, and of allowing each its proper role. Propositions and assertions speak to my intellect. Commandments speak to my will. Stories speak to all of me.

Because they address all of me, stories are a better gauge of this thing we call faith than propositions are. Am I a person of faith? Am I, more specifically, a follower of Christ—a Christian? The terms by which I answer that reveal a lot about how I conceive of what it means to put one's faith in something.

The propositional approach tends to say, "You are a Christian if you say yes to this set of assertions." If you *believe* them. If you agree that they are true. The exact assertions vary from one Christian tradition to another (*Ha! Even the Christians can't agree on what a Christian is!*), but they usually center on God, Christ, sin, confession, and the relationships between me—the one who believes—and all these things that one is expected to believe.

As a shorthand for something more profound, there is nothing wrong with this approach. But if this is all that faith is, or even if it is seen as what is most central to being a person of faith, it is woefully inadequate.

Assent to a set of propositions as proof of faith is like taking the exchange of wedding vows as proof that a couple has a good marriage. The vows are important to honestly affirm, but the proof will be in the marriage. The belief in a set of propositions is a place to start, and even to return to from time to time, but the proof will be in living out the story.

"Are you, Mr. Taylor, a Christian?" My answer is that I have committed myself to the Christian story as best I understand it, and am trying to live it, with God's help, as best I can. God have mercy.

This is the only way I can be a Christian. If you force me to give assent to a long list of propositions, and to abide by a long list of behaviors, I will have to ask what you mean by this and by that. That will require you to formulate further propositions, which will prompt further questions. Each of those further propositions will be more abstract, attenuated, and divorced from the everyday world than the one before it. Eventually we will be far removed not only from everyday life but from the story-centered assertions of the Bible. We will end up discussing angels dancing on the head of a pin. (*The good old days. Now those medieval guys could really argue!*)

I think the same is true of many of the dogmas, doctrines, and theological formulations of the church. I think they are extremely valuable, and usually worth defending, but they are also secondary to and dependent on the stories. C.S. Lewis says (do not be alarmed by his use of the word "myth") that doctrines are less true than the stories out of which they arise, being "translations into our concepts and ideas" of that which God has already expressed in the stories of actual things such as the Incarnation, Crucifixion, and Resurrection. Their historicity and telling is more important than the humanly made concepts that we abstract from them.

Okay, I am making myself a little nervous as I take this tack. Not because someone will criticize me (*I criticize you all the time—but it doesn't seem to make you any more reasonable*), but because a part of *me* is criticizing me. Here is what that part of me (my Inner Apologist?) is yelling:

"Are you saying it doesn't matter whether one thinks Jesus is the Son of God (in a way no one else can be) or thinks he's just a good man?"

"Are you saying that theology and doctrines are not important, only 'living' is?"

"Are you saying we should shut down our brains and simply swim around in the existential, emotive, relativistic soup?"

"Are you saying that truth is whatever your subjective story says it is?"

"Are you saying I memorized TULIP for nothing?"

No, I'm not saying any of those things. I believe we should use every tool at our disposal to better know and understand the human experience and its relationship to God. That includes reason and propositions and dogma. But I am saying that these three have their limits, and that the richer and more powerful paradigm is story—and that even the idea of story doesn't mean much in matters of faith until *a* story becomes *my* story.

Propositions and doctrines tend to be all or nothing. "Do you believe this—yes or no?" "Well, sort of" doesn't make anyone happy. Not the asker, not you. One round of qualifications—"Well, if you mean this, then yes, but if you mean that, then no"—is rarely enough. Every qualification raises the need for even further qualifications, and soon we are counting the dancing angels again. We argue distinction after distinction until after the cows come home, after the lights have been turned off, long after Elvis has left the building.

And we often argue about things that I believe God has little interest in us fully understanding—things like the exact relation between our free will and God's foreknowledge, the precise nature of the Trinity, what is happening to the bread and wine during the Eucharist, among others. These things are worth discussing, but we should hold our answers loosely, because they are *our* answers, not things God has chosen to make explicit. Not only do we not really know the answers, we probably have not even framed the questions correctly. (We are perhaps asking the theological equivalent of "How fast is a mountain?" or "What does truth taste like?")

Defining faith by propositions tends to create a bright line in the sand by which we can determine who does not belong—who can stay and who must go. Stories are more likely to let you stay—if you want to. The story of faith allowed Thomas to stay even when he couldn't, for a time, believe the good news of the Resurrection was true. The story embraces me when I believe and agree to the propositions, but it also allows me to stay when I doubt and question and whine, and even when I say some important assertion can't be true. The story never kicks me out. But it always allows me to choose to leave for another story, at which point I am genuinely no longer a believer.

This doesn't make the story weak or relativistic or wishy-washy or "merely" subjective. The *story* of faith is actually harder on me than propositions alone are. Those just require of me a quick yes (often disguising a hidden "why think about it?") and then I'm in—saved. Story, on the other hand, asks me a much more difficult question: "Why do you call me Lord, Lord, and do not do what I command?" It says my *life* has to be different, not just my opinions.

Truth is infinitely valuable; propositions are valuable only to the extent that they reveal truth and let loose its power in our lives. In matters of faith the ability of propositions and arguments and doctrines to do so is genuine but limited. We err on one side to deny the helpful role of reason and propositions; we err on the other to exaggerate their effectiveness and make them definitive. Give me all the truth that reason and proposition can muster, but do not forget to tell me the story on which they depend. Then call me to live it.

FAITH LOGIC AS STORY LOGIC

Starting at the beginning, Peter told them the whole story.

ACTS 11:4

I want to be clear that I am not simply saying that the Bible has a lot of stories in it. I am claiming that faith operates by the logic of story more than by the logic of syllogism. And because it does so, faith as story creates room for a Skeptical Believer in a way that a rationalistic understanding of faith does less well.

I realize that by saying the "logic of story," I appear to be stealing a word, "logic," from the realm of rational discourse that I seem to be belittling. Not so. I am not belittling the use of reason at all (again, I'm using it at this moment as best I can); I am simply trying to encourage its proper as opposed to improper use.

Further, the term "logic" simply means, in this instance, the coherent inward workings of something toward a goal. (*Distinctions and definitions! I love 'em! Guaranteed to put your reader to sleep.*) A car engine has an internal logic—these parts move in these ways to turn these wheels so the car will move. A political or advertising campaign has a logic that describes how it functions in working toward its goal. There is also a logic to a man romancing a woman. All systems have a logic of one kind or another.

Philosopher's logic consists of moving in an orderly and predictable way from premises to conclusions. It deals in assertions, claims, propositions, and inferences. It is, in fact, the science of inference—how one claim connects to another. And it can accomplish a lot of good things (including clearing away Smoke). But there are also a lot of places in life where it's not so useful.

Narrative or story has a kind of logic as well. It also is interested in making connections between things. It also has goals and conclusions. It is just as interested in inference as the logic of philosophers, though it is more likely to ask us to infer something from the look on a woman's face staring out a window than from the movement from abstract premise to abstract conclusion.

If rationalistic logic deals in premises and propositions, story logic deals in setting and character and plot. If one kind of logic asks me to think abstractly, remove emotion and personality, and become as object-like (objective) as possible, story logic asks me to become engaged, enter into a scene, bring my mind and emotions and individual experiences, and even to become a character in the story myself.

The goal of philosopher's logic is to accurately describe the relationship between various claims. The goal of story logic is to increase our understanding of the human experience. It does so by making meaningful connections between a depicted slice of life and our own lives. Story logic goes something like this: by sharing the experience of these people (or beings) in this setting, you will see connections between their situation, their choices, their actions, and their reactions that will illuminate your own situation, choices, actions, and reactions. That illumination may simply entertain you, but it may also cause you to change—to modify your present story or even to abandon it for another.

Consider the story of Peter and the sheet and the pigs (Acts 10 and 11). Cornelius, a Roman soldier (and therefore a Gentile), is visited in Caesarea by an angel and told to summon a man named Simon Peter from another town. The soldier sends people to do so. Meanwhile Peter, who has never heard of Cornelius, is praying in Joppa and has a vision in which a sheet is lowered from the sky, filled with what Jews like Peter considered ritually unclean and therefore inedible animals. God commands Peter to slaughter and eat from these animals, and Peter refuses because they are unclean. God tells him not to call unclean what God has made clean. It happens three times, and Peter is deeply puzzled by the vision.

The men Cornelius sent arrive and tell Peter the story of what the angel said, so Peter returns with them to Cornelius. He makes clear he cannot, according to the religious law, enter Cornelius's home and share hospitality with him. After hearing Cornelius tell the story of the angel, Peter realizes the meaning of his vision: God plays no favorites—the gospel is for everyone, including the Gentiles. He explains the Good News to them of peace with God through Jesus Christ. They are filled with the Spirit and speak in tongues, a sign that indicates to Peter that it is acceptable to baptize them, which he does.

When Peter later returns to Jerusalem, he is criticized by other Jewish followers of Christ for breaking the religious law by eating with Gentiles. Peter tells them the story of what happened—both his vision in Joppa and the baptisms in Caesarea—and recalls what Jesus had told them about the baptism of the Holy Spirit when he was with them. The Jerusalem believers cease their criticism and praise God for expanding the blessing of forgiveness of sins to the whole world, and there follows a description of believers spreading that message beyond Israel to distant places. These are story-changing experiences for everyone involved.

And now this story has the potential to change my story as well. There are stories within stories here, and each of them invites me to be a part of it. I see and hear in my mind the angel speaking to Cornelius, and I feel his fear. I see Peter's vision with him, and, on first hearing, I also do not understand its meaning. I go with Peter to Cornelius's house and see how uncomfortable Peter is at being welcomed (almost worshipped) by someone he considers a contamination. Peter doesn't want to break any rules, not even if God, the rule-maker, is telling him to do so. I perceive Peter's astonishment as he realizes that he is now living out the meaning of his vision. I sense his enthusiasm as he tells Cornelius's household the gospel story, his astonishment as they are filled with the Spirit, and perhaps his uncertainty as he baptizes them. And I go with him to Jerusalem and face the critics, watching as the truth dawns on them that God is doing something they had not expected.

Henri Nouwen writes of spending hours sitting in front of Rembrandt's great painting of the story of The Prodigal Son. Nouwen says he at various times sees himself as each of the characters in the painting—the prodigal son, the embittered brother, the watching servants, the forgiving father. He has had each of their emotions in his life; he has been, at one point or another, each of them. I feel the same about many a biblical story, including this one in Acts. I have been in each of their shoes—the seeker, the confused believer, the critic, the rejoicer.

Because the story of Peter and Cornelius makes me feel myself present in it, and because I see a part of me in each of the characters, the story makes a claim on my own story. It does not exist simply to entertain me or to give me information; it requires me to consider whether its insight or truth is a truth for me. I can critique this story, but it also critiques me and my life.

What do I, lifelong believer and rule-keeper that I am, consider unclean or unchangeable that God would have me think about differently? Is it an irritating or offending person, a rule or practice, a favorite doctrine, a beloved habit, a comforting formulation? For the Skeptical Believer it might well be a familiar rationalization or self-defense or comfortable excuse.

Whatever it is, it is more likely to be shaken up by a story than by an abstract argument. Notice that Peter, when criticized for breaking the rules, does not offer an argument (that will be more Paul's role in the New Testament). He simply tells them what happened—what he saw, heard, and said. He tells a story. He testifies. And the story persuades them, because they suddenly see how it fits into the larger story and into their own.

A KING, A BEAUTY, AND A PROPHET: HOW A STORY CAN CHANGE YOUR STORY

Then Nathan said to David, "You are that man!"

2 SAMUEL 12:7

If you want more evidence that stories involve us as whole persons—or that story is primary in the Bible—consider the story of David, Bathsheba, and the prophet Nathan as told in 2 Samuel. This is another example from within the Bible itself of how stories shape us. It also shows us how abstract commands—in this case against murder, adultery, and theft—carry more force when embedded in a story.

We start in the middle of an ongoing story. David has abused his power as king in order to sleep with Bathsheba and has made her pregnant. To cover his failure—morally and as a leader—he has her husband called back from war, assuming Uriah will sleep with his wife and thereby cover David's tracks. David, however, has not counted on Uriah's integrity and loyalty. When Uriah refuses the comforts of home because his fellow soldiers have none, David arranges for his death and brings Bathsheba into his household.

This is a powerful story in itself, and yet another story appears within the story that will signal a change in the direction of David's life and in that of the nation of Israel. God sends Nathan the prophet to David to tell him a story. The story is a trap—or, perhaps better, an instrument for revelation.

And Nathan tells it masterfully, with a storyteller's sense of timing and irony and pathos. It goes like this:

There were two men in a certain town—one rich and one poor. The rich man had great flocks and herds. The poor man had nothing but one little lamb he had bought. He raised that little lamb, and it grew up with him and his children. It ate from the man's meager fare and drank from his cup and slept in his arms like a baby daughter. One day a traveler arrived at the home of the rich man, but the rich man was unwilling to take an animal from his own flock or herd to prepare for the traveler. Instead, he took the poor man's lamb and prepared it for his guest.

Nathan's story has the "once upon a time" feel of fiction—"There were two men in a certain town"—more than of a recounting of an actual historical event, and yet David is totally engaged by the story. Historicity is crucial in some stories, but not in this one. Not all stories have to have happened to be true.

David is enraged by the actions of the rich man in Nathan's story and proclaims in all his royal indignation, "As surely as the Lord lives, the man who did this deserves to die!" All of David is engaged in this story: his intellect, his moral sense, his emotions, his will, and, yes, his body (his heart no doubt is beating faster). That is, he responds to Nathan's story as a whole person—and it is exactly the response Nathan must have hoped for.

At this climatic moment, Nathan unleashes the lightning bolt of revelation as only a great story can. We can picture him reaching out his arm and pointing at David as he shouts, emphasizing each word, "You... are... that... man!"

Nathan then makes explicit the connection between the story he's told and David's story:

David is the rich man and Uriah the poor.

David has been given much and yet has taken from the man who has little.

David has been blessed by God and has responded by breaking God's law.

David was a murderer, adulterer, and thief. But he only fully felt it when confronted with a story that made him see the wicked turn his own story had taken. That story revelation led him to repentance and a determination to repair the shalom of his own story.

How are stories like this helpful for the Skeptical Believer?

I will speak for myself. They are helpful to me because I find stories believable and compelling and directive in a way that I often do not find with rational arguments. My Inner Atheist dearly loves to argue. (*Just standing up for the truth, thank you.*) He is quite good at finding more leaks in the dike of an argument than anyone has fingers enough to plug. (*I'm flattered.*) When presented with a rational argument making big claims, I instinctively create in my mind counterarguments, even when I very much want to be convinced by the claims being made. Argue for the existence of God, something I long for you to succeed in convincing me of, and I will find reasons to object to your line of argument. Sometimes I will object so effectively that I will convince myself not to believe for a time the very thing I want to believe.

But it is more difficult to argue with a story. A story does not say, "Let me tell you what is true," but "Let me tell you what happened." When someone begins telling us what is true, especially in a cynical, relativistic age like ours, we are poised to say, "That may be true for you, but it's not true for me." But if they begin "Let me tell you what happened" or "Once upon a time," we shut up and listen, because nothing interests human beings more than news about what happened (even if it only happens within the story).

You can of course argue with a story if you like. You can say, "Nice story, but it isn't true. It didn't really happen (and therefore is not useful)." But by that time a really good story has bypassed the objecting part of your brain and seeped into your heart and bones. Do we dismissively say, "Nice story, but it isn't true" to *Moby Dick* or *Pride and Prejudice* or *Anna Karenina*? If so, we simply display our own stuntedness.

Or we can say, as some want to say of the biblical stories, "Nice story, didn't happen, but still useful." I heard that line recently about the story of Noah and the ark, with the suggestion that it was the same with the Exodus story of the Jews escaping Egypt. I could maybe see his point with the ark (or with Job), but how do you get a useful lesson from the Exodus story (about God's rescuing us from our troubles, for instance) if the story on which you base that claim is untrue? (The Old Testament writers refer repeatedly to the Exodus story as evidence of God's care for Israel, but if God didn't really rescue the Israelites, why should Israel believe God cares for them, and why should I believe he will rescue me?) And I didn't even want to know the speaker's explanation of the empty tomb ("Yes, each of us can have our lower selves be resurrected into our better selves." Gag.)

The faith story makes such big claims on our lives that surely it has to pass some sort of "it really happened" test. This is what C.S. Lewis realized, and why it was so important to his conversion when Tolkien and others convinced him that the Christian story was a myth, like all the other myths Lewis loved, with this difference, that it really happened. It was, in Lewis's words, a true myth.

But doesn't that just get us back to the rational argument stage—reasons for and against accepting that it really happened? It can, if you want it to and want to leave it there. And I certainly support Christian apologists making all the factual, historical, geographical, and philosophical arguments they can for why we should accept that claim. But I am also saying that I don't myself find life in those arguments. They wax and wane in my mind, pushing me first one way and then another. I find life in the story and my role in it. (And I find competing stories just as incapable of proving their truth claims—including the story that says I shouldn't believe anything I can't prove.)

I don't expect my stories—literary, biblical, or personal—to be hedged around with unassailable walls of fact and proof and impregnable argument. I allow them breathing room, space to grow and even change. The stories are alive, and that is why they can give life to me.

STORIES WON'T LEAVE US ALONE

The destiny of the world is determined less by the battles that are lost and won than by the stories it loves and believes in.

HAROLD C. GODDARD

The essence of story is characters making choices—especially characters in tough situations making difficult choices. We are drawn to (and into) story by the tension of plot ("What's going to happen next?") and the tension of choice ("What will she do now?"). And there is always the implicit question, "What would I do if I were in this situation?" Stories are about choices and their consequences—and so is the life of faith.

In the Bathsheba story, as we saw, David made disastrous choices and they had disastrous consequences: a woman abused, a faithful subject murdered, a baby dead, the integrity of the king compromised, and therefore the community put at risk. (Nathan tells him that because of his sin, Israel will never know peace in David's lifetime.) All because he wasn't satisfied with everything God had given him. He wanted more; he wanted something else.

This story also indicates another quality of story—stories have the power to change us. (And what is faith if it isn't about changed lives?)

David's failure and its consequences are revealed by a story, but Nathan's story also led David to repent. He is shown his own story within Nathan's story and, unlike his predecessor Saul, he reacts appropriately. He says, "I have sinned against the Lord." That confession spares his life. Though it does not save him and Bathsheba from the loss of their son, it makes possible the subsequent birth of Solomon, the son who will eventually carry on David's line.

Powerful stories have this potential to change us. They do not exist to kill time, but to give time significance. They are quite aggressive in a sense. They say, "You must be different because of what you have heard. Your life cannot be exactly the same now that you know this story." David could not hear Nathan's story—and Nathan's interpretation of the story—and pretend he could go about his normal business. He might be king, but kings too must pay heed to stories.

Stories don't just tell us that we have to change; they often tell us how we must change. (*Sounds like fascism to me!*) They are directive. Not just any change will do. You must change in a certain direction. You must be a certain kind of person, a certain kind of character.

Stories, as Alasdair MacIntyre points out in *After Virtue*, teach us our lines:

> I can only answer the question "What am I to do?" if I can answer the prior question "Of what story or stories do I find myself a part?"... It is through hearing stories about wicked stepmothers, lost children, good but misguided kings... youngest sons who receive no inheritance but must make their own way in the world, and eldest sons who waste their inheritance on riotous living and go into exile to live with the swine, that children learn or mislearn both what a child and what a parent is, what the cast of characters may be in the drama into which they have been born and what the ways of the world are. Deprive children of stories and you leave them unscripted, anxious stutterers in their actions as in their words.

Without stories to direct us, we do not know what to say or what to do. We cannot answer any of life's big questions. (*Questions are more fun than answers anyway.*) We, quite literally, do not know who we are or what lines to speak. Stories change us. Diseased stories change us for the worse. Healthy stories show us how to live.

Stories call us to action. Nothing kills a story faster than a passive protagonist. Characters must act, even if they act disastrously. If you think faith is primarily a set of propositions to be agreed to, then you might well think it is simply enough to say, "Yes, I believe those things. Therefore, I am a believer, a person of faith." If that were enough, then all the demons of hell would be creatures of faith, because we are told that even the demons acknowledge the truth about God and that they tremble (James 2:19). But obviously that does not make them people of faith. You and I are more likely to act in faith, and live out the life of faith, if we conceive of ourselves as characters within a story than if we think of faith as agreeing to a set of statements.

Each story we hear makes a claim on us, makes a claim on our own story. It says, "Here's what happened, what does this mean for your?" Sometimes a story means nothing more to us than the meaningless repetitions in *Waiting for Godot* meant to Vladimir and Estragon: "Well that passed the time." Sometimes a story means, "I must change my life."

The overarching biblical story demands the latter response, even though we are free to tame or reject it. But what is true of the large narrative is also true of the individual stories within the Bible. None of them is there simply to fill up space. Each makes its claim on us.

Take, for instance, the story of Peter speaking to the resurrected Christ on the shore of the Sea of Galilee. Three times Jesus asks Peter, "Do you love me?" Three times Peter says, "Yes, Lord, you know that I love you." Three times Jesus tells him to feed his sheep (or variations thereof).

My pastor preached on this story yesterday. I've already forgotten most of what he said, that is, most of his *assertions about* the story. But I haven't forgotten the story, nor at least one of the applications my pastor tried to make to our own stories.

He pointed out what we all knew—that Peter was a big-time failure, one of the biggest ever. Peter has gotten a key role in (drum roll) "The Greatest Story Ever Told" (cymbal!), and he blows it. While Jesus is being interrogated and tortured before the Crucifixion, Peter is hanging around in the shadows. A servant girl recognizes him.

"You were with Jesus the Galilean," she says.
"I don't know what you're talking about."
Moments later another servant girl sees him. "This man was with Jesus of Nazareth."

With an oath, "I do not know the man."

And shortly thereafter, a bystander comes up to him. "Surely you are one of them."

With curses and swearing, "I do not know the man!"

Cue the rooster. Three strikes and you're out.

Unless you are a character in Christ's story. In that story, three strikes, says my pastor, and you're put in charge.

Three times Peter had denied Christ. Now three times Jesus asks Peter if he loves him. Three times Peter, with growing exasperation, says yes. Three times Christ draws a similar conclusion, "Feed my sheep." My pastor encouraged me to find a place for this story within my own story. It wasn't hard. In a world where failure is leprosy, the story of Jesus says, "If you fail but you still love me, then I want you to do the job that I myself have been doing up to now, but will no longer be here to do—feed my sheep." Fail but stay in the story, and you get the boss's job. You get to do what Jesus came to do.

If I had wasted much of my life on drugs or drink or brokenness of any kind, I cannot imagine a more encouraging story than this. If I had hurt my parents or spouse or children or others I love, I would eagerly embrace Peter's story as my story. If I had spurned God or others in a single-minded focus on myself and my own needs, I would welcome with open arms the opportunity to repair the damage I had done.

And if I haven't done much of any of that, but have simply been a nice little run-of-the-mill, card-carrying believer with a lifetime membership, content to polish my pew and get on with my conventional life (as has been the case with me), then I should equally be astonished and delighted that Christ is saying to me, "Dan, do you love me? Feed my sheep."

"Feed my sheep" is a command. It is embedded in a story. It claims to be relevant to my story. It calls me to action. If I accept the claim, it will, among many, many other things, send me to prison to visit a fellow named John, as we will see.

STORY AND THE POSSIBILITY OF BEING WRONG

Apologetics runs the risk of creating the impression that showing the reasonableness of faith is all that is required.

ALISTER MCGRATH, *MERE APOLOGETICS*

What if I'm wrong? (*Yes, think about it. How distressing. Keep thinking about it. Then think about it some more.*)

It's a question that occurs to most reflective believers, but it especially haunts skeptical ones. What if, after all the reasoning and analyzing and evaluating and agonizing and risking and committing and living, it turns out I'm wrong? What if faith—the Christian faith—while a nice idea, simply isn't true? (*Don't you feel foolish now? Think how much time and struggle you've wasted.*)

"What if I'm wrong?" is a good question for everyone, religious or secular, to ask about any important conviction they hold. What if I'm wrong about abortion? What if I'm wrong about my position on the death penalty, or on war, or about race relations, or about whether I should quit my job, or go on with this marriage, or... ? What if I'm wrong about my any of my core understandings of life?

Here's how I think about that for myself regarding faith.

The possibility of being wrong underlies all important life commitments. As does the element of risk. I shouldn't expect it to be any different when it comes to God.

And if I am wrong about God, I will never know it. This is part of Pascal's infamous "wager" argument. Given uncertainty about God existence, it is more reasonable to bet that God exists than that he doesn't. Since this issue can't be settled incontestably until after death, says Pascal, the person who expects to meet God face to face on the other side will never know they were wrong because they will have no consciousness. The person who bets against God (and an afterlife), however, will discover, consciously and tragically, if they are wrong. (*But that's so far away.*)

That's a nice debating point, but personally it doesn't make me any more likely to make the leap toward faith. I don't find much comfort in never knowing I am wrong if in fact I am, any more than it would comfort me to be assured that anytime I run over a kid in the street, I will never find out about it. Seems to me like a philosopher's comfort, not one that makes me rest easier at night.

I am more interested in the consequences of belief or disbelief in this life, in my own life, than I am in the afterlife. What kind of story will I live if I take the risk of believing? What kind will I live if I don't? I don't think it's helpful to be theoretical here. Theoretically, I could be a good pagan, live a praise-gaining moral life, make contributions to the community here and there, keep my nose clean, and die believing my life had been worthwhile. Theoretically, yes. But in reality, I'm quite sure it would be otherwise.

When I look at my own life, not anyone else's, I know without question that my conviction that I have a part to play in the story of faith has called me to a better life than I would otherwise live. It has not just "made my life better" in the sense of more benefits for me, it has also called me to live at a higher level than I would otherwise demand of myself.

I'm a fine fellow and all, but my natural tendencies are to physical laziness, diffidence, detachment, and self-indulgence. (I forbid my wife to quote this back to me.) If I followed my inclinations ("instincts" for you Darwinians), I would weigh four hundred pounds, smoke cigars and read books all day long, watch sports on television and snack all night, and let the rest of the world go, literally and figuratively, to hell. You wouldn't want to bring your problems to me. (*You're too hard on yourself. You probably wouldn't be a pound over three fifty.*)

If I actually live a little better than that, it's because I have a story. I have committed to the story of faith even though I know I could be wrong about it. That story tells me I have a role to play that will get me off the couch and out of myself. That story tells me that when Jesus was reading in the synagogue out of the book of Isaiah, he was saying the lines that I must say for myself:

> The Spirit of the Lord is upon me,
> for he has anointed me to bring Good News to the poor.
> He has sent me to proclaim that captives will be released,
> that the blind will see,
> that the oppressed will be set free...

Maybe I haven't brought all that much good news to the poor or set many oppressed free, but my story has at least called me to do so. And it has not been totally without effect.

In fact it was after reading similar words in the Gospels that I was nudged to a small act of transient obedience. When Jesus is speaking of separating the sheep from the goats in Matthew 25, he says some will "inherit the kingdom" because of their service to him: "For I was hungry, and you gave me food; I was thirsty, and you gave me a drink; I was a stranger, and you welcomed me in; naked, and you gave me clothes; I was sick, and you cared for me; I was in prison, and you visited me."

When those listening ask when they ever did this (or failed to do this), Jesus says, "I tell you the truth, in doing it for the least of these my brothers and sisters, you did it for me."

Having been a church attender since infancy and a Bible reader only slightly less long, I had heard those words many, many times. But one time, as a young man, I heard them as if for the first time. I heard them the way a character in a play hears lines spoken by another actor who then looks for my reply. Those were the lines spoken to me; what were my lines in response?

Could it be that "I was in prison and you visited me" was not a hypothetical example but a command? Might it not be that as someone who called himself a believer, one of the places I should be was in prison? I couldn't see any way around it. So I looked in the phone book—or perhaps I responded to an advertisement—and I found an organization (secular) that worked with prisoners, and next thing I knew the prison door was sliding shut behind me and I was on my way to meet John.

We seemed to have as much in common as fire and water. I was white, John was black. I was a professor, he was a thief. I was free, he was in prison. I had a future, he had a past.

But we found we had at least two things in common: we were both human beings, and we both had a story.

Over the months we talked about a lot of things. We talked about wives, and he marveled when I mentioned my seventh wedding anniversary coming up. "Seven years?" he smiled. "Seven years with the same woman? I can't imagine that. I can't imagine seven whole years with the same woman." He shook his head and laughed softly. No, there was just no way he could get his head around being seven years with the same woman.

We talked about kids. I had two, then three, during that time. He had a child too, a son, and he worried about him. His son and the son's mother lived a long way off in the South. He worried about her violent boyfriend. He worried for the life of his young son.

We talked about sports, and politics maybe, and whatever else came up. He was trying to prepare himself for something better when he got out. He was taking computer courses inside and learning to write software. It seemed a long shot to me—John the thief becoming John the software engineer—but I thought it at least boded well that he was trying. He told me he was determined to change his friends and his clock. In the past, his day began in the afternoon and ended around dawn. He knew if he hung out with the same friends when he got out, he would live the same life and would eventually be back inside.

I found him to be a gentle, thoughtful man. And quiet. Sometimes I felt the tension of not having enough to say. Fifteen minutes into an hour-long visit and all the usual topics had been exhausted. And then there were the times, like when he told me that, yes, his son had been murdered as he feared, that all words seemed empty and unprofitable. It didn't seem to me I had much important to say to John.

But I must have said something.

Because twenty years later the phone rang. It was John. He wanted to talk. He hadn't much wanted to talk when he had gotten out, within a year or two of when we first met. In fact, I had written off my little exercise in gospel obedience as a failure because the support I was supposed to offer once John had gotten out was support he didn't want (similarly with another prisoner I visited). We hadn't talked since shortly after he got out of prison, many years before.

But he wanted to talk now. He wanted to tell me about his life and to thank me for my part in it. He said he actually had gone back to prison not long after getting out. He had gone into computers after all, but he was in the business of stealing, not programming, them. He was quite successful, and prided himself on dressing nicely when he pulled off his crimes—a gentleman thief—but eventually he got caught and went back to prison.

Somewhere in those years he found Jesus. He got a new direction to his life that job skills alone couldn't give. He discovered a new story. When he got out again, he founded an organization that got dads in the hood reconnected with their kids. He walked around the neighborhood at night with other fathers and talked to kids who were hanging out on street corners.

He wanted me to know. He told me I had played a role. I couldn't think of anything I had done or said to make it happen. He assured me that he remembered some things, even if I didn't.

What's the point? What does this have to do with the fact that I could be wrong about God?

The point is simply this. Without my believing that God was telling the world a story that included me, I wouldn't have been in that prison. I would have read a few more books, or watched a few more games. I would have been so afraid of being wrong in what I believed that I would have played it safe and believed in nothing except what I could prove. In shuffling off to see John for a while, I did no great thing. It was a very small act. But add it to other small acts, of varying sorts, and I end up with a different, and better, life than I would otherwise be living. And so does John.

Other people, of course, do much better things than this with no religious story at all. But I'm not talking about other people; I'm talking about me. I know myself. I'm not naturally a good person. Nor am I now good. But I am a better person than I would otherwise be. I am much more likely to live a significant, outward-looking, risk-taking life because of my story of faith.

I don't offer any of this as a proof for the truth of Christianity. (*That's good, because it doesn't prove anything—at all.*) But for me it is an evidence, a small rock that goes with others in building a foundation. And it makes me feel easier, knowing that my story has called me to something higher, even accepting that I may be wrong.

What is the worst-case scenario if I am wrong about my commitment to God? I will have lived by a view of reality that calls me to a higher plane of living than I would otherwise embrace.

What is the worst-case scenario if I allow uncertainty to lead me away from God altogether? I miss the purpose for which I was created: to know the one who made me.

WHO INTERPRETS THE STORY?:
SATAN AS LITERARY CRITIC

Now the serpent was more shrewd than any wild animal that the Lord God had made. And he said to the woman, "Did God really say, 'You must not eat from any tree of the garden'?"

GENESIS 3:1

And beginning with Moses and all the Prophets, Jesus interpreted to them the things concerning himself in all the Scriptures.

LUKE 24:27

"When *I* use a word," Humpty Dumpty said in rather a scornful tone, "it means just what I choose it to mean—neither more nor less."
"The question is," said Alice, "whether you *can* make words mean so many different things."
"The question is," said Humpty Dumpty, "which is to be master—that's all."

LEWIS CARROLL, *THROUGH THE LOOKING GLASS*

A story is just words until someone interprets it. We cannot make any sense of a story at all unless we understand the meaning of the words, and we cannot understand its larger significance unless we come to some conclusions about what the action of the story adds up to. Who gets to interpret the story, and what protection is there against distorted or malevolent interpretations? Remember, Satan was the first literary critic.

In the Eden story, God tells Adam and Eve that they can eat from all of the trees except one—the tree of the knowledge of good and evil. Satan offers Eve an interpretation of what God has said. He begins with a deception, asking her if it's true that God has forbidden them from eating from all the trees. He doesn't state that as a fact but nudges Eve in the direction of error by hypothesizing a falsehood. Eve corrects him by accurately reporting that God only forbade eating from one particular tree.

Satan then moves to his more serious distortion, one less easily corrected, a misreading of what the story means. He contradicts God directly, telling Eve that she and Adam will not die if they eat of the forbidden tree. No, they will instead become like God himself, knowing good from evil. Eve accepts this interpretation of the story—and the rest is history (a long, long history with a lot of pain). Even good stories are susceptible to diseased interpretations. And there are plenty in the history of faith.

My Inner Atheist is often quieted by stories, but he can get very excited about interpretations. (*Children get "excited." I sometimes get, shall we say, animated.*) Interpretations, after all, move us toward assertions, propositions, claims, and arguments—meat and potatoes for any self-respecting Inner Atheist. (*And for any self-respecting, reasonable person, which I would like us to be.*) Like our first literary critic, he will grant me the story but will try to control the interpretation. (*I'm just sayin'—as they say.*)

My answer to the question about who gets to decide the meaning of stories does not satisfy my Inner Atheist, nor did it satisfy me for many years. But it is an answer that I have made my peace with. *I* am the one who decides what a story means, in conversation with my communities and in light of other stories—all of which is ultimately judged by God.

I have claimed that God is telling the world a story. He is telling the story to me. And he is requiring me to make a decision about the story—to reject it or to join it. (He is not asking me if I merely agree with it.) If that sounds too individualistic, or arrogant (*Or delusional*), I can only say this is my interpretation of the story. When Jesus says, "I stand at the door and knock," I hear a rapping on my own front door.

God is telling the story to me, for me to come to a decision about, but he does not leave me without help. In fact, God has supplied story interpreters from the very beginning. Abraham, we are told, left his homeland without knowing where he was going, but knowing what he was looking for—a place promised and built by God (Hebrews 11). He accepted a great deal of uncertainty in his life because he had placed his hope in the story and the Storyteller.

Moses does the same, and before his death he offers the people a reminder of God's faithfulness (and hope for the future) by retelling and interpreting the stories of their time together (Deuteronomy). So do Joshua, David, all the prophets, Jesus, Stephen, and Paul. Each one is both a storyteller and an interpreter of the story. And each of them was, at the same time, living the story and calling others to do the same.

The entire New Testament, in fact, can be seen as an interpretation of the stories of the Old, just as the Old Testament is an ongoing interpretation of earlier stories stretching back to creation ("Remember, you are the people who were rescued out of Egypt"). The disciples looked at the old stories and saw them as pointing to Jesus as the Messiah (not so, say the Jewish leaders of the time, with a different interpretation). Jesus says he did not come to change the stories (including the Law), but to fulfill them. The disciples accepted Jesus' interpretation of the story; the Pharisees did not. You and I face the same choice.

And I do not claim that the choice is transparent or easy. Neither the ultimate choice between God and no God—and Jesus as God versus Jesus as good (perhaps mythical) guy—nor the less central but still contentious choice between one interpretation of church doctrine or practice and another. How does one know, at the time, a false prophet from a true prophet? How does one discern when a reading of the story of faith is a call to greater faithfulness and when it is a siren call to destruction or banality? How does one know the difference between reformation and renewal on the one hand and disobedience and heresy on the other? And, again, who decides?

You do. But you could not decide wholly on your own, even if you wanted to. Whether you know it or not, your decision is influenced by centuries of storytelling and interpreting, since biblical times and up to the present moment. Many voices, many views, many lives lived, many lives lost—all contributing to how the stories are presented to you and how the questions are framed. You cannot decide alone because the stories belong to everyone who values them, and each one has a say. (*Right, so who's to say which is correct?*)

And you cannot hide behind the multiplicity of views as an excuse for not deciding. That favorite relativistic evasion—"Who's to say?"—doesn't work. Because Jesus is asking the question of you, as he did of the disciples,

"But who do *you* say that I am?" (Not, "What is the range of opinions on who I am?") For you *not* to say is, in fact, to say. It is to say, "Not convinced, Jesus, that you are worth the risk."

And so I interpret the story, listening closely to what my community (or communities) have said over the centuries and are saying now, pondering (like Mary) these things in my heart, seeking the guidance of the ultimate interpreter—the Holy Spirit—and then making my choice, with my life. God ultimately judges my decision. (There is a "who," after all, in the "Who's to say?") But what if there is no God to judge any of our stories and our interpretations? Then we are left with a narrative that says we are a cosmic accident of colliding atoms and that, as far as meaning and significance goes, we are making it all up. I would accept that story and make the best of it if it could prove itself true and my story false. But it can't and so I don't. Why settle for so little when there are so many reports of so much more?

At this point in my life, and I hope to my life's end, I answer Jesus' question, Skeptical Believer and all, as Peter did: "You are the Messiah of God" (Luke 9). And I try to live accordingly.

FAITH AND SUSPENSE: LIVING IN THE MIDDLE OF THE STORY

We are always coming in on something that is already going on.

EUGENE PETERSON, *UNDER THE UNPREDICTABLE PLANT*

Wait for the Lord;
be strong and courageous
and wait for the Lord.

PSALM 27:14

Living the story of faith is not unlike the experience of being halfway through a great novel. The scene has been set, the characters introduced, the central conflict identified. Characters are up to their eyeballs in some kind of trouble, usually with no clear or easy way out. Whether the novel is plot-driven, character-driven, or centering on clashing ideas, there is a "what happens next?" quality to even the most subtle stories. We call this "suspense," and it is a quality that we find in our lives as well as in our novels.

We feel suspense even in stories that we have read or heard many times. There is an "unfolding in the present moment" quality to even the most ancient of stories. The story draws us into the scene being enacted once again in our presence. We are witnesses. Better yet, we are participants—because we listen and evaluate and judge and make decisions about people and events in the same way as the characters themselves. And we feel it all in our emotions and will and desires as much as or more than in our intellects.

And because we are not static characters ourselves, our sense of a story will change over time. Reading *Huckleberry Finn* or *Jane Eyre* as a twelve-year-old is not the same as reading them at twenty-five or fifty-five. None of the words have changed, but experientially it's not the same story. I am different, and so the stories are different. This is why great stories—including the stories of the Bible—are never finished. They are filled with potential energy—as the term is used in physics—and they explode in our lives at unpredictable times and in unpredictable ways.

We are also in the midst of our own story. We literally do not know how it's going to turn out. (*I'll tell you: Cold and dead, briefly remembered by others who will soon themselves be cold and dead.*) We are not completely clear even about what has already happened. As an audience for our own story, we try to sort things out, evaluate, make judgments, come to some understanding of where we have been, where we are, and where we are headed. We experience *suspense* about our own story, wanting to know what it all means, what's coming next, and where it will end. And, of course, we wonder about *after* the end.

That is where both you and I are at present. I am in the fourth quarter of my life. (*Feeling a bit cold?*) I grew up in fifteen different houses in eleven different towns in three different states (a restless father). A common denominator throughout was church and communities of faith (too many to count). I had good school teachers (four different ones in four different places in third grade) and a good education. I vowed to read books before I could even read, and I approached grade-school reading contests like an addict snorting cocaine. Books have been filling my head with thoughts and feelings ever since.

I married well (in every important sense), have raised four better-than-I-deserve children, and am now the old grandpa to a growing number of new votes for the importance of the future (that is, grandchildren). I taught literature for almost four decades, getting paid—modestly—for my addiction to books. (*What a scam!*)

And throughout it all, I have always wondered what it all means, what's going to happen next, and how it will all end. And so have you.

We are all characters in our own story, and we have only a limited knowledge of what's coming next. I find myself playing many different roles at the same time in my own story. I am narrator, character, audience, and critic. I find the tone of my narration alternately hopeful, doubtful, confused, engaged, detached, mournful, joyful, and bemused. As a critic and interpreter of my own story, I am sometimes harsh, but mostly grateful. I find connections between things that give me a sense of my life having a meaningful plot and the realistic hope of a desirable conclusion. Overall, I have a very strong sense that I am living a better story than I deserve.

Not everyone feels this way about their story. Some feel cheated, or put upon, or victimized, or tormented, or otherwise treated unfairly by life. Others feel they had good chances but have failed themselves and others. And a lot of people are just confused, uncertain, or not thinking about such things at all. One can find Skeptical Believers in all these categories and others.

We Skeptical Believers tend to want to know more and to know it sooner than life seems willing to grant. We want a story to prove itself before we commit to it. The questions are always in our heads, "But what if it isn't true?" or "How can I know for sure?" or "What about the claims of competing stories?" In essence, we want to know how the story ends while we are still in the middle. Because knowing, for certain, the end would remove the tensions of the middle.

But I think that's cheating, and it's not an available option anyway. In reading a novel we often want to skip ahead to see how things are going to turn out, and some people do. I think doing so is a character flaw. Being willing to accept incomplete knowledge for a time is part of the implied contract between a storyteller and an audience. "I will tell you a story, but you are going to have to hear it in the way and at the pace that I tell it." Skipping to the end is bad faith.

I think it's much the same with the story God is telling you in your own life. We don't know what's next. We don't even know for certain that we're in a truthful story. And we *want* to know. Yesterday, my three-year-old granddaughter Stella wanted something sweet to eat, but she had already had an ice cream cone not long before. When her mother said no, Stella replied with a drawn-out, plaintive cry against the universe, "But I *want* it!" She hasn't figured out yet (as Ayn Rand never did) that the universe is at best only mildly interested in what she wants.

Some folks will say, "We *do* know how it will turn out, because the Bible tells us how." But that won't help the Skeptical Believer much, because whether the Bible speaks accurately or not is precisely one of the issues. (*See, you can be rational when you try.*) And even for those of us who accept the Bible's description of the ending—because we have accepted the risk of being in the story—knowing how things turn out in general does not answer pressing questions about how things will work out for us specifically, in the day-to-dayness of our own lives.

My advice is to accept (and even enjoy) the suspense of the faith story as one does in a good novel. Much has been revealed to us. More things will be revealed. Some things never will be. This is the human condition, and it does not disappear for believers—it simply occurs on a higher plane with more at stake. Rather than wondering what next random, arbitrary thing will happen to me and those I love (which is all the materialist can legitimately wonder), I ponder what will be the next development in this story God has been telling since time began and which God is telling me personally in the details of my own life.

Because there is another element in the implied agreement between storyteller and audience. And that is that the storyteller will not waste your time. The storyteller will tell a story worth hearing. God does not tell stories to pass the time, but to redeem the time. There is suspense in your story and mine, we would prefer to know now, but, as with all good stories, the ending is worth the wait.

STORY, SHALOM, AND (RE)THINKING FAITH

"For I know the plans I have for you," declares the Lord,
"plans to prosper [shalom] you and not to harm you,
 plans to give you a future with hope."
JEREMIAH 29:11

Peace I bequeath to you; my peace I give you. I do not give to you as the
world gives. Do not let your hearts be troubled or be afraid.
JOHN 14:27

I find, as I move from getting older to being old, that life is simplifying itself. Or at least my understanding of it is. Fewer things seem important to
me, although those that remain so are more important than ever. I want
less stuff in my garage; I also want less stuff in my head.

Which is a prelude to saying that two words dominate my thinking
about faith in recent years—"story" and "shalom." I think of story as the
form faith takes and shalom as the primary theme of that story.

I've spoken a lot about story already. Let me say a few words about
shalom. Some form of the word appears 270 times in the Old Testament.
It has many related meanings, including peace, prosperity, wholeness,

health, good relationships, and blessing in general. It is closely associated with righteousness and justice and is often linked to obedience. The New Testament shalom word is *eirene*, and it contains in most of its ninety-one uses the Old Testament associations. The whole message of the New Testament is called "the gospel of peace" (*eirene*/shalom), and Christ is seen as its embodiment.

Shalom is the state of all things and all people doing what they were created to do. It is nothing less than God's intention for his creation. In a fallen world, shalom is always falling apart. Our job as people of faith is to be always repairing and extending it. The concept of shalom offers a core principle by which to make decisions within our stories. We should repeatedly asks ourselves, *What, in this situation, most contributes to the repairing and extension of God's shalom?* What action, what attitude, what use of money, what vote, what words?

These two concepts have changed the way I think (-ology) about God (theo-) and the life that God calls me to lead. Here, in the briefest brush-strokes, are some examples.

Sin is any act or attitude which undercuts God's shalom. It is not best thought of as hurting God's feelings by breaking his rules; it is an offense against wholeness, justice, and righteousness. As such, it is always harmful—to the self and to the community and to the Story. (*Aiii! Metanarrative alert!*)

Salvation is to accept one's place in the story of faith whose theme is shalom. It entails the forgiveness of sins, but the reason sin needs to be defeated is so that you can be what you were created to be—a contributor to shalom. We are "saved" from many things, but one of those is from missing the purpose for which we were created—to be rightly related to God and to the work of God in the world.

The Church exists to embody and extend shalom: in worship, in discipleship, in love for each other, in evangelism, in repairing the world (see Luke 4:17-21).

Evangelism is telling others the Good News of the story and inviting them to join in its blessing (shalom). It is an act of narrative criticism—first of one's own story and then of inviting others to assess their own. Its primary strategy is storytelling—testimony. The paradigm is the simple declaration of the healed man in John 9: "I was blind, now I see." Evangelism is an invitation in light of a story.

Baptism is a public announcement of one's commitment to the story of faith. It reenacts symbolically the story of Christ's death and resurrection, which (along with Creation) is the supreme shalom event.

Communion is the shared reenactment of that same event—a retelling of that story in ritual. It puts us with Jesus and the disciples in the Upper Room. We do not simply live in light of those Easter events, we participate in them through the Eucharist.

Creeds are the distillation of key aspects of the story—both events and concepts—into a form that allows us to recite the story together and to judge our living of it.

Orthodoxy is the accurate and life-giving telling of the story. To be meaningful, it must result in orthopraxis, the daily practice of the story.

And so on.

Both story and shalom are central to me as a Skeptical Believer. Thinking of faith primarily as a story disarms my Inner Atheist (*Not so cocky—when disarmed, I always rearm*) and discourages my tendency toward overanalysis, navel-gazing, and paralysis. Seeing the main theme of the story as shalom gives me a lifetime of useful things to do.

TELL ME THE OLD, OLD STORY?
YES AND NO

Tell me the old, old story of unseen things above,
Of Jesus and His glory, of Jesus and His love.

A. KATHERINE HANKEY

This is my story, this is my song.

FANNY CROSBY

Tell me the story of Jesus,
Write on my heart every word.
Tell me the story most precious,
Sweetest that ever was heard.

FANNY CROSBY

I once was speaking at a Christian college about faith as story. The young worship leader asked me ahead of time if there was a song I would like the students to sing together before I spoke. I mentioned a couple of hymns that centered on my theme, including "Blessed Assurance" (*Pabulum!*) and "We've a Story to Tell to the Nations" (*Arrogant triumphalism!*). After the obligatory rock band played the obligatory mumbled worship songs

(*Dinosaur!*), the young fellow got up and asked the students to turn to a page in their little-used hymnals. Just before starting one of the hymns I had suggested, he blew upon the page, as if trying to blow away the accumulated dust of irrelevancy. (*Touché!*)

"Tell me the old, old story"? Yes and no.

Yes, tell the old, old story—it is God's story, and it has not changed since before the day of creation, nor since it was lived out in the lives of those who have gone before us.

No, do not tell the old story in the old way—as though it is fossilized in one set of words and concepts and deeds. The story is alive and growing and changing. Tell it as it is today, and let it change and grow some more tomorrow.

Ezra Pound, a thoroughly pagan poet, expressed a useful concept for believers in master stories. "Make It New!" he says. Poetry should not ignore the past, nor should it merely repeat it. Instead it should take whatever is vital and still useful from the past and reforge it in new forms and sensibilities, letting it live anew in the latest poetry. Sounds to me like the story of faith over the centuries.

The twin temptations of people interested in the story of faith are to petrify it and to dissipate it (Emil Brunner). The petrifiers turn faith into rules and rigid conventions that are defended at all costs in the forms into which they have been cast. The dissipaters cast the story to the winds of current thought and feeling and jettison anything that might offend contemporary tastes and ideologies. With one extreme you get a leaden anvil, with the other a miasmic cloud.

So how should the story be told instead? With fear and trembling, I think. With deep respect for how it has been told in the past, yet with boldness about how it must be told now. With an awareness that some things must change, combined with a conviction that some things must never change. With an eye for how old truths (like old wine) can be expressed in new ways (like new wineskins). With an awareness of how a living, unchanging God is also a living, changing God (always changing being one of things about God that does not change).

One can argue that God never changes, yet constantly reveals himself in fresh ways that change our perception of him or of what he is up to. In fact the change/doesn't change question is probably an obtuse one on our part. It misstates the reality. Of course God changes. Of course God doesn't change. Make It New!

And even if God, in some senses, never changes, certainly the story does. Not least because you and I are living it now for our first and only time. The story is different because we are part of it (or is different because we choose not to be). Each of us (a word to leaders, especially) is a keeper of the story—a story steward. It is our job to leave the story healthier than we found it (or it found us), to increase the shalom of the story. To make it new. This is what every great leader of Israel and of the New Testament and of the church has tried to do. It is what you and I should be trying to do as well.

One thing the story has never allowed and never can (because then it's something else)—the claim that it is just another story, just one among many. That is a recent claim about the faith. It is also one of the oldest claims.

There are many gods, said the nations surrounding the Israelites. "The Lord is one," answered Israel.

There are many gods, said the nations of the Roman Empire in Jesus' time. "I am the way, the truth, and the life," said Jesus, adding, "No one comes to the Father but by me." (*I can explain that away!*)

There are many paths up the mountain, say many good people in our time. "As for me and my house, we will serve the Lord," says Joshua. That last answer is an old answer, one that, when I declare it myself, is also new.

MY STORY WITHIN THE STORY

Then David said to Goliath, "You come to me with a sword, spear, and javelin, but I come to you in the name of the Lord of hosts, the God of the armies of Israel, whom you have defied."

1 SAMUEL 17:45

There was once, long ago, a young boy and a giant. Everyone was very afraid of the giant, but not the boy. He thought God would help him defeat the giant. The boy did fight the giant and killed him with a small rock. Then he cut off the giant's head. Everyone was glad. (*Not the Philistines.*)

This was the story of a small boy told nearly three thousand years later to another small boy. The story did not have to beg for belief. It was obviously true. I knew about giants. I knew about fear. I knew that even your parents can't always keep the giants away. Knowing all this to be true, it followed logically that God needs to be stronger than giants. It was also clear to me that sometimes it would be me, not David, who had to fight the giant. Clearly, I needed to keep God on my side.

A few years later, when I was eight, I heard another story, this one not from the Bible but from a magazine—and then from the pulpit. It was a story about a man who wanted to tell people about Jesus who had never heard of him before. He and some other men learned of a tribe in South America that had no contact with the rest of the world and that killed any stranger who came into their part of the jungle. The men dropped gifts to them from an airplane and later landed and spoke with them. Things seemed to be going well.

Not long after, the tribal people speared the men and killed them. (*Sic semper imperialists.*) The adults who told me about this were very sad, but also very proud of those men. They called them martyrs. They told me that one of the men, named Jim, once said the following: "He is no fool who gives what he cannot keep to gain what he cannot lose." I wasn't sure what that meant, but I thought about it for a long time. I decided that I didn't want to be a martyr, but I thought maybe I would have to be. I thought I needed to be ready just in case.

When I was eighteen, I came across another story, a made-up story that never happened. But then again, it was a story that had been happening for quite a while in my own life. The man who made up the story had a strange name—"Tolkien"—and the story was filled with strange creatures and strange happenings.

But there was something about the story that wasn't strange at all. It was a story about good and evil and having to make choices and not being sure which choices were the right ones and knowing that choices had great consequences. That was something that was happening in my own life, and the story deeply impressed me with the desire to choose bravely and well. And though the story never mentioned God, I knew that God and good were among the things I was given to choose or not choose.

The stories, and my response to them, grew more complex over the years. But the basic pattern of call and response did not greatly change. The stories of faith—from the Bible, from history, from my family—made their story claim on my mind and imagination and will. They said, "Here was the situation. Here is what people are like and what some of them did. Here is what God is like and what God did. How about you?"

In this pattern is the essence of all story, including the story of faith: people making choices under difficult circumstances—and then dealing with the consequences. And making more choices. In that repeated pattern we have all the elements of story that we have already discussed in this book: setting, character, plot, and theme—all related by a narrator to an attentive audience.

Ultimately, in the story of faith, that narrator is God. Ultimately, that audience is me—you and me. God, I have said, is telling the world a story. More relevantly, God is telling *me* a story. And, as with all important stories, he is asking me for a response. Is this story to be my story, or will I choose another?

If life in general presents itself to us as story, as I have argued, so, in my case, did the life of faith. No one asked me to believe anything; they simply told me stories of belief. The people who told me these stories loved and cared for me. The stories themselves rang true. The only conscious challenge of faith was to live up to the stories.

But at some point in adolescence, I got the message that true faith did not reside in my accepting the stories—and joining in them—but in agreeing with certain statements about faith and about the nature of things. To be a believer was to believe these statements. Ironically, perhaps, I got this message as strongly from within my community of faith as I did from those outside it.

If faith was to be based on accepting statements, I of course needed to decide if those statements were true. (*Very astute.*) Truth, all my education told me, required assessment of evidence. The rational analysis of evidence was the basis of proof. And so I became ravenous for evidence and for proofs.

I was a sucker (*Well put!*) for any speaker, book, or system that offered, finally, once and for all, to nail everything down. If there were still leaks after reading a book, I was hopeful that the next tape series would plug them. If I found myself confused and uncertain, I told myself I just didn't know enough yet. I would find somebody smarter, somebody wiser to learn from. I would, like Descartes, start at square one, reason carefully to square two, make no mistakes in getting to square three, and eventually, at some ever-receding point in the future, arrive at the throne of God.

It never happened. I now know it never could have happened, at least not for me. What is clear to me now, and only really clear at this moment that I write these words, is that *I was trying to believe the propositions separate from the story.* And it is not possible. I had come to believe that the propositions were the main thing. I had to prove them true, beyond any reasonable doubt, or I could not honestly call myself a believer. I found that I could not prove them true, not with certainty. There was plenty of reasonable doubt, oceans full of it.

I have since come to think of propositions as the powdered milk of reality. I weighed ten pounds and two ounces at birth, which made me the smallest of the three Taylor boys. The doctor told my mother we should drink powdered milk or we would end up round balls of fat by the time we went off to school. I still remember clearly but without fondness those watery glasses of blue-white, would-be milk with little islands of powder floating in them.

Well, propositions are to stories (and to reality) as powdered milk is to what comes from the udder. Propositions are dried-out stories with much of the vitality removed. They may say something technically true, just as powdered milk is still technically a form of milk, but they do not win our hearts and are not enough on which to nourish a life. (*So reasons aren't important, then?*)

That does not make them unimportant. I want to make clear what I do and do not believe about truth and the relationship between truth, story, proposition, and creed. I will do so with a series of propositions.

I believe that truth exists independently of any of us or all of us, and that we do not just make it up. I believe our knowledge of this truth is both partial and damaged. I believe, nonetheless, that it is better to know truth partially and imperfectly than to act as though it doesn't exist at all. Therefore, the most worthy and worthwhile human enterprise is the pursuit of truth (in which I am including for the moment concepts like justice, goodness, and beauty). My contention is not that story is better than truth. It is that story is the single best *way* to truth. In our finite state, story is the form in which truth most fully and powerfully reveals itself. If you value truth, you must value story. In the end, they cannot be separated.

But back to my own story (which I will tell more than once in this book). It appeared to me, as a young man, that my two choices were rationalism or fideism—proof or "just believe." And yet neither was any longer possible for me; both were prescriptions for the starvation of my soul. In his mercy, God showed me a third way, a way that I took without understanding it and that I am using this book to try to explain to myself.

That third way was to return to story and to faith as a story.

The only true test, I decided, was not a logical test, nor a belief test, but a life test.

And I would not—and still do not—worry that I have no crushing response to those who say this is not proof (*That's not proof*), that other religions or no religion can accomplish the same thing (*Other stories can do the same thing*), or that I am being entirely too subjective (*You're being entirely too subjective*). Subjectivity is simply a synonym for being human. I don't seek to be anything other than human.

The idea of faith as story has enjoyed a renaissance among theologians since the later twentieth century. Many embrace it because it lets them off the hook of defending biblical accounts as factual. Personally, I'm not interested in using story as a refuge from the darts of skeptical minimalists. I have enough fundamentalist left in me to enjoy the offense some people take when the Bible doesn't reinforce all of their up-to-date convictions. (*Fundamentalists don't enjoy anything—they just get mad.*) I embrace story because I think it the best way to genuine, red-blooded truth, and because it's the foundation on which proposition and creed and command are based.

If you agree with a set of statements, some would say that you are a believer and call this faith. I don't think this is enough, or even much. It is like saying "I believe the poor should have enough to eat" yet never lifting a finger to make it happen. Don't tell me what you believe. Show me what kind of character you are in what kind of story. It's not that your behavior earns you salvation; it's that your commitment to the story demonstrates you have actually chosen it and not something else.

It became clear to me that I had to spend less time on Christ's most fundamental question— "Who do you say that I am?"—and more time on obeying his most relevant command—"Come, follow me." The question called to my intellect. The command called to my whole life. It isn't that the question is unimportant; it is that responding to the command is the only meaningful answer.

4. OBJECTIONS TO FAITH

REASONS AND RATIONALIZATIONS FOR DISBELIEF

Truth is so obscured nowadays and lies so well established that unless we love the truth we shall never recognize it.

BLAISE PASCAL

But as Paul was discussing righteousness, self-control, and the coming judgment, Felix became frightened and said, "Go away for now, and when I find time I will send for you." But after two years had passed, Felix was succeeded by Porcius Festus...

ACTS 24:25, 27

One of Aesop's fables is titled "The Wolf and the Lamb." A wolf comes across a lamb who has strayed from the fold. Wanting to appear a reasonable and just wolf, he gives the lamb reasons for why he is going to eat it, ranging from "you have insulted me" to "you have eaten my grass." The innocent lamb refutes each accusation. Frustrated, the wolf declares, "Well, I won't miss my supper, even though you refute all my arguments!" And he eats the lamb. Aesop's moral is that a tyrant will always find a pretext for his tyranny. Pragmatism trumps both principle and logic.

It is much the same in matters of belief and disbelief. When pressed as to why we believe or disbelieve something (secular or religious), we will usually come up with reasons. Whether they are convincing, to ourselves or to others, is less important than that they create space for us to continue living and believing as we deem desirable.

Skeptics are particularly good at this, and so are Skeptical Believers. More than most, they want to have reasons—arguments, evidence, facts—for why they believe or disbelieve as they do. Ask about their convictions and they will crank up the "reasons generator" and churn away. I do it myself all the time. (*Meanwhile, I'm cranking away with my "on the other hand" generator. Great fun!*)

I am focusing in this section of the book on objections to faith. I do not pretend to raise them all or answer most of them. I do not claim even that all of them *can* be answered in conclusive, uncontestable ways. I raise them because I think it is useful for the Skeptical Believer to inspect some of the objections he or she entertains as reasons for not fully committing to the story of faith. Simply stating and inspecting them reduces the power many of them have to keep us from living the story as we ought. It will not necessarily keep the wolf from eating the lamb anyway, but it may make us more honest in how we live.

Most of the objections to faith fall under one of the following categories or combinations thereof:

- "I do not find it credible."
- "I do not believe it valuable."
- "I do not believe it relevant to my life."
- "I do not sufficiently desire to live by it."
- "I am not able to live by it."
- "It's not convenient for me to live by it at this time."

There is nothing inherently wrong with any of these categories of objection. Most are exactly the reasons I disbelieve in a lot of things, including things that others believe passionately. These responses are only a problem if the thing not believed in *is* true, valuable, relevant, desirable, and livable.

When something is so, then one's reasons for disbelief (or failure to act on belief) become one's rationalizations. *A rationalization is an excuse masquerading as a reason.* And human beings are full of them. They then become not just objections, but obstacles—obstacles to the richest, fullest, most truthful life that one can (and is created to) live. At that point, we are no different from the wolf in Aesop's fable. Actually, we are much worse than the wolf, for the wolf is only following its nature, while we are denying ours.

I will attempt (with mixed results) to treat most of these objections with respect, something apologists often do not do. For some are the objections of my own heart. And others are the objections of people I love.

OBJECTIONS TO FAITH — NO, NO, A THOUSAND TIMES NO!

It ain't the parts of the Bible that I can't understand that bother me, it is the parts that I do understand.

MARK TWAIN

Oh, Adam's sons, how cleverly you defend yourselves against all that might do you good!

ASLAN IN C.S. LEWIS, *THE MAGICIAN'S NEPHEW*

At the very end of the Gospel of John, the evangelist makes a famous observation: "Jesus did many other things as well. If they were all written down, I suppose the whole world could not contain the books that would be written" (John 21:25).

If we knew them all, there would be more chapters to the story of Jesus than could possibly be written down. The same could be said for all the objections to that story and to the larger story that it defines. There are as many ways of refusing this story as there are people who have heard and refused it. Disbelief, like belief, is as individualized as one's fingerprint, but there are some large categories into which most objections to faith fall, and I think it is helpful to reflect on them. For now I will mostly list them. My reflections and ruminations on some are scattered throughout the book.

Since this is a book addressed to people who process much of life through their minds, I will begin with the intellect, though I do not think it contains the most important objections even for intellectuals. What follows is mostly an overlapping list, with a few clarifying comments. It is far from complete and includes terms subject to a variety of definitions.

SOME CATEGORIES OF OBJECTIONS TO FAITH

INTELLECTUAL OBJECTIONS

These are the objections that arise from systems of human thought—some ancient and lasting, some newer and fleeting—that find the claims of Christianity objectionable on the grounds of offense to their understanding of reality.

- *Offenses to reason*—the general charge that faith involves believing things that reason demonstrates are false, illusory, or highly improbable.
- *Offenses to naturalism and materialism*—the more specific charge that faith is incompatible with the truths proven by the scientific method.
- *Offenses to historicism*—the objection that faith refuses to acknowledge that it is the product of particular cultural and historical forces and not a response to anything transcendent of human culture.
- *Offenses to relativism*—the broad view, which lurks beneath the surface in many contemporary views of reality, that all truth claims are simply assertions of opinion and desire and power, having neither universal nor eternal validity.

EMOTIONAL/PSYCHOLOGICAL OBJECTIONS

These are objections based on highly personal, interior states of feeling (which may or may not have an intellectual component).

- *Objections based on pain*—one's own suffering and the suffering of others in the world makes Christian claims unbelievable and even offensive.
- *Objections based on unanswered prayer*—God does not give me the things I pray for, thereby calling into question God's existence or goodness or promise keeping.
- *Objections based on one's own sense of worthlessness or failure*—one feels inadequate or undeserving of God's love or attention.
- *Objections based on self-esteem*—one feels competent, independent, self-actualized, and therefore not needing the things faith offers.
- *Objections based on self-determination*—Christianity violates one's

right to choose what to believe and how to live.
- *Objections based on irrelevance*—the claims of faith do not feel relevant to one's daily life and commitments.
- *Objections based on busyness*—the day-to-day demands of life are so pressing that spiritual considerations seem too distant to be central.
- *Objections based on indifference*—the claims of faith are simply not interesting or attractive.

OBJECTIONS BASED ON THE HISTORICAL EXPRESSIONS OF CHRISTIANITY

These are objections based on the history of the church and the actions of individual Christians.
- *Objections based on failures of the church*—the church has so often been the source of injustice, violence, and ethical failure that its claims are not credible.
- *Objections based on internal divisions*—the church is so often fragmented and has so often attacked other believers that its claims are not credible.
- *Objections based on comparative ethical performance*—Christians are no better than anyone else, and often worse, thereby undercutting their claims.
- *Objections based on diversity of views within the church*—Christians don't even agree with each other about their basic claims, thereby rendering their claims difficult to establish, much less embrace.
- *Objections based on political association*—Christianity is too often tied to conservative (status quo) politics, which undercuts its own ethical claims.

OBJECTIONS BASED ON SPECIFIC CHRISTIAN TEACHINGS

These are objections, some intellectual and others more visceral, to specific points of Christian theology and instruction. Following are a few of the more familiar examples.
- *Objections based on the doctrine of hell*—ethically and conceptually offensive.
- *Objections based on the doctrine of election*—offensive to a sense of fairness.
- *Objections based on the doctrine of sin*—seems antiquated, judgmental, and psychologically unsophisticated.

- *Objections based on belief in miracles*—offensive to scientific reason and common experience.
- *Objections based on Christian claims of absoluteness and universality*—an offense to pluralism and diversity.
- *Objections based on confession and self-denial*—offenses to notions of self-worth and self-esteem.
- *Objections based on the view of God*—too authoritarian, vengeful, patriarchal, and generally unattractive.
- *Objections based on the Incarnation of Christ*—too mythical, exclusive, and culturally rooted.
- *Objections based on the uniqueness and divinity of Jesus*—a moral teacher perhaps, but nothing more, and only one among many.
- *Objections based on the Christian view of history*—too linear, insular, and teleological.
- *Objections based on the Christian view of persons*—too negative, psychologically primitive, and generally unappealing.
- *Objections based on response to the Bible*—full of errors, self-contradictory, and merely a cultural product of its times.

OBJECTIONS BASED ON TOLERANCE
Objections based on a complex of related contemporary values.
- *Objections based on tolerance*—offenses to the value of affirming the equal validity of widely divergent worldviews and values.
- *Objections based on open-mindedness*—offenses to the value of consciously seeking out views that might challenge and change one's own.
- *Objections based on flexibility*—offenses to the value of holding all convictions tentatively and being able to readily change in light of ongoing experience.

OBJECTIONS BASED ON THE ZEITGEIST.
These, like some of those above, are objections based primarily on the dominant ideas, values, and ways of seeing of our particular moment in history.
- *Objections based on the notion of progress*—offenses to the sense that we are wiser, more informed, and further along developmentally than those who went before us.
- *Objections based on the priority of time over eternity*—offenses to the (existential) sense that this world is the only reality that we have and need to address.

- *Objections based on the priority of the physical and material over the spiritual*—offenses to the conviction that reality is entirely physical and that talk of the spiritual is illusory and harmful.
- *Objections based on the suspicion of overarching explanations*—offenses to our skepticism about any ideology or story (metanarrative) that claims too much, especially if those claims impinge on our own ideologies, metanarratives, and stories.

OBJECTIONS BASED ON LIFESTYLE AND PERSONAL EXPERIENCE
These are objections based on one's specific life experience.
- *Objections based on pragmatism*—the "it doesn't work for me" objection, varying from "I tried it and it didn't work" to the conjectural "That would never work for me."
- *Objections based on how one has been treated by Christians*—testimonies to mistreatment by individual churches and by individual believers.
- *Objections based on passing, informal experience with Christians*—off-putting experiences with Christians in the workplace and other shared spaces.
- *Objections based on one's overall image of Christians and Christianity*—formed by media, word of mouth, the views of colleagues and friends, and other personal sources.
- *Objections based on impact on one's lifestyle*—a recognition of Christianity's view of how one is living and the perceived impact of having to live differently.

OTHER CATEGORIES OF OBJECTION
- *Add your own.*
- *Add others that you hear around you.*

(*Well done. And I thought you weren't listening. Oh me of little faith. Ha! I find myself very amusing.*)

Why is any of this important for the Skeptical Believer? First, because Skeptical Believers seriously entertain many of these objections. Second, because even when not fully embracing such objections, Skeptical Believers often allow some of them to diminish their own commitment to the Christian story. Third, because identifying the nature of your objections to faith—as opposed to a vague, ongoing dissatisfaction—can help you more honestly consider the possible responses to these objections, theoretically and in your own life. It's worth knowing why you believe something, and also why you don't—so that both can be more thoroughly tested than is generally the case.

I think many of these objections are specious—logically and otherwise—and that there are good responses on the part of believers to even the strongest of them (see earlier reflections on the nature of "answers"). But some of these objections are ones I have or have had myself. None of them is trivial if they keep you from seriously considering the story of faith or send you fleeing.

My general plea is only that you probe any of these objections deeply, that you look for the best responses to them that you can find, that you test them to see if they are really impassable barriers to belief. I think many are legitimate challenges to those who claim faith, but none of them make faith impossible, illegitimate, or irrational. They are primarily challenges to believers to live a better version of the story of faith—individually and collectively—than is presently the case.

The Bible is full of people who object to what they are being told, including by Jesus. Each of them has reasons that seem convincing to them. My story does not ignore or attack the objections or the objectors; it includes them. It invites them to be part of the story and to find their answers within it.

WHO'S THE HYPOCRITE?
MOST EVERYBODY

I asked God for a bike, but I know God doesn't work that way. So I stole a bike and asked for forgiveness.

UNATTRIBUTED

You can sincerely believe there is no God and live as though there is. You can sincerely believe there is a God and live as though there isn't. So it goes.

FREDERICK BUECHNER, *WISHFUL THINKING*

One of the very few moral principles still held in common in our culture is disgust with hypocrisy. It is one of the rhetorical spitballs hurled most frequently in the culture wars, often at traditional Christian believers (not infrequently by other Christians). Better to be a baby killer than a hypocrite. "At least I'm not a hypocrite" is the squeaky defense of many a moral mouse.

Well, let's face it: you are a hypocrite. And so am I. And so is anyone who makes significant claims and commitments in life. The only way to avoid being a hypocrite is to make no claims, have no commitments, assert no oughts, no right and wrong, no protests against the way things are—in short, a virtue toad. (*Mouse and toad—you're on a roll. Cockroach next.*)

Hypocrisy is measured largely by the gap between what we say we believe and value and how we actually live. If there is no gap, you are either a saint or a moral moron, the standards of your commitments being much too low. (And saints often report they feel themselves the biggest hypocrites of all.) When someone says to me, "Christians are such hypocrites," I typically respond (in my head, of course), "That's true—*somebody* has to keep you company."

We Skeptical Believers are especially defensive when charged with hypocrisy, because it is a favorite accusation we like to make of others. We tend to think that our playing it safe (intellectually and otherwise) protects us from claiming much and therefore from being held accountable for very much. We have, using our keen observational and reasoning powers, "seen through" a lot of Smoke and mirrors, avoided the pitfalls of the naive and overeager, and therefore armed ourselves against the charge of hypocrisy. Which leaves us free, then, to make the charge frequently against others.

All Smoke. First, as we have seen, skeptics are wide open to the hypocrisy charge regarding their failure to be skeptical of their own skepticism. Skeptics live in glass houses like everyone else.

Second, no benefit accrues to you for having found hypocrisy in someone else. It doesn't do you or your "position" any good to find that someone else doesn't live up to their own announced standards. It doesn't make your way of living and thinking any truer or more moral or more defensible. Finding hypocrisy in others doesn't get you anywhere. If I think most abortions are the unnecessary taking of innocent life (which I do), that position is not strengthened if I manage to point out the hypocrisy of people who support abortion but shed tears over the destruction of eagle's eggs or violations of human rights. It might score debate points and make me feel morally superior (and I do believe some positions are morally superior to others on all kinds of issues), but it doesn't show I'm right. Similarly, if hard core secularists (or wavering Skeptical Believers) find hypocrisy in the church or individual believers, that doesn't add a shred of logical support for their views about God or no God.

Hypocrisy hunting is an entirely unrewarding enterprise unless it is directed at oneself. Chopping down others by pointing out their hypocrisy may well only make you the loudest cockroach among the mass of cockroaches. (*Cockroaches. I knew it was coming! But "loudest"?—do cockroaches make noise?*)

So am I defending hypocrisy or suggesting we should take it lightly? Not at all. Hypocrisy is a distinctly bad thing, but the charge against others, or against the church, shouldn't be used as a cover for one's own lack of commitment. If you find hypocrisy anywhere, your job is to live with as much integrity as you can muster, not to use hypocrisy as an excuse for your own tepidness (or your own hypocrisy).

Actually, hypocrisy is a quite useful concept when used on yourself. Being called (or calling yourself) a hypocrite can be morally bracing, if it causes you to assess your own life and reduce the gap between it and your expressed commitments. A few hours ago my wife told me I should go out and help my neighbor shovel his driveway from the eighteen inches of snow we just received. I didn't want to. I wanted to work on this book. I tried to think of reasons why I didn't have to. Given the story I say I live by, I couldn't muster a reason that convinced even me, eager though I was to be convinced. So I went out to help. (*You don't earn good boy points with that lousy attitude, buddy.*)

One of my favorite Britishisms—which I initially experienced on recorded messages in London subways—is "Mind the gap." The first time I was about to step onto a rail car in the Underground, this pleasant and proper recorded female voice intoned, "Mind the gap," and I had no idea what she was talking about. A little reflection helped me realize that "the gap" referred to the distance between the platform and the rail car, and that "Mind" meant "be mindful of"—the British equivalent of "Watch your step."

That's the useful part of the charge of hypocrisy—when I direct it at myself. Be mindful of the gap between what I say I believe and how I actually live. I've already told the story of visiting John in prison when I realized there was a gap between Jesus' expectation and my own life. In visiting John, I closed the distance slightly between belief and action. The gap subsequently widened a bit, since after a few years I found myself no longer visiting prisoners. (Note the subtle rationalization of my verb selection here—"I found myself"—as though it "just happened," rather than was the result of a conscious choice. Even in confessing hypocrisy, I try to defuse the charge.)

In sum, you can't avoid being a hypocrite except by being a moral toad. So aim high. Choose the best story you can, with the highest standards, then keep the gap between your life and those standards as small as you can. One of the nice things about the story of faith is that it knows you can't meet those standards and offers you help and forgiveness.

MANY STORIES, MANY RELIGIONS— WHO'S TO SAY?

If Christianity were the truth it would have to be offending and correcting your [and every culture's] thinking at some place.

TIM KELLER, *THE REASON FOR GOD*

If the Lord is God, follow him; but if Baal is, follow him.

1 KINGS 18:21

"Yes, faith is a story. That's why you should keep yours to yourself." So says, in so many words, the critic of my faith story. So says my Inner Atheist. (*Actually, I don't say keep it to yourself. I say ditch it all together.*) And the admonition to keep it to myself is one I am constitutionally inclined to embrace. By temperament and personality, I am more comfortable with sitting out of the way in the corner, thinking my own thoughts, puffing on my own mental pipe, than I am with working the room and telling people what they ought to think or do. (*So why, Mr. Modest Guy, are you writing this book?*) But my story won't let me.

One argument against my conviction that my story is *the* Story goes something like this. There are many different ways of understanding and living in the world—many stories, if you will. When people start claiming that their story is more true or good or real than other people's stories, bad things happen—tension, conflict, hatred, oppression, even war. Since there is no agreed-upon way of deciding whether one story is more true, good, or real than another, we do best to allow all stories to be told and lived. And we should suppress (in a tolerant, nonviolent way, of course) those people who disagree with this view. (*"Suppress" is such an unpleasant word. Let's say we should "discourage," through good reasoning, the acceptance of contrary views.*)

There's a lot to like in this line of argument, and it echoes some of my own favorite themes—humility, openness, story. But there are also some deadly traps. It contends, illogically, that since truth is contested, it's illegitimate to claim to know the truth. (While at the same time declaring truths of its own.) Implicitly, it suggests that claiming the truth of your own story is bad manners (unless it agrees with the truth of other people's stories). What it calls "tolerance" is not tolerance at all, but a kind of soft (or not so soft) relativism. (True tolerance requires you to believe someone else is wrong about something.)

I am a firm believer in the marketplace of ideas (more coming), but I also believe that some of the apples being sold are riper than others. And a few are downright rotten.

I want to address one particular strain of this debate about stories and truth—the existence of many religions—but the issues and arguments are similar when talking about how one navigates among the claims of all stories in all areas of human life.

Let's start with definitions of a few terms (*Not definitions again. What's on television?*), recognizing that my definitions may not be exactly someone else's definitions. (*Right, so why do you think you're going to convince anyone of anything?*)

"Pluralism" is simply the awareness and acceptance of the fact that there are many different ways of understanding and living in the world, coupled with the conviction that society should allow those differences to peacefully coexist. I'm a pluralist in this sense.

"Relativism" is the view that no one way of understanding the world is truer than or superior to any other way of understanding the world. No one genuinely believes this in its most undiluted form, but a great many people affirm softer versions of it, especially when it comes to things like religion. I'm not a relativist.

"Religious pluralism" can mean a number of different things. It can mean the view that all religions should be tolerated, even respected, or it can mean the more openly relativistic view that all religions are equally valid (*Or invalid, says I*), equally true, and equally saving (*Whatever that means*)—and that one should therefore not argue for one's own religious story over another. I am a religious pluralist in the first sense, but not in the second. (*As though anyone cares. For the record, I treat all religions equally—they're all foolish.*)

In what follows, I am going to use the term "religious pluralism" in this second, more relativistic, sense, and I am going to argue against it. I think this second sense describes those who most commonly embrace the term, even though all of them would deny earnestly that they are relativists. In the long run, the terms are much less important than the kind of relationship to God that different ways of thinking and living lead to.

One great attractiveness of religious pluralism—the view that most all religious stories are equally true and equally paths to God—is that you don't have to argue. Your story is good for you, my story is good for me, everybody's story is good for them. No unpleasantness, no ugly disagreements, no chosen people and not chosen people, no one being carted off to hell, everyone gets to play, everyone gets a cookie. (Though everyone in the conversation has to be a religious pluralist for it work this smoothly.)

Sounds good to me. Until I think about it too much. It's not my Christianity that is offended most (Christianity, and Judaism before it, grew up surrounded by many gods and are used to this kind of pluralism); it's my sense of logic. (*You spend page after page running down rationalism, and now you're going to invoke logic?*) It seems clear to me that the religions of the world make radically different and often mutually exclusive claims about almost everything: the human predicament and human nature; the central problem that needs overcoming; the manner in which that problem should be overcome; the nature of God or transcendence (and even the existence of either); the social implications of religious faith; and on and on. Judaism and Christianity put sin at the heart of any explanation of the human condition; other religions deny the very concept. Islam says there is only one God; other religions say there are many. Christianity says Christ is indispensable to any notion of salvation; other religions (and the nonreligious) say Christ is only Jesus and is, at most, one ethical teacher among many, and deny, by the way, that there is anything to be saved from or to.

I don't have a premodern view of truth (emphasizing authority) or an Enlightenment view of truth (emphasizing logical certainty), but I can't shake the conviction that the Law of Noncontradiction still holds up pretty well. (That is, two genuinely contradictory propositions cannot both be true at the same time and in the same sense).

Does it really not matter that the monotheistic religions of the world claim there is only one God, that the polytheistic religions claim that there are many gods, and that some quasi-religious outlooks, such as forms of Buddhism, claim there is no personal God or god at all? If these are all equal paths to the same place, it is not clear to me what that place is. (This evokes the favorite "many paths up the mountain" analogy of religious pluralists, my response being that most of those paths never make it to the top, and more than a few lead off cliffs. So much for analogies.)

Many argue that the place everyone is trying to get to is goodness. They argue that the point of religion is to make us better people. (*The point of religion is to make gullible people easier to control.*) They claim that if you stand back far enough from the details (way, way back, it seems to me), you can discern an ethical core in each religion that is very similar to every other religion. This is what we should focus on, they suggest, not more peripheral matters about whether there's a God or whether sin is moral failure or simply ignorance. It's sort of the Sesame Street approach to religion—let's all learn to share, take turns, and play nicely. (*That's the second time you've invoked Big Bird. Hmm. God as Big Bird. They have a lot in common: big, imaginary, feelings easily hurt...*)

This is a point at which I think religious pluralism fundamentally misses the boat. My story of faith tells me that the purpose of my faith— my worship, my commitment, my life—is not to make me a good person. It is to put me in a healthy relationship with the God who created me. Better behavior might be a *result* of the relationship, but it isn't its primary goal. And my story tells me that God, not I, determines the healthy nature of that relationship, and that the key to that relationship is Christ.

This is where I become persona non grata. This Christ stuff. *Jesus* is fine—a great model even—but the *Christ* part, all that Creator and Messiah stuff, has to go. It's too exclusive, too triumphalist, too intolerant. Too *Christian*, you might say. Because while you can manufacture a Christian-flavored religious pluralism (it comes in many flavors), there is no pluralistic, relativistic version of the Christian story (or of Judaism or any other religion, for that matter) that does not empty terms of their traditional meanings. Jealous God, Christ for everyone, and all that.

I also can't make sense out of the pluralist idea that no one should try to convert anyone else to his or her religion. We don't say that about any other area of human thought or endeavor. We don't say no one should try to change anyone else's political views. We don't believe everyone should be left with their own truth when it comes to racial equality, women's rights, or gay marriage. In almost all other areas, most people believe in the so-called "marketplace of ideas"—where individuals make, weigh, and test claims and counterclaims and then make up their minds, perhaps hewing close to views of their parents and community, perhaps not. We don't pretend all political views are equal. We advocate freely. Why do we pretend all religions or all stories are equal? Or that it is improper to advocate for one as opposed to another?

People say that others already have their religion and shouldn't be proselytized by someone from another religion. This is arguing that one's core convictions should be set by one's parents and birth community. Christians should stay Christians, Hindus stay Hindus, atheists stay atheists, Republicans stay Republicans, Yankee fans stay Yankee fans. (And cultures that do not grant women basic human rights should, of course, be encouraged to maintain their traditional views?) No one should be involved in persuading others to change their story. Really?

Religious pluralism, in the sense I am using it, markets itself as the champion of inclusion and the friend of all religions. I think, instead, that it is the enemy of all religions, because it rejects the central truth claims of all of them. At some point pluralism says to every particular religion that it must give up any claims that are offensive to other religions. And eventually that will require giving up a claim that the religion itself considers nonnegotiable, something at the core of its very being. For orthodox Christianity, that includes the claim that Christ is the world's Messiah, not just another local god.

For in my view, religious pluralism is another form of the oldest temptation in the history of my faith tradition: add another god. Just to be safe. Add the local god, the household god. "Who knows? Maybe the local god is just a hunk of wood, but no harm in including this god too. Everyone else is doing it." No harm except to your soul. Pluralism is adding all the local gods—from around the world. It covers all the bases. But nothing is a greater rejection of the one God. (There's a reason the First Commandment is first.)

Some stories are like marriages: you can't have more than one at a time. Maybe other people can make it work with multiple wives and multiple gods, but I can't. I'm barely adequate for one each.

Compare adding the local girlfriend. You are wedded to the wife of your youth, who is, perhaps, no longer young. At least she is no longer new. There are other women out there. Does it honor your wife to add the local girlfriend? Not in my case. Not in my story. I hope not to follow after additional girlfriends. I hope not to follow after other gods, no matter how reasonable and tolerant it may seem to some.

When I most want to be a pluralist, I picture myself announcing it to Christ. What do I say? "Yes, you are the one who created us all and everything in the universe. Yes, you are God come to dwell among us, your creatures. Yes, you were despised, crucified, died, and rose again—for my sake. But I hate to break this to you, Jesus (your *real* name), you are irrelevant to most of the people of the world. We Christians worship you for who you are and what you have done, but, well, the rest have their own stories. It wouldn't be right for us to tell them about you. It would be, well, exclusive; it would be intolerant." That's not a speech my story allows. If I believe it, I'm not living the Christian story. I'm putting my chips on the local gods.

Christ is only for Christians? When Christ came, there *were* no Christians. So was he intolerant to say, "Come, follow me"? You can argue that Jesus never thought of himself as anything other than a good Jew and that he never intended to start something called Christianity. But you can't say that from within the story, because that assertion empties the Christian story of all significant meaning. It is the death of the story, and trying to remake it as ethical pabulum will not bring it back to life. (*So let it die then. Good riddance.*)

So what is a Skeptical Believer to think about other religions? I will only state what this one Skeptical Believer thinks, admitting that I likely have not thought about it enough. I respect all committed attempts to discern and live by transcendent spiritual truths (with more respect for those committed to a different religious story than for those who claim to be committed to them all—or to some misty core of generic ethics that supposedly derives from them all). I am a pluralist in the sense of not wishing to silence the many voices speaking in the marketplace of ideas, nor wanting any special favors for my own. I am not a relativist in that I believe truth (including spiritual truth) to be something real, independent of human culture, and at least partially knowable. I believe in common grace, one manifestation of which is that all human beings, cultures, and religions are capable of insight, including into spiritual truths. I believe Christianity provides the most accurate description of God and God's relationship to the world, and that, in whatever form that relationship takes (including forms I may not know or understand), Christ is at the center of all reconciliation between God and the creation, including us.

Intolerant? Not at all. Tolerance is putting up with the objectionable, not, as some would have you think, affirmation of the diverse. Objectionable, in this context, means assertions I do not agree with. I put up with, even respect, many people and positions that I think are wrong (in politics, my family, my own religion, and other religions). I may argue against them, but I do not try to silence them. I am as tolerant as the day is long.

Exclusive? Quite the opposite. We speak of an exclusive country club or other private organization as one that carefully restricts its membership. Would you call a country club exclusive that went around the town knocking on doors and imploring people to join it—for free? Most critics of Christianity wish it would *quit* trying to get others to join and would restrict itself to its present members—that it would be *more* exclusive.

And please don't claim that it's exclusive to believe you're right and others are wrong. You just embarrass yourself. Is not the pluralist claiming that his or her approach to religion is right and that the so-called "exclusive" fundamentalists are wrong? Every systematic claim about the nature of things, including religion, is exclusive in the sense of thinking itself right and opposing views wrong. Otherwise it would not make its claim.

Proselytizing disrespectful? No, it's showing the ultimate respect. If I have something that I believe is helpful and good and will benefit others, how can I justify *not* sharing it? If I have a vaccine that will cure a plague, do I not offer it to others, even to people who do not agree they are sick or reject the vaccine because they think it useless or harmful? If someone urges on me something they think will genuinely help me, I am grateful for their interest and concern even if I do not agree with their advice.

The question is not why do Christians proselytize; it is why do others not? Why don't they care enough about others to share what they have found to be true and good? Do they not care, or do they not believe what they have found is genuinely true and good? (If the latter, then why not listen carefully to those who testify that they have found such a thing?)

I can't even conceive of how a Christian can oppose the call to evangelize. Christ came to teach a story that no one needed to hear because they already had one? Paul was wasting his time going to the Greeks and Romans because they already had a lot of gods? Jim Elliot and Nate Saint should have left the Aucas alone because they were perfectly happy to be spearing their enemies?

Actually, of course, people *do* believe in proselytizing. Our culture is soaked in it (think advertising, political campaigning, human rights and environmental activists). We're not against proselytizing; we simply want to convert others, not to be converted ourselves. (Or we are indifferent to others.) Arguing against proselytizing is itself an example of proselytizing. Religious convictions are no different from political, social, ethical, economic, or other convictions in this sense. In a free society, everyone has the right to try to persuade others, and everyone also has the right to resist persuasion—by saying no, hanging up the phone, slamming the door, changing the subject, or arguing back for a different position. I'll talk with you about God or the weather—you decide—but I'm not apologetic about doing either.

Everything about me as a Skeptical Believer predisposes me to a pluralistic, relativistic approach to spiritual things. But I've decided it's weak tea. Practically, garden-variety pluralists often use their supposed respect for all religions as an excuse for not practicing any religion. Philosophically, they neuter every religion by pretending that all of them are, at the most important level, really the same.

They aren't the same, not even close. Personally I choose to live the full-blooded version of the Christian story (too bloody for some), or not to live it at all. My culture is constantly proselytizing me to abandon my story—or to dilute it beyond recognition. I'm not buying. I will either live the story as it has been passed down to me—resurrections, miracles, Second Comings, preaching the gospel, and all—or I will give up on the whole enterprise and be the philosophical stoic I am most inclined by temperament to be. Anything less feels like the sin of Cain—offering God vegetables when he requires my life.

I do not believe this makes me arrogant. I respect anyone who won't settle for anything less than genuine transcendence—be they Jew, Hindu, Muslim, Christian, or questing secularist. Anyone playing the game of life for anything less than ultimate things is playing for toothpicks. If you are looking for something beyond getting and spending and the brittle bones of the material world, you have my respect. But I am not, after long thought, a pluralist in the relativistic sense.

I see the appeal of asserting that everyone is pursuing the same ultimate being but with their own names and rituals. Pursuing, yes. Finding, no. I can't convince myself of the truth of it. I am a Christer—as we have been derisively called. I will accept that label as a badge of honor. My story began before the world was made, it stretches into an eternal future after the world is ended, and it reached its pivot point on a wooden instrument of torture and in an empty tomb. I cannot live in the universalist story that claims that event was meaningful only for some people, for the Christers, but not for anyone else.

My story tells me that whenever people in another story find the truth, that truth will, in one way or another, be named not just Jesus, but Jesus the Messiah, that is, the Christ. That belief prompts some people to call me bad names. I can't help that. It's the story I have been invited into. It's the story I have tried to find my place in. I will live no other.

BAD CHRISTIANS, BAD POLITICS—
TWO BAD REASONS TO BE A
BAD BELIEVER

We have to fight evangelicals and their agenda. Truth, education and science are their enemies. They grow and thrive in the darkness of ignorance, and they wither and die in the light of knowledge and truth. It's our job to shine a light into that darkness.

CRAIG JAMES, ANTI-RELIGION BLOGGER, *THE RELIGION VIRUS*

I seemed to hear God saying, "Put down your gun and we'll talk."

C.S. LEWIS, *GOD IN THE DOCK*

When I was a kid I heard a lot in church about "the wrong crowd" and how I shouldn't get "in" with such people. I wasn't sure who they were, but I got the impression that they were to be found on street corners, perhaps even smoking cigarettes. Some people were just bad for you. (*Wine-bibbers and publicans I think they were called in the day.*)

Turns out, according to what I hear now, it was those church people who were the wrong crowd. They were the ones who were the bad influence, with all their judgmentalism and intolerance. (*And narrowness and hypocrisy and smugness and ignorance—shall I go on?*) At least that's what I hear from a lot of my fellow Skeptical Believers. They tell me that one of the big obstacles to their fully embracing the story of faith is all the bad Christians they see—in history, in church, on the air waves, even in the White House. If these people call themselves Christians, who would want to be one?

Fair enough. But let me put the same question in a different context. Some people who advocate for justice for the oppressed are exploitative, self-serving egotists (I won't name names). Do people say, "If this is the kind of person who works for justice in the world, I don't want to join"? It's easy to see the fallacy in that. It should be just as easy to see why the "bad Christians" argument is a weak one.

One can reject the bad Christians argument while agreeing fully that Christians are very often bad. I know enough history. I've spent all my life in churches and seen what goes on. I hear what is said on radio and television. I see what is done in legislatures and oval offices. And I also see what goes on within my own heart. I will stipulate, to use a lawyerly term, that Christians are often bad.

Then I will say, "So what?"

How is it that I even know we Christians are often bad? Only by my Christian story. My faith tells me what shalom is, what goodness is, what makes for a healthy society, and what destroys a society. It tells me my responsibilities to the poor and the oppressed, my duty to my children and neighbors, how I should behave in business and in relationships with the stranger and the opposite sex. Without it, I don't even know what bad is, and a materialistic, relativistic, secular culture certainly isn't going to help me.

My point is that Christianity can be self-correcting for those who stay within the story. Who put an end to the Inquisition, that fabled example of Christian intolerance? Other Christians. Who fights against Christians who equate God's blessing with prosperity and power? Other Christians. Who ended the slave trade that many Christians participated in? Other Christians. Who fights against the unreflective linking of faith with status quo politics? Other Christians. It is faith that tells you that judgmentalism, indifference to the poor, greed, hypocrisy, and so on are wrong. Secularism may tell you the same, but it got those convictions from religion (not from its own materialistic assumptions), and yet it denies those convictions any foundation other than mere opinion (more later in "Who Has the Right to Speak of Right and Wrong?"). Meanwhile it perpetuates enormous moral failures of its own.

So, do you find too many bad Christians, people whose behavior contradicts their stated values? Then be a good Christian yourself. Start your analysis of the health of the faith community with yourself. If you are pleased with yourself, then keep it up. If you are not, then do better. But don't use the weakness of other Christians as an excuse for your own weak contribution to the story of faith.

One derivative of the bad Christians argument against faith, or against wholehearted commitment to faith, is the bad politics objection. I hear it myself most often from young believers. It discourages them that theologically conservative Christianity is so thoroughly identified (accurately or not) with conservative politics—especially in America. To put it in that context, they get the message that being a Christian these days means voting for people who are for many things your are against and against many things you are for. And who, by the way, are also stiff and pompous, and have questionable hair. (Mostly puffed or waxed—bad hair suggests bad politics and bad theology).

Again, "So what?"

If Christians with conservative politics bug you, then associate yourself with Christians with liberal politics (if you think they are substantially better). Or don't associate yourself with politics at all, while still doing the things your story tells you to do (which will often have political implications—politics, by definition, involves a community of people). You really don't want to have that conversation with Jesus in heaven that goes, "I would have followed you much more faithfully, but, you see, there were these people called Republicans, and... " Imagine the puzzled look on his face.

It is helpful when discouraged by the number of bad Christians in the world to spend equal or more time thinking about the good ones. If you are a sports fan, do you go to an important game thinking of all the lousy amateur athletes there are? If you want to be a doctor, does the number of lousy doctors keep you from wanting to be one yourself? Do you abandon your political convictions because someone who shares them does foolish things? So why fill your head with examples of lousy Christians, except as a caution against being one?

Fill your mind, instead, with those you admire who have lived faithfully and well. Create your own cloud of witnesses, living and dead. Who is the best Christian you know? What makes you say so? How can you be more like that person? What person of faith do you admire from history? What writer or artist or thinker? What church leader? What politician?

I refer to my own guides frequently in this book—from biblical figures to historic models to my own teachers to simple but faithful people sitting next to me in the pew. I take these people as guides and mentors and spiritual directors. They show me what is possible, including the possibility of recovering from failure. They model perseverance, risk-taking, commitment, integrity, and love. They destroy a favorite rationalization for not embracing the story of faith as I should. I know it to be an evasion to use bad Christians as an excuse for my own flaccid faith. There are too many good ones calling me to join them in the story.

SENDING YOURSELF INTO EXILE: FIFTY WAYS TO LEAVE YOUR LOVER

I have been away from God for a large part of my life...
I had gone into exile of my free will.

WIM WENDERS

You just slip out the back, Jack
Make a new plan, Stan
You don't need to be coy, Roy
Just get yourself free
Hop on the bus, Gus
You don't need to discuss much
Just drop off the key, Lee
And get yourself free

PAUL SIMON, "FIFTY WAYS TO LEAVE YOUR LOVER"

Why would anyone who has ever known God choose to walk away?

That other verbs come to mind—wander away, edge away, work away, slink away, suffer away, sprint away—indicates that people take leave of faith in many different ways. There are, as the old song says, "fifty ways to leave your lover."

Only a few people, a very few, leave faith at a clearly defined point. Fewer still leave God because they have reached the conclusion, after careful thought and testing, that God does not exist. Most people who have ever been part of the community of faith don't so much consciously choose to leave faith as they live themselves away from faith.

By "live themselves away from faith," I mean they simply make more and more life choices, tiny ones more often than big ones, that do not take God or the story of faith into account. These choices might range from whom to marry, what to value, what to do when in trouble, how to raise kids... to how to vote, what to buy, whom to have as friends... to what books or films or activities to soak in, whom to admire, or what to do on a Sunday morning.

Some people suffer themselves away from faith. Their life is simply too painful for them to hold that pain and the goodness of God in their head at the same time. (While others are driven *closer* to God by pain.) Some move from faith because they surround themselves only with people who find faith irrelevant or pernicious. It takes more strength of mind to live at odds with the views and values of our immediate companions than most of us possess.

And one of the great deadeners of faith is simply the busyness of life. So many demands fill up the foreground—school, friends, coming and going when one is young; careers, marriage, raising children, getting and spending when one is older—that God is pushed to the background. Or even into another world that we visit only occasionally, if at all. And these demands are mostly good things—or at least necessary things—and few of us have the luxury of not paying them attention.

Faith dies by a thousand cuts more often than by a single fatal blow. In this it is like other forms of love. We can fall in love in an instant, including with Jesus. We are less likely to fall, precipitously, out of love. More often we edge away from love as we are distracted by other things. We do not say, "I choose no longer to be in love." We don't say anything. We rather innocently devote our attention to other things, and at some point realize, "I am no longer in love." Maybe we are in love with something or someone else instead, but more often we are simply "out of love" and floating.

The Irish poet W.B. Yeats, in one of the most quoted passages of poetry from the last century, writes of the collapse of civilizations, but he could as readily be speaking of the movement away from faith:

Turning and turning in the widening gyre
The falcon cannot hear the falconer.
Things fall apart; the centre cannot hold...
The best lack all conviction, while the worst
Are full of passionate intensity.

The falcon is trained to hunt, flying in circles over the head of the falconer, responding to verbal commands or whistles or arm motions. But as it flies, the circles get wider and wider. The voice of the falconer is farther and farther away. Now I barely hear it. Now I don't hear it all. Did I, the falcon, consciously choose to fly off from God, the Falconer? Or did I simply fly too far, farther and farther from the Falconer's voice, until, perhaps without even noticing, I am flying on my own?

And am I now free, as the secularist would say, free from the stupid rules and narrow constraints of childish faith? Or am I merely without a center? Am I one of those who now "lack all conviction," not believing anything in particular (or only the things those around me believe), playing it safe, going in whichever direction the wind is blowing? Is it enough for me now to be, as so many claim as an adequate goal in life, "a good person"?

Wim Wenders, I think, has it right when he says, "I had gone into exile of my free will." God exiles no one. Many choose, one small choice at a time, to exile themselves. As the church bulletin board asked, "If God seems distant, who do you think has moved?"

Many of us never officially leave faith; we simply move to the edge—just inside faith, or just outside it—and take up residence there. We are neither fully in nor fully out. Like T.S. Eliot's spiritual sleepers, we live dormantly, buried under "forgetful snow, feeding/ a little life with dried tubers."

But can I be "just outside" faith? Is faith like being pregnant—you are or you aren't—or is it like being a sports fan—ranging from fanatical to indifferent, with at some point, known only to God, not being a fan at all? Some fans are fair-weather fans and jump back on the bandwagon when the team makes it to the championship game. With faith it's often the reverse. We are foul-weather fans, becoming interested in God only when life turns stormy and God seems useful.

We are like the prodigal son. Give me my inheritance so I can live life the way I want to live it, away from the burdensome voice of the Falconer. Our life without a center falls apart—or perhaps simply declines into emptiness—and we wonder if we can come home.

The answer, always, is yes. We can come home. It has been pointed out that "The Story of the Prodigal Son" is misnamed. It is not primarily a story about the son's failure, but about the father's welcoming forgiveness. It should be called "The Story of the Forgiving Father."

But returning home is a choice. It will not be forced upon us. Some return home in one giant step, moved by the power of the Spirit to repent and commit again. Others will return as they left, one small step at a time, in a long journey of small acts of belief. And, of course, some will never return at all.

But whether in a moment or as part of a long journey, those who choose to return will find the forgiving father, not just waiting but scanning the horizon, eager to forgive, eager to kill the fatted calf, eager for a celebration.

JUST NOT INTERESTED

Christianity..., if false, is of *no* importance, and, if true, of infinite importance. The one thing it cannot be is moderately important.

C.S. LEWIS, "CHRISTIAN APOLOGETICS," *GOD IN THE DOCK*

Because of this many of his disciples turned away and no longer walked with him.

JOHN 6:66

There is one, and only one, response to the claims of faith that leaves me with nothing to say. That response is, "I'm not interested." Tell me that its claims are not true, and we have grounds for a discussion. Tell me that the Bible is a crock, and we have something to talk about. (*The Bible is a crock.*) Tell me that God or the church has let you down, and I will listen. Tell me that you have a better story to live by, and I will ask you about your story. But tell me that you just don't care, and I am mute. We may as well move on to what's for lunch, our favorite football team, or the weather.

A person who is not interested is not a doubter, nor necessarily even a denier of the things of faith. He or she is terminally indifferent, the furthest possible distance from belief. (T.S. Eliot argues that even blasphemers are closer.) This is relevant to the Skeptical Believer because indifference is only a couple of steps beyond skepticism. Skepticism is not indifference, but it is a virus to which the skeptic is susceptible.

One can say to the person who does not care, "You *should* care" or "Someday you'll wish you had cared"—both true—but neither is effective. Indifference is its own defense. If one is indifferent to a claim, one is automatically indifferent to supposed consequences.

I know this because I am myself indifferent to many claims that people around me make. (*Right, including my claim that you should think more clearly.*) They have their ideas of what makes for a successful life, and I have mine. Sometimes I think them wrong, but sometimes I simply am not interested in the things that interest them. So I include myself, at times, among the indifferent.

The main issue, then, is not whether one is indifferent, but what one is indifferent about. I can understand when someone thinks the claims of my story are false. I have a much more difficult time understanding why anyone, in any state of life, is indifferent to the consideration of ultimate things. Which is the case, as I look around, with countless of my fellow human beings—including many of those that our society would call the most successful. Pascal says it is reasonable to serve the God one knows, and it is reasonable to search for God if one does not know him, but it is not reasonable to be indifferent to the possibility of God, or to cease looking for an ultimate meaning in the universe. I think he's right.

One cannot force people to be interested in the things that should interest them, as anyone who has raised an adolescent knows. Interest and indifference is a measure of valuing. If you value diamonds (and what they bring), you will bore great tunnels in the earth to find them. If you value ultimate things (and what they bring), you will devote a great part of your life to seeking them. And you will not stop seeking because they are hard to find or understand, or because someone else says there are no ultimate things.

Not to value the things of God is, perhaps, related to what the Bible calls the sin against the Holy Spirit, for which there is no forgiveness. (This is pure speculation on my part.) (*Oh, now you're going to tell us what is and isn't forgivable. Very modest of you.*) Perhaps it is to say, having been told the story of what God has done, "I don't care." It is not that this angers God and he therefore punishes you. It is that by voluntarily treating the story as of no significance to you, you freely refuse its offer.

This way of putting it will cause no concern for the indifferent person, because he or she is just that—indifferent. But it should terrify the Skeptical Believer. (Substitute a milder word if you think "terrify" too sensational.) I believe God can work with my skepticism, but I believe he will allow me the fruits of my indifference, and those fruits are bitter indeed.

The pursuit of ultimate things should never end. If one has looked and not found, then keep on looking. Anything less is foolish. If one has once tasted God but wandered away, then taste again. If one has accepted God's story, then never stop exploring and living it. If someone you love is indifferent to the things of God, pray that circumstances in their life will break through the white noise of their indifference and send them on a quest whose ultimate end is the one who made us all.

STORY AND THE PROBLEM OF PAIN

Some questions are so big they can only be lived with, lived in, lived through.
VIRGINIA STEM OWENS

Sickness is… more instructive than a long trip to Europe.
FLANNERY O'CONNOR

Perhaps truth is the ultimate test for any life story. But suffering is a close second. A story that can't help us live with suffering is too thin to be useful. Because, God knows, as did Job, that "people are born for trouble / as surely as sparks fly upward."

Sometimes we suffer ourselves, sometimes we must respond to other people's suffering, which, if you are compassionate, involves pain for you as well. Any helpful response to someone else's suffering must start with listening. Then silence. Perhaps a touch. Often shared tears.

A reaction to suffering that gets too quickly to an answer is only itself a cause of more suffering. As is any that is too cocksure, too neat, too sealed up tight, too bowed and ribboned. Or any that moves on too quickly to other things. Or that is impatient, overly pious, or sentimental. Or any of a thousand other things.

Our suffering is a measure of our valuing. If we didn't care, we wouldn't suffer. It is an acknowledgment that something or someone valuable has been hurt or lost, that some good has been diminished, that shalom has been ruptured. Human beings do not wish to be relieved too quickly of their suffering, nor should they wish it when they suffer from what ought not to be. Many, many things in a fallen and twisted world ought not to be. This is no small thing. Feeling pain for it is as it should be.

We have had, since the time of Job and before, explainers of suffering. Some do it professionally or piously, many to comfort others, some to protect themselves: "Your suffering raises the possibility that I have no defense against suffering myself, and so your suffering must be explained... away... quickly."

Reasonable, rationalistic answers to suffering are, I find, the least helpful. They are like the admonition to a child with the skinned knee, "Come on now, that didn't hurt... shake it off... be tough... you're going to be okay." Maybe I'm going to be okay, maybe I'm not. In the midst of my suffering, it isn't a helpful observation.

It's especially unhelpful when these explanations are generic and prepackaged—when they are crafted as a response to (trumpet fanfare) "The Problem of Evil" rather than to my specific loss at this specific moment. This is so for those who use suffering to defend God and for those who use suffering to abuse God. When people use suffering in the world as a reason for not believing in God, they usually invoke someone else's suffering or suffering in general. I think they should speak from their own. When they invoke other people's suffering (who, by the way, often interpret their own suffering differently) as a reason for disbelief, I am inclined to argue with them. When they invoke their own, I am inclined to listen to their story.

Listening to the stories of suffering is where we must start. And often the best response—at an appropriate time—is another story. Story is better suited to both convey and respond to suffering than is reason alone. Why?

Among other things, stories have more room. They have room for the unresolved, the uncertain, the ambivalent. They also have room for the scream, the shaken fist, the refusal to accept or make peace with, the *j'accuse*. In other words, room for all the emotions and reactions that pain stirs up in the human heart and mind and body. Stories don't have to explain everything; many times they just present what is, and sometimes how we think and feel about it.

Logical argument, on the other hand, demands a conclusion—an assertion, a this and not that. Its goal is precision, clarity, and, in many cases, certainty. This is what a reasonable person must accept, because I—Explanation Man—have gathered together solid propositions and handled them carefully and arrived at an unassailable conclusion. Problem acknowledged. Problem solved. Next question?

The next question is likely to be a repeat of the first question: "Why did this happen?" followed by the second, "How do I go on?"

Stories insist on the legitimacy of human emotion. Tears and extremes of emotion get in the way, we are told, of rational thinking. But they are the very source of story. No pain, no story. (In all significant stories, something has gone wrong.) Here, again, is an example of story's inclusiveness, its appeal to the whole person.

Stories also spread out over time, the most important ones over all of time and eternity. A telling of the story may end, but the story itself never does. This is important for dealing with suffering. Suffering may come to an end in one form, it often never ends altogether, certainly not its effects. When we convey our suffering in story, we use a form that will last as long as the suffering does, without attempting to deny it. When we respond to suffering with story, we offer a balm (not a solution) that can last as long as the pain.

I have said that story works better with suffering than assertions, but so far I have only made a raft full of assertions myself. Clearly I must tell some stories. I don't know which to choose, there being, sadly, so many painful stories. Being a believer, do I first tell biblical stories? Job is the classic story of suffering. But Job doesn't feel fully "storied" to me. It seems more like a profound, extended illustration—an example—told to decorate a mostly logical assertion ("God is God and you ain't"). I am being too cavalier. Job is a story, and it rewards deep study, but it is too rich to make use of briefly.

The story of Naomi and Ruth works better. Just eighty-five verses long, it is one story of suffering among hundreds in the Bible (is there anyone who doesn't suffer in the Bible?). Naomi suffers from as many different calamities as perhaps anyone in Scripture. The Bible tends toward understatement, not exaggeration, when it comes to suffering, and oceans of pain are often reduced to a single, simple declarative sentence. In the first line of the book of Ruth, we are told that Naomi and her husband and her two sons left Judah for Moab because of famine. No elaboration. But think of how bad it must be for a family to leave everyone they know and love because they are in danger of starving.

Then we are told that sometime after settling in Moab, Naomi's husband died. Again, no elaboration. The person she had married and then depended on in a foreign land was dead. How much pain did that cause? We can only guess.

Her sons, at some point, marry local women. A good turn for Naomi? Maybe. But two sentences after, we are told that both sons died. The story doesn't tell us how Naomi felt—it is not modern in that sense. Perhaps it doesn't believe it needs to tell us. How would you feel—a survivor of starvation, a foreigner, a widow, now childless? In a society that granted no status or protection to someone in your shoes. Stories leave some things to the imagination.

Her prospects are so dim that Naomi decides to return, more than ten years after leaving, to her ancestral place in Judah. (You could say she returns to her original story, and that story takes a new turn.) Ruth, her widowed daughter-in-law, insists on coming with her, declaring her loyalty in famous words that begin, "Where you go, I will go... " The two of them return to Bethlehem, at which time Naomi, devastated by the direction her story has taken, asks the women of the town not to call her Naomi (meaning "pleasantness") but Mara (meaning "bitterness"). "I went away full," she declares, "but the Lord has brought me back empty."

Who has not felt something like that emptiness? What believer has not thought, even if only fleetingly, that the feeling signaled an abandonment by God?

The story then turns more to Ruth and her "redemption" by Boaz. Naomi is an adviser and confidant. She shares, at least indirectly, in the good fortune of Ruth. She had never blamed or cursed God, but had felt deserted by God, someone without any blessing in her life. Now, hearing of Boaz's favor toward Ruth, Naomi blesses Boaz and declares that the Lord "has not withdrawn his kindness to the living and to the dead."

Ruth marries Boaz and has a son. Interestingly, the story tells us that the women of the town declare "a son has been born to Naomi" rather than to Ruth. This is Naomi's story, and it ends with all the women celebrating that Naomi has been granted "a renewer of life and one to sustain you in our old age." To make things even better, we are given a genealogy and find that Ruth's son will be a direct ancestor of David, the greatest king of Israel.

This is a story about suffering. It is powerful and instructive not because it has the proverbial happy ending. It is instructive because it claims that suffering is not the final word. Even had Naomi died before seeing Ruth redeemed and a son born, the hearer of the story would see that Naomi's story was full of meaning and value, because without Naomi's suffering in Moab, Ruth would not have come to Bethlehem and King David would not have been born.

Nothing in this story dismisses Naomi's pain. The ultimate outcome of her story and Ruth's did not return her husband or her sons to life. It did not make that suffering "go away." It didn't even redeem it in the sense of turning it into something else. That suffering is still what it was, and its ache would never entirely end.

What it did say was, "That loss is real, and so is this blessing." The story tells us that suffering does not have to be the final word. That there is more to the story during and after the intense pain.

Can we be certain of that in our own stories? No. You can't be certain. Maybe the human experience is random, as many say. Maybe it's just luck—you're lucky for a while, then unlucky. Sorry, mate: life sucks. You may go out full, but you'll come back empty.

Or maybe the biblical stories are true. Maybe the same God who does not prevent us from suffering nevertheless "has not withdrawn his kindness to the living and to the dead." Maybe suffering is a word, but not the only word, not the last word.

Stories, unlike arguments, offer us choices. "Believe me or not," they say. "Bring me into your life or keep me out. Here's the story. You decide what to do with it."

CONSIDER NATALIE: FURTHER REFLECTIONS ON SUFFERING

The starting point for many things is grief.

BELDEN LANE, *THE SOLACE OF FIERCE LANDSCAPES*

If stories of God and suffering, such as Ruth's, were found only in the Bible, we could deal with them quite adequately. We would be content to limit the issue to our minds, one of many problems to be solved in due time. But suffering is as much a part of our everyday experience as breath. It does not go away, and it is not solved.

Consider Natalie.

Natalie is the daughter of the friend, Phoebe, who told me if I was going to write a book like this one, I had better write about suffering. I took her to mean, if you can't say something useful about suffering, you don't have much useful to say. She's right. (I once read the following somewhere: "You haven't suffered? Then what do *you* know?")

This is not a story about the most severe forms of suffering. The most severe stories stun us into silence (or should). They take our breath and our answers away. This is a story about genuine suffering of the kind that many can understand because it is in a sense the kind of suffering common to the human condition (while not at all "common" in a dismissive way).

Phoebe understands suffering. She once watched her unstable father beat her mother, and, early in life, she put herself in between them. She suffered for years with a debilitating illness. And then there was a long respite. She is now suffering with something similar again, only worse. She has stories, told reluctantly, about these things and more.

But she also suffers because of the suffering of someone else—her daughter Natalie. Natalie was conceived out of season. Phoebe had a viral infection, and the doctors said she should not get pregnant while it was being treated. Despite redundant precautions, she became pregnant anyway, and Natalie was born with significant mental and physical disabilities. Whether they were connected to Phoebe's illness or the drugs she was taking is impossible to say.

Natalie today is a young woman. She has tremors. She has trouble with balance. Stairs are doable but only with the energy and focus that most of us would use to climb a cliff. Thoughts in her brain do not always link the way they should. Reading is difficult. Understanding fully or making herself fully understood is sometimes a challenge. The drugs she must take make her heavy. They harm her at the same time that they help. It is unclear whether Natalie will ever be able to live alone.

Natalie has a sense of a brokenness within herself. She has asked, "Why doesn't my brain work?" "Why did God make me this way?" She has suffered not only in body over the years but from the social isolation of being rejected by other children and now by being different from other young adults. She wants to be whole and yet accepts that she isn't. She both yearns for something that is not and accepts what is, a paradox of sorts that is not simply resignation.

That is one word about Natalie. Here is another.

Natalie is as kind as any person I know. She has a gentle spirit that wishes everyone blessing. Her own suffering has made her highly sensitive to the suffering of others. She prays fervently and effectually for those who need prayer. She offers a comforting word to those who are sad, even though she is sometimes quite sad herself. She is, I often think, in touch with parts of reality that others of us know little of.

And she is cute—with light brown freckles, soft, brown hair, and a fetching laugh.

Is Natalie's a sad story? Yes.

Natalie suffers in body and mind. Phoebe feels deep grief most every day at the affliction that keeps her beloved daughter from being whole.

Is Natalie's a happy story? Yes.

She laughs often. Many people live better because she is in their lives. Many with better health live much less happily.

Should I wish her story were otherwise? I don't know.

Certainly, were it in my power then or now, I would have given Natalie health and Phoebe peace of mind. There is no question that all suffering is a break in shalom, in how things ought to be. I do not romanticize suffering.

But neither can I confidently wish it away. I cannot bring myself to wish that this Natalie, the one who prays and blesses and, yes, walks unsteadily, were not here. I cannot confidently say, "Take away this Natalie and give me one who has been healthy from birth." Because I do not know that Natalie. I do not know that she would be as gentle and accepting and concerned to bless others. I do not know that, rid of her troubles from the beginning, she would even be as happy. I can imagine her story turning out differently— and not as well. More healthy in body, perhaps less healthy in spirit.

One can claim that Natalie's afflictions prove there is no God, or not a good one. Or one can be angry with God for not protecting Natalie from harm and Phoebe from grief. One can say that God stuttered when he spoke Natalie's story. But I can't say that myself. I know that disability was a first word and is an ongoing word. It does not seem to me that disability is the only word, nor the most important word—nor is it the last.

There are other words that describe Natalie today: compassionate, gentle, comforting, prayerful, and kind. These do not erase the suffering, but they surround it and, dare we say, give it the potential for meaning. A word was spoken about Natalie at her birth; it is still a word about her life; but it is not the word that tells her who she is.

MY OWN STORY OF PAIN

I feel sometimes
we are his penance
for having made us. He
suffers in us and we partake
of his sufferings.

R.S. THOMAS, "COVENANT"

When Jesus tells us about his Father, we distrust him… but when he
confides to us that he is "acquainted with Grief," we listen, for that also is an
Acquaintance of our own.

EMILY DICKINSON

I have put off doing what I have said that anyone who speaks of suffering
should do—that is, speak from my own.

I hesitate largely because I know I cannot do so with any authority or
conviction. My overwhelming sense about my own life is of blessing and
grace, not of suffering and hardship. Someone with a different temperament might be able to take a few of the circumstances of my life and con-
coct a narrative of woe, but it's not one I'm peddling or buying myself. I've

heard too many other stories—in history, in literature, in today's newspaper, in the lives of those I love—to think myself as anything but blessed.

But I have committed myself by my own reasoning to telling a story from my own life, and so I will. This is a very condensed telling of a story about my mother. (See my *Creating a Spiritual Legacy*, Brazos Press, for the entire story.)

I tell my mother lies.

Sometimes three or four times a day.

I lie mostly about money. That I've sent it or that I'm just about to send it. Or that surely I will send it tomorrow. My mother waits for money like the bums waited for Godot.

One day she called seventeen times. So said the long-distance bill. But I admit I stopped answering after seven or eight, and the rest went on the answering machine. That's not as cruel as it sounds—because each call was new for her. She didn't think, My son refuses to answer my calls. *She thought,* I need money. I'll call Danny. *Seventeen times.*

That's what most every call is about these days—money. It starts with, "Well, what you doing up there?" "Up there" *means Minnesota, where I live. She lived for twenty years in Memphis, and "up there" made sense. Now she's in North Dakota, farther north than I am, but she sticks to the old mental map. Good for her.*

"Is that wife of yours still running up and down the steps?" She doesn't risk using my wife's name—Jayne. Names are booby traps these days. Try a name, and you may reveal the secret—the secret that everyone knows but you.

But eventually—very quickly, actually—she gets to the point. "Listen, honey. I am desperate for some money." *And she* is *desperate. That's the stabbing part. She is desperate. You can hear it in her voice. It's full of anxiety and appeal. And you want to do something about it. Your mother is desperate, and you want her not to be. You want her to be okay. You want her to be peaceful—full of peace. Because you know that she has earned it, and because she is your mother.*

My mother has had to worry about money most of her life. She married an irresponsible man. A talented man. A charming man. In many ways a generous man. But a man you couldn't trust with money. If he had money, he spent it—often on himself. You could send him out for bread and milk and he'd come back six hours later with a new television set. Or three new suits (he wanted to look good even when he got fat), or five books (he read to find the world he needed to live in), or, one time, six of those newfangled transistor radios ("If one breaks, then we've always got another one").

My father didn't make as much as he spent—at any of his fifteen different jobs. We lived, unbeknownst to three trusting little boys, on the ragged edge of insolvency. We were never officially poor, but we sometimes toured the neighborhood. My mother fended off the creditors with monthly five-dollar payments on ravenous debts.

So she went to work, becoming a school teacher when I was ten. She got up at five in the morning to clean the house, woke the rest of us at six-thirty, went off to a day of teaching, and then came home to make supper and wash clothes. Teaching brought in the dependable income, but it couldn't quite keep her ahead of my father.

So the last thing I want my mom to worry about is money. She's got almost enough herself, and I've got more to back that up, so money, for the first time in her life, shouldn't be an issue.

It's an issue.

"I've got a list of nineteen things I've got to get. And I haven't got a penny to my name."

It's always nineteen things. Never seventeen, never twenty. Sometimes I ask her what's on the list. It's not a fair question. If she actually has a list, and she probably does, she isn't sure where it is, and asking her to remember what's on it is like asking Mrs. Lindbergh about her baby. (I'm sure hairspray is on the list—she has seven cans of it in her closet.)

"What good does it do me to have $38,000 in the bank if I can't spend any of it?"

I take it as a rhetorical question. I don't know where she got the number 38,000. I guess it will do as well as any. It's as good as nineteen—twice as good in fact.

And then the question I dread from the moment I hear the phone ring. "Will you send me some of my money, son?" (She doesn't risk my name anymore either.) "I've just got to get some clothes for summer"—or whatever season, about which she is often wrong. "Will you send me some money?"

That's when I lie. It's the only thing I've knowingly lied to anyone about, and it's painful. I try to lie quickly, so we can move on to something else.

"Yes, I'll send some money. No problem, Mom."

But she wants details.

"When are you going to send it?"

"Today, Mom. Tomorrow at the latest."

"How much are you going to send? Can you send fifty dollars?"

"Mom," I want to say, "I'd send fifty thousand dollars. I'd send you the world. If I thought it would do you any good. Even if I thought it would do you good for an hour. But it won't. We've tried. And it won't do you any good at all."

This is the beginning of a longer story I've written about my mother and the relentless dissolution of her mind. Among other things it is, of course, a piece about suffering. About her suffering anxiety over a world that is slipping away from her, and, indirectly, about my suffering from watching it happen and knowing there is nothing I can do about it.

Nothing except be present to it. Be a witness. Call. Show up. Say the things that can be said. Go through it with her.

Maybe sing together.

Once when I was visiting her in the nursing home in North Dakota, the name of a hymn comes up. I start to sing it, thinking only to croak out a few bars. But my mother looks at me with a smile and picks up the tune. She is harmonizing underneath my broken melody. She used to do the same with my father, sometimes in church, her sitting at the piano—he the handsome preacher, she the dutiful pastor's wife.

Her voice is tremulous, partly from habit—a traditional way of hymn singing, I think—and partly from age. My memory of the words runs dry— dry, that is, until the words are needed. From somewhere deep inside me come the words just in time for the next phrase. "There shall be showers of blessing; this is the promise of love." What's next? "There shall be seasons refreshing. Sent from..." My mother finishes, "The Savior above."

It is a sweet moment. Singing with my mom. Something I haven't done since I was a child. I don't look at her as we sing, for fear I might cry.

"Showers of blessing we need." That's certainly true, Mom. We do need them. How can I, given how you are now—and how I am—be a blessing to you? What can I do that will last for more than a few moments?

"Mercy drops round us are falling. But for the showers we plead." Maybe that's the most I can hope to do for you, Mom—mercy drops. A call here, a visit there, a book of beautiful photographs that might, if you remember to look at them, take you briefly to other places. The doctors say you can only get worse, steadily and inexorably, as surely as winter follows fall. But even in winter, perhaps, there can be mercy drops.

Telling even these tidbits of my mom's story makes me feel guilty again. I feel guilty because even while I create the nice phrases about calling and witnessing and being there with her, I know I do not call or witness or go there enough. The ten hours of driving, her instant forgetfulness of my visits, and the repetitiveness of the calls are enough to allow me to let myself off the hook, but not enough to completely erase the guilt.

Maybe that's one reason to tell each other these stories. I can comfort others about their guilt, and they can offer me solace about mine. And maybe then each of us can move on to more useful emotions and actions. Story leaves open that possibility. It also tells me that the God who made my mother loves her, does not wish her mind to crumble, and will not allow this, even if it is how her life will end, to be the last word about her life.

I have a final thought, for now, about suffering and story. One of the things my faith story tells me about God is that God suffers too. He does not just watch us suffer. He does not even watch us suffer and then sometimes intervene. God also suffers, more than you or I, because his suffering includes all of ours and more. (We often ask, "Why does God allow suffering?" I think there is a prior question, "Why does God allow himself to suffer?")

God suffered before we did. God may (this is speculation) have suffered before he ever created the world. Suffering, it seems to me, is part of the nature of God. Our being made in the image of God may include, among many things, being capable of meaningful suffering. The thing that makes suffering most unbearable is the suspicion that it is meaningless. Having a story that includes suffering raises the possibility that suffering doesn't have to be so.

One difference between God's suffering and most of ours is that his is voluntary. Somehow and for some reason, God allows himself to suffer—and it seems mostly for our sakes that he does so. (It is no small thing that we are told that the Christ was "despised and rejected, / a man of sorrows and acquainted with suffering.") My story of faith makes the scandalous claim that love is at the center of the universe. Maybe love is at the center because suffering is not far away. Though we wish it otherwise, perhaps love cannot come into being any other way.

But now I am back to trying to make it work out logically. In Dostoyevsky's great *The Brothers Karamazov*, the atheist Ivan uses the fact of suffering to make an unanswerable attack on the idea of a good God. His gentle, believing brother, Alyosha (I think of Natalie), answers him the only way he knows—with a kiss. Reason's question is "Why do I suffer?" Story's response is a showing of love. Or at least that is my story's response.

"Some questions are so big they can only be lived with…" I cannot solve the problem of evil. I no longer try. I don't think I am being escapist or irrational. I think I am reasonably recognizing that one can only answer some important questions, not with an argument, but with a life. The story answer to the problem of evil is "together we go on, we remain hopeful, we continue to live—as other sufferers have lived—within this story of faith, believing that the last word is love." God help our unbelief.

THE BIBLE—WHAT TO MAKE OF IT

The Book rusts
in the empty pulpits above empty
pews, but the Word ticks inside
remorselessly as the bomb that is timed
soon to go off.

R.S. THOMAS, "WAITING"

"Really—the Word of God?"

So asks my friend, trying hard not to add, "How crazy is that?" (*I'll gladly say it: "Staggeringly crazy. Padded-cell crazy. Dangerous-to-self-and-others crazy."*)

Crazy indeed—filled with stories both fetched and far-fetched. Stories of six-day creations, parting seas, walking on water, universal floods, naked prophets marrying prostitutes. And worse, commands to kill men, women, children (and livestock too) (*What, the sheep didn't pay their Temple tax?*), and hate your father and mother. And crazier still, stories of raising the dead, stopping the sun, and—changing everything—an empty tomb. And, perhaps craziest of all, God becoming one of us, a human being (*Supersized*), walking around in our midst. Just like you and me—though different too.

What is a Skeptical Believer to make of the Bible? So much to be skeptical about from so long ago.

A different friend, this one a doctor and a believer, says to me in Ireland regarding the miracle stories associated with the Celtic saints, "Obviously bogus."

I say, "You believe in the miracles of the Bible, including floating axheads. Why are you sure these later miracle stories are bogus?"

He replies, "I *have* to believe the Bible stories, because they're *in* the Bible, but I don't have to believe these stories about the saints, and I don't."

Not a very satisfying answer, I think, certainly not to a Skeptical Believer who is suspicious of all "have to" arguments. Actually, you don't have to believe the Bible or its stories (most don't). You don't have to believe anything at all. (Though everyone does, in fact, believe many, many things—most of which they cannot themselves prove.)

A few minutes ago, I received an e-mail from a stranger whose faith is shaken by having to believe in a talking snake in the story of the Garden of Eden. Here's how I responded: "Regarding the snake: no requirement that I can see to believe a literal snake is talking. I know this opens Pandora's Box, but humans opened that box a long time ago. If I choose to move away from belief, I don't want it hinging on the question of talking snakes or no talking snakes." (I could also have said, but didn't, "If one already believes in a God who created the galaxies, why is it harder to believe in a snake that talks?") (*True enough. Once you drink the Kool-Aid, all things become possible.*)

The Pandora's Box, of course, has to do with how we are to read the Bible. I know generally the issues involved in this question, and I know they are not trivial. I am willing to go to the mat over whether or not there was an empty tomb, because I think there is no meaningful Christianity without it, but I simply am not going to put much weight on the question of talking snakes. (And, no, I don't believe that believing one requires me to believe the other in the same way.)

The point isn't talking snakes or no talking snakes; the point is that one's reasons for leaving (or dismissing) something as all-important as faith in God should be commensurate with the enormity of the consequences. If Christianity is untrue, then the consequences must be accepted, for good or ill. If Christianity is true, then to abandon it for inadequate reasons (like talking snakes) is the ultimate tragedy. (*Excellent! So how about we argue a bit about whether it's true or not. Just for old times' sake? Just for a few minutes? You make a point and I'll make a point. Whadda ya say?)*

I have spent a good hunk of my life working on Bible translations (looking out for the English, not the Hebrew or Greek). I have read these stories with the eye of a stylist-translator, something quite different from reading them with the eyes of faith. I have also tried putting myself in the shoes of someone who reads them purely as ancient stories, and I can easily see why they would find them "rusty" at best (to borrow from R.S. Thomas above).

Actually, reading the Bible from cover to cover as an eighteen-year-old precipitated one of my most significant crises of faith. It knocked me off the pedestal of my more or less comfortable adolescent belief, and I have never been able to climb back on that particular pedestal (nor should I want to). It did not, to be clear, give me a deeper faith; it made me question the whole enterprise of faith. (Parents—do you hope your child will spend more time reading the Bible? Be careful of what you hope for.)

So, to return to my friend's question, is the Bible the Word of God—and if so, in what sense? You have a lot of answers to choose from, and of course are free to create your own. The spectrum runs from "Yes, literally the very words and Word of God, spoken directly to human beings who copied them down, and sitting on the page (translated or untranslated) in front of us" to "No, the words of culturally bound human beings, assembled from various now lost sources, reflecting the worldview and prejudices of their times, like any other ancient document." And every point in between: "Yes, the Word of God but conveyed more in story and metaphor and symbol than in proposition," or "Yes and no, *containing* the word of God but also containing error and human speculation," or "I don't know exactly; all I know is reading these words changes my life like nothing else I've ever read."

I don't know where R.S. Thomas stood on all this, but I am drawn to his observation that the Bible sits in churches, now largely empty in many parts of the world (though bursting at the seams in others), ticking away "remorselessly" (unaffected by our theories), a bomb ready to explode.

It is a bomb that has already exploded countless times, including in my own life. It blows up our thought systems, our carefully constructed explanations of things, our stays against confusion and our walls we have shored up against our ruin (two poetry allusions), our culturally constructed definitions of success, our sense of accomplishment, our securities and insecurities, our political and social commitments, and all our tenuous philosophies of life.

I can describe the Bible, but I can't define it. I can't get my head completely around it (and would value it less if I could). I am not inclined to spend large hunks of my life defending it against attackers (though I respect those who do). I do know that it helps me see; that it helps me love; that it helps me live—perhaps forever. And it tells me the Story by which all other stories are to be understood.

For this Skeptical Believer, that's my answer to the question, and that's enough.

GOD TELLS YOU ONLY YOUR OWN STORY

"Child," said the Voice, "I am telling you your story, not hers.
I tell no one any story but his own."

C.S. LEWIS, *A HORSE AND HIS BOY*

One of the most common charges against Christianity is that it is unfair. It bothers people, including believers, and it used to bother me. The most common form of this charge is "What about those who never hear—of God, of Jesus?" Or, put another way, "What about people of other religions?" It's a respectable question—sometimes asked out of sincere concern, but often asked as a way of deflecting Christianity's truth claims. Respectable and worth discussing, but also highly theoretical and abstract. Good for people who like to speculate and debate. (*My kind of people!*)

When I think of this question, I also think of Aslan's rejoinder in one of C.S. Lewis's Narnia stories: "I tell no one any story but his own." I think it's disingenuous to use the supposed injustice of God in supposedly condemning those who haven't heard the gospel as an excuse for rejecting the gospel yourself. You have heard. God is telling you your story. The person who hasn't heard will be treated according to what they have heard. So what are *you* doing with what *you* have heard? (*Either rejecting it, I hope, or mulling it over forever.*)

The biblical passage that comes to mind is Jesus speaking to Peter of Peter's future death at the hands of others. Peter asks about John, with the suggestion that John might get a better deal than Peter is getting. Jesus answers, "If I want him to remain until I return, what is that to you? As for you, follow me" (John 21:22). The vernacular paraphrase might be, "Mind your own business." And Peter does have important business to mind. And so do we.

The "unfair" accusation is actually a charge against God's character. It says, "God can't handle this. He can't work it out. He doesn't have what it takes to be a fair judge." Really?

Everything I know about God (from the Bible, from the testimony of others, from my own experience, from my reason) renders the charge groundless. Fairness is one expression of God's love, and God's love is the defining quality of God's character.

Then again, fairness is an inadequate concept to express God's character. God is not fair in the sense of giving people what they deserve. Human beings in general, and believers in particular, should *not* want what is fair. We need something much greater than fairness—we need grace. We need to receive much better than we deserve or have earned. I am the last person to ask God to be fair to me, or to anyone else.

I believe God is telling each of us our own story and showing us how we are part of God's story. The sometimes frustrating additional fact is that he only reveals the details as we need to know them. We know the overarching plot of our past, present, and future—and that is our hope—but we don't know how it is going to be worked out today and tomorrow—and that can be our frustration. We'd like to know more. Sooner. But God only says, "As for you, follow me." It makes for a heck of a story.

I want everyone to hear this story because I think it is the story of the universe. I do not worry any longer that God will be unfair to those who never hear it. I do worry that some hear it and turn away. I do worry that some of us hear it and live it tepidly.

5. ARGUMENTS FOR FAITH—
ALL OF THEM RESISTABLE

BELIEF, DISBELIEF, AND THE FAILURE OF THE IMAGINATION

Imagination is more important than knowledge. For knowledge is limited to all we now know and understand, while imagination embraces the entire world, and all there ever will be to know and understand.

ALBERT EINSTEIN

The imagination is not highly prized, generally speaking, among the following: religious conservatives, rationalistic atheists, naturalistic materialists, and math teachers ("Show your work"). It ought to be. A constricted imagination is at the heart of the following: intolerance, judgmentalism, indifference to others, coldheartedness, legalism, fundamentalisms, and bad Christmas presents. (*My imagination works fine: "Imagine there's no heaven / It's easy if you try / No hell below us / Above us only sky."*)

At the heart of the imaginative faculty is the ability to picture things differently (think image-ination). Differently from what? From how they are usually pictured, by yourself or others, or by tradition. A bare minimum of imagination is necessary for survival—my ability to imagine falling off this cliff keeps me from getting too close to the edge. A *limit* on imagination is also necessary for survival—I imagine myself flying if I jump off this cliff, and so I jump. A healthy imagination works in partnership with the other faculties to create a world that is fully realistic (the imagination being as useful for discovering and creating reality as is observation and analysis) and, at the same time, one in which I can flourish.

Two areas in which the imagination is essential are personal relationships and life assessment (discovering how best to live). The failure to get along with others, including spouses and companions, is largely a failure of the imagination, especially of what in the eighteenth century was called the sympathetic imagination. The sympathetic imagination is the ability not only to conceive how others are feeling and seeing things, but to actually participate in those feelings and understandings—to the extent that one escapes the cocoon of one's own feelings and ways of seeing for a time and becomes that person (or even object).

We have a number of common expressions that describe this action—"walk a mile in someone else's moccasins," being in someone's shoes, "I feel your pain" (the words "sympathy" and "compassion" both meaning "to suffer with"). My wife and I have very different temperaments and needs. (*Mars versus Venus. Potato chips versus salad.*) The only hope we have of living well together is to be able to imagine how the other is seeing things and to act and react accordingly. ("What, she wants to talk this over yet again? Okay, we'd better talk.")

A failure of the sympathetic imagination is at the heart of our culture's current list of big sins—racism, sexism, homophobia, environmental indifference—but is also foundational in strident secularism, all culture wars battles, and intolerance in general. The opposite of the sympathetic imagination is seeing those who understand things differently as some combination of ignorant, stupid, and evil. (*The Holy Trinity!*) These are the three qualities ascribed to one's opponents if one is a fundamentalist of any stripe (including secular ones).

Intolerance is rooted in a failure to imagine how any well-meaning and intelligent person could assess and live in the world differently than you do. Such a failure of the imagination is not to be admired. It is not commitment or sincerity or faithfulness. It is a disability. And it is widespread in our time, as it has always been.

It is not difficult to understand why the imagination, including the sympathetic imagination, is often not highly valued by the extremely committed. The imagination can be threatening to orthodoxies of all kinds because it increases the possibility of seeing the legitimacy of non-orthodox perspectives. (What if atheists are more moral than we thought? What if some

Christians are as smart as we are? What if not all capitalists are heartless? What if profit isn't necessarily the ultimate good?) (*What if nobody gives a fig about what you think about anything?*) If you encourage people to start using their imaginations, you never know where they'll end up.

They might end up as they did in the book of Judges, where, lacking a central authority, "everyone did what was right in their own eyes." The unrestricted imagination is its own authority and doesn't willingly submit itself to verifications and tests of any kind, including the pragmatic survival test. ("I can fly!") Thus the claim that the imagination must work in combination with the other human faculties, all of which must be used with a keen awareness of their limitations.

Overall, those who devalue the imagination think it more likely that the imagination will create false realities—illusions—than that it will discover true realities. And since, as with all human faculties, there are healthy and unhealthy uses of the imagination, this fear is not groundless. (Though, by this line of reasoning, we should not use logic or experience or tradition or revelation either, all being subject to abuse.)

I am invoking the imagination in this overall discussion of belief in our time because, first, I think it necessary for healthy faith, and, second, because I think it offers help to the Skeptical Believer. I do not think it is possible to have faith in anything, much less in God, without an ability to perceive and value realities that are beyond the very limited perceptions of our senses. If you can conceive as real only that which you yourself can touch, taste, smell, see, and hear, then you will cut yourself off from huge areas of reality. If you value and trust only the mind's manipulation of these sense data—through reasoning or scientific testing, for instance—you may discover many interesting and worthwhile things (and even be thought a genius), but you will never get far beyond surfaces.

Isaac Newton, one of the half dozen most important scientists of all time, said the following: "I seem to have been only like a boy playing on the sea-shore, and diverting myself in now and then finding a smoother pebble or a prettier shell than ordinary, whilst the great ocean of truth lay all undiscovered before me." One could apply this comparison to many things, but I would say that science is exploring the shore, while art and religion are exploring the ocean.

We Skeptical Believers are, for the most part, a cautious lot. We are more afraid than most of being fooled or of looking stupid. When other believers wax rhapsodic about their conversations with God, their confidence in unseen things, or their joy in the absolute truths of the Bible, our innate caution arises and we ask (either aloud or to ourselves), "What about us who do not have such experiences or such confidence? And what if you are wrong?"

And we react similarly, or at least I do, to the confident claims of disbelief. When the secularist says, "You can't prove that" (*You can't, you know*), I say (aloud or to myself), "Yes, and I cannot prove that love is not illusory, or that justice and compassion trump self-interest, or that beauty is necessary, or that truth is more useful than illusion."

My own ability to believe—in God and many other things—depends on my ability to imagine and is related to my belief in the power and truth of stories. The story of faith tells me that certain things have happened—inside time and space and out—that I must pay attention to, and that I ignore at my great peril. Many of those things resonate with my own experience—giving them a subjective credibility—and some of them do not. Because the story limits my freedom (limits on freedom often being a good and necessary thing), there are limits on my opportunity to pick the things I like in the story and discard the others. I am not free, for instance, to pick the reassuring things (the primacy of love and grace) and the ethically pleasing things ("Jesus was a good person and offers us an example") and ignore the hard things (resurrection from the dead, Jesus for everyone, sin, judgment). The story doesn't give me that choice, any more than the feminist narrative allows me to value women but believe they are inferior to men.

I see with my own eyes and my own experience only the tip of the iceberg of faith and of God. Science assures me that the tips of nature's icebergs are only one-ninth of their full reality. My imagination—in the best sense—is necessary for me to believe in great areas of faith that I have not experienced or cannot prove. I myself cannot prove that the scientists are right about the hidden mass of the iceberg, but I take their word for it. There is also much that I cannot prove about my faith, but the beauty and truthfulness of the part that I have experienced is so powerful that I accept the truth of the rest without complaint. Which is not to say that I am not also aware of the human distortions that have been imposed on the story, not all of which I am likely to detect.

Nor is it to claim there is no possibility of my being wrong about this story. (*There are many other stories.*) I do not need to be reminded that there are other stories making contrary claims. That my imagination and reason approve this story does not make it true. But since any significant story is a risky one, why not take my chances with one that offers me so much? The greater the promises a story makes, the greater the risks of being wrong. But the less a story promises, the greater its insignificance if it is the only truth. I would rather bet my life on a story that promises a universe built on love than on a story that promises only what I can see and prove. My story encourages me to imagine more than I can prove. I'm all in.

I am sympathetic with any genuine inquirers who have come to different conclusions than I have. I am not sympathetic with people (believers or unbelievers) who think those who believe differently than they do must be either fools or devils. Discovering the truth about the human condition is hard. But accepting the proper role of the God-given imagination encourages me to believe in the whole iceberg.

AN AESTHETIC ARGUMENT FOR FAITH

"Beauty is truth, truth beauty,"—that is all
Ye know on earth, and all ye need to know.
JOHN KEATS, "ODE ON A GRECIAN URN"

How beautiful on the mountains
are the feet of the messenger who brings good news,
who proclaims peace and salvation,
the good news that your God reigns!
ISAIAH 52:7

We can be sure that whoever sneers at [Beauty's] name, as if she were the
ornament of a bourgeois past,… can no longer pray and soon will no longer
be able to love.
HANS URS VON BALTHASAR

Okay, Keats was wrong. "Beauty is truth, truth beauty." That is not *all* we
need to know, nor do people even agree on what he meant by it. But he's on to
something nevertheless. There is some link between beauty and truth (and
goodness, too, though Keats doesn't mention it). One of the reasons I choose
the Christian story is that I find it beautiful. (*Looks can be deceiving.*)

I know, I know—looks can be deceiving, Satan was an angel of light, not all that glitters is gold, supermodels are sometimes superficial. (*Higher cheekbones than IQ, but who's counting?*) Still, I think, given that all choices of stories to live by are inherently risky, one may as well choose one that is beautiful. The more beautiful it is, in fact, the more risk I am willing to tolerate in order to be part of it.

But is the Christian story a beautiful story? (*Inquisition, Crusades, sin, hell, double-knit suits—you decide.*) Some have made a living claiming it is not. Any single answer depends on what the genuine story is, on the nature of one's relationship with it, and on the wisdom of the person doing the judging. There's too much in all this to unravel briefly, so allow me simply to cast a few large nets.

There are as many versions of the Christian story as there are tellers of the story. No two are exactly the same, nor should they be. I can't even tell the story of what I did yesterday the same way twice in a row. Why should I expect there to be only one version of what happened when God created the earth, put the human experience in motion, joined intimately with that creation, and is now bringing it to fulfillment? Too much for too long and with too much mystery for finite human beings ever to tell or understand more than a sliver of the whole. We need, therefore, many tellers. And much conversation. (*So why not all religions and all stories then? I know, you already discussed that. But I like returning to my favorite questions.*)

Some tellings of the story, however, are too ugly for me to believe—or even to want to believe. When I hear those versions, I say to myself, *If that were what God and faith are all about, I wouldn't be a believer either.* So an early question for a doubting believer, or for someone outside belief who is seriously investigating, is "What version of the Christian story are you talking about?"

If you are living in or considering a perverse or truncated or warped version of the Christian story, then by all means reject it. (*They're all warped, and I don't know what "truncated" means, so I do reject all versions of the story. I am, in fact, a master rejecter, a veritable Potentate of Rejection, if you like.*) Do what Jesus would do (*Now there's a catchy bit of advice*), as when he rejected distorted versions of faith in God that he encountered in his own life (think money-changers, legalistic religious leaders, exploiters, thrill-seekers, and so on).

But do not, in rejecting an enfeebled form of faith, think that you have said anything significant about faith itself, about the story in its most beautiful and winsome forms. That is like deciding that music is worthless because you hear *me* play the piano. Don't decide based on my playing, but based on the playing of a master.

This may require some effort on your part. We are offered lazy caricatures of faith all the time—by its enemies and proponents, and by our Inner Atheists. (*Caricatures? I just tell it like it is, baby.*) To get past the caricatures, you may have to work a bit, including observing the lives of the best—not the worst—believers around you and in the past. Because any life story should be judged by the kind of life it is capable of supporting, not by how badly it can be abused.

Judging the beauty of a story is also influenced by the nature of one's relationship to it. The judgment will be affected by whether you are living the story as you assess it or treating the story merely as an object for contemplation—a puzzle to be solved. My use of the word "merely" indicates my preference, and why this book is aimed at the Skeptical Believer more than the person on the outside looking in.

One is more likely to realize the beauty—and truthfulness—of the story of faith if one is engaged in living it, just as one is more likely to perceive the beauty or goodness of a person with whom one is in close relationship. The more I work out within my own life the implications of the story to which I have committed myself, the more I see its beauty (as well as its logic), and the more I am willing to risk to be part of it. I cannot commit myself to a story that I know to be false. But I can commit to one that has only the *possibility* of being true—just as I have committed to a marriage that could have turned out poorly, and to writing books that could have self-destructed, and to friendships and causes that could have failed.

On the other hand, the more I make this story a quiz question, an abstract problem to be solved, a theoretical construct, the more the life of it fades. I find myself feeling superior to the story—I am its judge, its examiner, its critic. I begin expecting it to please me, to satisfy me, to heel at my command. I put the story up against other life stories and list the pros and cons, as though comparing two brands of washing machines. I start enumerating what I like and don't like about the story, as though God were tailoring a coat for me or giving me a haircut to suit my tastes.

Faith in God is not a matter of "figuring it out." It is an illusion to think that the most honest and useful approach to matters of faith and doubt is carefully sifting evidence until the truth makes itself clear. That approach is an invitation to a lifetime on the treadmill without ever getting anywhere. (*What's the hurry? I have loads of time. Shouldn't rush these things.*) The truth will make itself clear in your life before it makes itself clear in your head.

I am not arguing that one should not probe and evaluate a life story—in fact, I have been arguing that you should and that beauty is a legitimate aspect of the evaluation. I am simply saying that engagement with the story, rather than distant contemplation, will *affect* the evaluation. It's the difference between asking someone what the pie tastes like and tasting it yourself.

Furthermore, the person within faith who is struggling mightily with doubts often makes the mistake of suspending the *practice* of faith while he or she is struggling. It is not unlike a person swimming for her life in a raging river who stops swimming in order to ponder whether she will make it. Keep swimming, keep doing the acts of faith, and in the process you may discover the beauty of being able to swim and making it to shore.

I suggested that a third factor in judging the beauty of the story of faith is the wisdom of the judge. I am not arguing that you have to be intelligent to judge correctly, but I do claim that you have to be wise. Wisdom is practical knowledge about the relative importance of things in life combined with the will to choose accordingly. Right priorities and right choices yield a life well-lived.

It strikes me as wise to include aesthetics—the beauty of things—in one's ultimate commitments. Many thinkers and artists besides Keats have explored the interweavings of beauty and truth, and also justice, grace, and love—and the expression of these things in physical and spiritual form. They seem to be different, but intimately related, expressions of some ultimate reality, one that so far surpasses mere matter that to limit oneself to the senses and measurement and syllogism seems tragically obtuse.

I do not say that all intelligent and well-meaning people will choose the story I do. I do say that anyone who chooses a story for the only life they will get that does not adequately account for ultimate things has not chosen wisely. And I will claim that my story's doing so is an evidence for its Truth. (I move to the capital letter to show that I believe in such a thing, even if I do not believe I understand it perfectly this side of eternity.)

If I cannot prove that this story is true, I also, of course, cannot prove that it is beautiful. I can only testify. And others will testify differently. The most important testimony, always, is testimony rooted in a story, because story addresses us as whole persons, including our sense of beauty.

Evaluating a story to live by in terms of beauty does not eliminate, even for a time, the consideration of truth—or of goodness. They actually are each part of the other, as each member of the Trinity is in inseparable fellowship with the other. Isolate any one aspect from the others and it begins to lose its life, like taking a starfish out of the sea (as I learned as a young boy). Consider Gregory Wolfe's wise reflections:

> Truth without beauty is fleshless abstraction.
> Goodness without beauty is moralism.
> Beauty without truth is a lie.
> Beauty without goodness is frigid and lifeless.

One of the things that contributes to a story's beauty is its truth. (It's also what makes it a "good" story.) A story that is true (in the deepest senses) is more beautiful than one that is not. And beauty (in the deepest senses) is a quality of truth. Keats was on to something. So too, many centuries before, was the prophet who equated beauty with the bringing of good news.

CALLED BY NAME

You formed my inmost self,
knit me together in my mother's womb.
PSALM 139:13

I ask myself: "Why do I believe in God, Wim?"
"He called me by my name."
WIM WENDERS

Samuel had it easy. He's lying in bed as a boy and God calls him by name: "Samuel." Why doesn't that happen to me? I think. (*You snore—wouldn't hear it anyway.*) Then I would know for sure about God and be a very, very good person. (*Right—and you'll start your diet right after Christmas.*)

Then again, maybe it wasn't all that easy for Samuel. We're told in the biblical story that "word from the Lord was rare in those days, visions were uncommon." Perhaps not all that different from today.

And at first Samuel doesn't realize it's God calling. Three times he gets out of bed, goes to Eli, and says, "Here I am."

Then the story tells us something a fundamentalist kid like I was could understand: "Now Samuel did not yet know the Lord, for the word of the Lord had not yet been revealed to him."

Yes, I knew about the need to know the Lord. We talked about it at church all the time. You had to have Jesus in your heart, to have your own walk with the Lord, to accept Jesus as your personal Savior. Jesus was sort of a combination valet, schoolmarm, policeman, judge, and, somehow, friend. (I could dimly understand the roles of provider, teacher, and enforcer, but friend always seemed a stretch. Friends with the one whom to look upon was to die? It still seems a stretch.)

And I also knew about "the word of the Lord." Adults talked a lot about "getting a word from the Lord." I never questioned it, although like the young Samuel I hadn't gotten any words myself. Maybe that came after you had read the whole Bible and become a deacon or something. (*Or when you stop taking your medication.*) Anyway, it sounded a bit too much like a television commercial: "And now a word from our sponsor."

Besides, maybe it wasn't so bad not getting words from the Lord. Even though God sets Samuel up with a little teaser—"Watch, I am about to do something in Israel that will make the ears of everyone who hears it tingle"—the word from the Lord in this case is not pleasant: it's all about the curse that the sins of Eli's sons had brought upon the family.

No, all things considered, it was just as well that God talked to other people, not to me.

Still, there is something haunting here. Being called by name. Being known personally. Having been known and loved since before time began. To a young kid it was like thinking of Michael Jordan looking at the television camera while holding his championship trophy and saying, "This one's for you, Dan." Maybe even better.

This idea of being called by name makes no sense to many. It's not something they expect, nor an idea they like. I remember as a teenager seeing the real Maria von Trapp, of *The Sound of Music* fame, on a television talk show. A woman from the audience asked with a smile, "Are you a Christian?" It was taken as an insulting question, as it would be today. "I am a Christian, of course," she answered with some indignation. "Austria is a Christian nation." Maria von Trapp clearly hadn't been raised in my churches. The question made almost no sense to her. She felt called, perhaps, as part of a nation, as part of Western culture; apparently nothing in her theology or experience led her to expect to be called by name.

Nor was that part of the expectations of an atheist friend of mine who has long since substituted science and career for any "word from the Lord."

Trying to answer her questions about what I believed, I said something about believing the main reason we existed was to be in a relationship with our Creator. She laughed. "God wants a personal relationship with me? Nobody ever told me *that* before." She didn't seem to find it either believable or attractive. (*Smart woman!*)

Do I?

Most days, yes. It is too deep in my bones to extinguish. And I don't think it's just because I was raised among the literalists. I think it's in everyone's bones. From the compelling description of the pub in *Cheers*—"Where everybody knows your name"—to tribal naming ceremonies, to the biblical idea of being one of those "whose names are written in the Lamb's book of life," to our antipathy to being numbered rather than named, there is something fundamental about being called by name.

It doesn't require any great insight to see why. To name and be named is to value and be valued (that's part of what Adam's naming of the animals was about). Names both individualize us—*this* child, not just another child—and tie us to a community: "You are named after your aunt on your father's side, the one who went to Africa and never came back." Names are something we have to live up to ("Do us proud!") and to protect ("That is not something that we Smiths do!"). In many cultures, names are considered destiny. And when people do something special, or when something special is expected of them, they are given a new name: Jacob becomes Israel, Saul becomes Paul, Frodo becomes Ring Bearer.

Can I move from these self-evident assertions to the claim that one of the evidences for faith is hearing your name called? The boy Samuel heard his name called—so the story tells us. It was a call that determined the course of his life. Paul heard his name called on the road to Damascus, and the rest is his-story. Many a medieval mystic heard her name called in anchorages and prayer cells, and thought it nothing fantastic.

But we live, like Samuel, in an age in which words and visions from the Lord seem "uncommon"—especially to Skeptical Believers. I know people well who have visions, and since I respect them in other contexts, I have no inclination to question the validity of their experience. But I have no visions of my own. I do not hear my name clearly called. We're told God spoke to Elijah in a "still, small voice." God's voice, to me at least, is a little too still, and a little too small, to be unmistakable.

And yet, I must have heard something. Somewhere. I have long since passed the time when I believe anything just because my parents did, or because I was raised at a certain time in a certain way, or because some politician or expert tells me so. And it's not as if faith has been for me in the last fifty years some uninspected given in my life that I accept without question. I have inspected and questioned it nearly to death. I have picked, probed, pushed, and pulled at it. I have weighed, measured, and dissected it. I have praised and ignored it; kicked it away and retrieved it; tested it; treated it with reverence, with fear and trembling, and with weary indifference. Something, it seems, has been calling me. Here I am, after all, writing another book. Trying once more to hear my name.

All right. I find I cannot end these particular reflections so diffidently. My bones won't let me. This calling of my name has been indirect, but it has not been impersonal. Once upon a time, I was sitting with my brothers in the front pew of a strange church on a Sunday evening. I was five years old. My father was the visiting preacher and had brought the family along. Whatever he talked about led me to consider my own distance from God. My father gave an altar call, a sort of name-calling ritual in my church tradition. I didn't "go forward," as we used to say, maybe because I was already sitting at the front. But my father must have seen something in my face. He must have heard someone calling my name. Because he came to me during the altar call and asked if I wanted to have "Jesus as my personal Savior"—the language of my version of the story. Unlike Maria von Trapp, I wasn't insulted. I cried. I said yes. I answered the calling of my name.

What to make of that now, so many years and so many experiences later? I don't know. I think I'll just accept it. I think I'll keep my ears open, to see if anyone is calling my name still.

STORY IN A PROVIDENTIAL UNIVERSE

Life can educate one to a belief in God.

LUDWIG WITTGENSTEIN

Few things irritate a convinced materialist as much as the notion that the universe is designed. Worse yet, that it is designed for the ultimate well-being of you and me. Strange how good news can be so aggravating to some. Then again, no one initially sees something that overthrows their whole explanation of their lives as good news.

And it *is* pretty hard to swallow. All these galaxies, all this space, all these ungraspable stretches of time, not to mention all the things happening on our tiny little planet (many of them lamentable)—and you want me to believe that it's all here so I can find God? Seems like more than a stretch. Seems like a whopper. (*Glad you occasionally recognize the obvious.*)

And yet there's a whole school of apologetics that uses just this scenario as evidence—some think as proof—for the existence of God. It involves the idea that anything that exists has to have had a cause, and it uses huge exponential numbers (including the number of electrons in the universe!) and calculates the odds against there being life *anywhere* if there is no designer God. And it is really quite impressive, and I hope that it is so. But, truth be told, I don't know enough to evaluate these claims. (I'm not sure anyone does, actually—including the experts.) I know there are some very good number crunchers who don't buy it at all. They merely shrug and say, "We're here, so we obviously beat the odds." I don't know who is Blowing Smoke in this case—maybe everyone.

I'm in no position to evaluate the numbers and their significance, but I do have a brief story to tell. Not a very impressive story, actually. It doesn't prove anything at all. No one would decide to believe in God because of this story, not even me. But it helps me, in a small way, to believe that we may actually live in a providential universe—one with at least a touch of design. Here's the story (drawn from another book of mine, *Tell Me a Story: The Life-Shaping Power of Our Stories*).

Sometimes we are shaped by people (characters) we never knew existed, and by stories we have never heard. Quite a few years ago now, I was invited to speak at John Brown University in Siloam Springs, Arkansas. I had never heard of John Brown University. Wanting to know a little about the place and people, I asked the chaplain to send me some information on the school.

I discovered that John Brown had been a traveling, Southern, tent-meeting, sawdust-trail evangelist of the early and middle part of the twentieth century. He had traveled along the South, as far west as California, saving the lost and admonishing the saved, and at some point had started a little school.

I will admit to a flicker of condescension when I read this sketch of the school's founder. I am just old enough to have witnessed a sawdust-trail tent meeting or two. These are not the Augustines or Pascals of religious faith. I also know something about idiosyncratic institutions that are dominated by the personality of an eccentric founder, sometimes well after that founder has passed on. I did not make any sweeping judgments, but somewhere in the back of my mind I prepared myself for the possibility of a few days in a backwater place with backwater people.

Shortly before leaving for Arkansas, I was talking on the phone with my father. He asked me what I was up to, and I mentioned I was going to a place called John Brown University. He replied, "Oh yes, John Brown. Your grandfather Nick was saved under John Brown."

It was one of those moments when God reveals to you in great clarity how stupid you are.

My father then told me a story I had never heard. My grandfather Nick had left a crowded and troubled home in Indiana when he was fifteen or sixteen. It was shortly before World War I, and he had nowhere to go, so he jumped on a freight train heading west.

Eventually he ended up in Los Angeles—lonely and without direction. One night he wandered by a revival meeting being led by John Brown. He went in, and there he met God. And because he became a Christian, in a personal and life-directing way, he later looked for a Christian woman to marry, and they chose to raise their only child—my father—as a Christian, and he chose a Christian woman to marry, and they chose to raise me and my brothers as believers.

So I discovered that this man, John Brown, whom I had safely pigeon-holed as someone far removed from and of no relevance to my life, was in fact an important link in the chain to my own salvation.

It was a story I needed to hear.

One does not have to be sympathetic to Christianity or religious belief or the idea of salvation to understand how a story like this might have some influence on me even as an adult. I didn't just hear this story, I accepted it—made it a part of who I was and how I thought about myself and life. It reinforced my sense of living in a coherent universe, of belonging to something important that has stretched over time, of being a link in a chain—indebted to many in the past, mostly unknown to me, and responsible to many in the future, who likewise will not know who I was.

Was the universe created for your benefit and mine? Do we live in a providential, rather than a random, cosmos—one whose arc, ultimately, is toward love? Preposterous and childishly naive, says the materialist and cynic. Maybe so, says the Skeptical Believer, but so is the belief that there can be justice in the world. I believe both. My stories tell me so.

BELIEVING TOO MUCH VERSUS BELIEVING TOO LITTLE

Those who can never be fooled will never be delighted.
ALAN JACOBS, *THE NARNIAN*

Cheerful insecurity is what Our Lord asks of us.
C.S. LEWIS, *LETTERS*

Friedrich Schiller, the eighteenth-century philosopher and poet, once wrote that given the choice between pursuing the truth and possessing the truth, he would take the pursuit. A fitting sentiment for a Romantic such as he was. I can see the line of reasoning—pursuit, quest, excitement, striving—versus, one supposes, mere knowledge, boring orthodoxy, repeating what everyone already knows. I have said elsewhere, however, that it seems disingenuous to say that you are pursuing something if you disparage the having of it or presuppose the impossibility of having it. It would be like telling your love that you want more than anything to be married but never getting around to proposing. You cannot convincingly say you love the truth if you are never willing to say, "This is true." (*Love only breaks your heart. Don't you ever listen to country-western music?*)

Despite my misgivings, however, I want to propose a Schiller-esque dichotomy. (*I love it when you use -esque formulations, so deliciously intellectual-esque.*) Given the choice between believing too much and believing too little, I choose to risk believing too much. Both choices are risky, but believing too much seems to me far more rewarding (and reasonable).

I am talking about believing in the context of the real choices life offers us, not belief or disbelief as part of an academic exercise. Time and again I am asked to commit to something in my life that may or may not reward the commitment. Invest in this, spend time doing that; read that book, declare this major; love this person, help that one; vote for this politician, work for that cause; tote that barge, lift this bale ("Old Man River"). Sometimes the result seems worth it; sometimes not. But what is the alternative—never to choose at all? (*Why put it so categorically? Just wait a bit longer, until you get more decisive information.*)

I once took my family on vacation to an area of the world where relatively rich people (like me) are served in resorts by relatively poor people (like most of the locals). At one meal, we exchanged affable conversation with our waiter. I decided (perhaps in a fit of white guilt) to bless him with an excessive tip. He had spoken of his wife and children, and I imagined them celebrating with him when he revealed to them his little taste of passing prosperity. It reminds me now of my variation on a comic line from a favorite movie of my family (I do not quote exactly): "There are maybe three great humanitarians in modern times: Albert Schweitzer, Mother Teresa, and... Daniel Taylor."

I basked in the look of joy on his face when he beheld the tip. He then exclaimed, "Boy, am I going to get drunk tonight!" Ouch. I had believed too much. I was thinking I had blessed his family, and it looked as though I had only condemned them to dealing with a drunken husband and father.

But looking back, I do not regret it. I had made a choice based on a real possibility—that the man would share his blessing with someone else. It was not irrational or mere wishing; it could well have happened. My choice gave him the opportunity to make his own choice—to spread the blessing to those he loved or to get drunk. I increased the *possibility* for blessing in the world even if I didn't succeed in actually blessing anyone. It still seems to me the right choice. And who knows? Maybe he changed his mind and brought the kids some ice cream.

This is also how I think about the things of the spirit and of God. As Kierkegaard warned me, my mind can generate just as many reasons to disbelieve as to believe. I can weigh and re-weigh the evidence and arguments for and against, and reach a different conclusion each time. I can pursue, pursue, pursue the truth until I am exhausted. But at some point—at every point, in fact—I believe I must choose. Not to choose is itself a choice—the choice of being a passive spectator.

Peter Elbow, a famous educator, has talked about the doubting game and the believing game. He says that Western thought has for centuries emphasized the doubting game, believing (yes, *believing*, not knowing) that doubt, questioning, skepticism, and analysis were the best (for many, the only) way to truth. Elbow suggests that one should also play the believing game—entering wholly, at least momentarily, into the world that a writer or argument creates. One does this for the truth's sake, realizing that we blind ourselves to some truths if we treat them always with suspicion. (If, for instance, I am suspicious that my love does not truly love me, my suspicion may destroy my beloved's love. My *approach* to the question *changes* the truth rather than *revealing* it.)

I am looking for a principle here—not being an enemy of principles and propositions when they are genuinely helpful. Perhaps it is something like this: *With anything that would make things better, believe as much as you can—then believe a little more.* I don't think this is wishfulness or mere hoping; I think it is a reasonable and pragmatic response to a complicated and uncertain world.

And so I choose to believe in God and in the Good News that has been offered me. I have good reasons—reasons good enough for me, perhaps not for you. If it turns out I have believed too much, so be it. I am voting with my life for the possibility of blessings, for the possibility of grace, for the possibility of significance—ultimately, for the possibility that the universe is organized around love. If this proves not the case, I have believed too much. I like my chances. I like the life it gives me.

A BRIEF DEFENSE OF RISKY BELIEF

Even a Proverb is no proverb to you till your Life has illustrated it.

JOHN KEATS

I realized that as much as I liked witty satire and withering critiques, I couldn't sustain a life on that. I had to create, and I had to live in a certain kind of hope.

GREGORY WOLFE

Disbelief has not been as common as belief through human history, but I suspect it is at least as old. As soon as there was someone, somewhere saying, "I believe... ," there was also someone saying, "Fiddlesticks" (or its ancient equivalent). Very possibly it was the same person saying both. (And we've already looked at Satan's role in the Eden story as Disbeliever-in-Chief.)

Belief and disbelief are the yin and yang of the meaning-making process. They feed each other, they steal from each other, they call each other names, they punch each other in the nose, they make up and hug, they finally go to sleep in the same bed—to start all over the next morning. (*Such violent images. I prefer to think of it as Reason (moi) speaking Truth—okay, truth—to Foolishness (tu), with a slight French accent.*)

Even my Inner Atheist believes a lot of things. (*Yes—in Reason, Modernity, Tolerance [except of fools], and Progress [as defined by me].*) He is not all Disbelief. He even believes some of the same things I do (*Every loss by the New York Yankees is evidence for the possibility of justice in the world*)— because, as I have said, he *is* me. That is, a part of me. He and I are both a churning mix of belief and disbelief.

But because I am finally on the side of belief (in many things, of many kinds), I will not agree that they are equals. I am not neutral about the comparative value of belief and disbelief (or doubt).

As we saw earlier, philosophers point out two very different goals when it comes to knowing things. One goal is to *maximize truth*—to believe in such a way that we miss out on the fewest possible truths. The goal of another approach is to *minimize error*—to believe in such a way that we affirm the fewest possible errors. The first approach will let in more error than the second approach, but it will also let in more truths. And I am arguing that the truths it allows in are much more important than the errors that may sneak in too.

The maximum truth approach casts a wide net. It allows for many forms and expressions of and pathways to truth: reason, intuition, imagination, tradition, revelation, informed conjecture, and so on. The minimum error approach narrows both its methodology (rationalistic logic, experiment) and its results (limited largely to what is certain or nearly certain).

On the surface, the maximum truth approach is more risky. It cannot be sure that everything it affirms is actually true. By allowing uncertainty, it has cracked the door wider for falsehood. (*Yes, Dr. Astronomer, please take a seat there beside Ms. Astrologer?*) The minimum error approach, on the other hand, can say, "We may miss some truths, but we are more sure that the things we affirm as true *are*, in *fact*, true." (*Hear, hear.*)

The minimize error approach seems less risky, but I think it actually much more risky. The price of minimizing error at all costs is too high. In business it means missed opportunities for profit. In relationships it means missing the risky rewards of love. In art it means safe repetition instead of the exciting and revealing new form. In the things of the spirit it means missing transcendence and ultimate significance and God. Risky indeed. There are many things, of course, that we should not believe. There are illusions. There are falsehoods. There are lies. There are partial truths masquerading as whole truths. It is healthy to have enough disbelief in you to detect such things.

Disbelief helps minimize error. But disbelief *as a way of life* is sterile. It creates nothing. It nourishes nothing. It takes no risks. It plays it safe (seemingly). Ultimately, disbelief on its own is boring. And potentially deadly.

Belief can be healthy or unhealthy. It can be profound and wise, and it can be naive and foolish. So can disbelief. But belief, unlike disbelief, has life-giving possibilities. Belief sees the part and intuits the whole. Belief witnesses a minor act of goodness and says, "Why not more?" It finds a little truth and looks for deeper truths. It is delighted by something fleetingly beautiful and wonders if there is not more beauty nearby.

Disbelief sometimes protects us, but without the windows of belief it is the protection of the dungeon. Disbelief *keeps out* certain kinds of harm, but belief opens doors and windows to the fresh air and *lets in* the light.

Belief builds a home we can live in.

HEALTHY AND DISEASED STORIES OF FAITH

There are two kinds of people one can call reasonable; those who serve God with all their heart because they know him, and those who seek him with all their heart because they do not know him.

BLAISE PASCAL

I am often amazed, and saddened, by the reasons people give for abandoning their commitment to the story of faith. Not because there are no reasons, or because I lack empathy, but because their reasons often seem so insubstantial. I readily understand why someone outside of faith might not be interested or attracted—there are endless other stories in the world—but once someone has lived the story from the inside, tasted even slightly the miracle of grace, forgiveness, purpose, and meaning that the story offers, how can they discard it for anything less than a better story? (*Getting rid of a bad story is a step towards finding a better story. So there!*)

And most who leave do not, in my experience, describe a better story they have found. They mostly describe what they find off-putting about their experience within the faith story they have left behind. And those descriptions, almost without exception, are of a diseased version of the Christian story. Some make little effort to find and live a healthier version.

It is enough that they have been disappointed in the particulars of their own experience, and so they move away, quietly or loudly, from a story which offers them life. (*Other people in other stories live quite well.*)

In formal argument, it is understood that one should defeat opposing views as expressed in their strongest form. To do otherwise is to construct a "straw man," easily defeated but with no great reward in the victory. If I argue for my political views by creating and then attacking caricatures of opposing views, I have accomplished nothing outside my own head and those of fellow true believers. Hence the wisdom of the rule invoked in Benjamin Franklin's debating club: "You cannot oppose a position until you have stated that position to the satisfaction of the one who holds it."

The same should apply when considering the story of faith, especially as one debates it within oneself (and with one's Inner Atheist). (*The point of arguing is to win, is it not?*) You should seek out the story in its healthiest, most winsome forms. If you are experiencing some truncated (*That word again*) or diseased form of the story, recognize it as such and keep looking and living.

I spoke recently with a young man who stopped calling himself a Christian because he found the Christians in his life so disappointing. He cited a pivotal event in which he was working with others to put on a play for his church (Archibald McLeish's *JB*, a retelling of the Job story). Members of the church board, undoubtedly alarmed by the controversial possibilities of such a play, came to the group and told them they would not be allowed to perform the play at the church.

This was not the only reason he left the faith, but it was symptomatic, and he identified it himself as a turning point. My response to his story was mixed. One part of me said, "Yes, many Christians are fearful of having their tidy version of faith challenged, and you had every right to be offended, discouraged, and angry at this display of timidity on the part of fellow believers." But another part of me thought, "Really? You come up against narrow-mindedness and fearfulness in your church, and so you throw over God, the Good News, the Incarnation, and the empty tomb?"

Let's see. How is this conversation going to go on Judgment Day? "Well, God, I would have liked to have continued that relationship with you (you're really first-rate), but, you see, these people at my church, they didn't like our play, and we had really worked hard on it, and..."

Consider your own conversation with God based on your own negative experiences with the church (with churches, actually, a different thing).

"I would have continued in the story, but I experienced..." legalism, or hypocrisy, or judgmentalism, or stupidity, or irrationality, or lack of love, or consumerism, or political obtuseness, or arrogance, or bullheadness, or indifference to the poor, or... fill in the blank. (*Don't mind if I do—bad hair, bad art and architecture, bad books, bad potlucks [think lime jello with marshmallows]. I could go on.*)

All of these things may be justifiable reasons for leaving any particular church or church tradition. None of them are adequate reasons, in my view, for abandoning faith altogether, not least because most of them will also be part of any other story you substitute for it. (Really? You think religious people are the only hypocrites?) And you cannot simply leave a master story like the Christian story without, whether consciously or not, becoming part of another story, with its own attendant failings.

I am not arguing that the Christian story is without challenges—to the mind as well as in everyday living. I am also not arguing that one cannot, with integrity, ever decide against it. I am arguing that it is the responsibility of anyone who has ever called themselves Christian to seek out and to live with all possible commitment the healthiest, most attractive, most fully engaging version of that story that is available. I am arguing that if you don't find that in the community of faith you have been in, then it is your responsibility to either work to make that community more whole, or to search diligently—in history as well as in your local surroundings—for a healthier version of the story which is worthy of your commitment.

If you do, that conversation with God will go a whole lot better.

FAITH AS NOUN, FAITH AS VERB

Believing in [Jesus] is not the same as believing things about him... Instead, it is a matter of giving our hearts to him, of come hell or high water putting our money on him, the way a child believes in a mother or a father, the way a mother or a father believes in a child.

FREDERICK BUECHNER, *SECRETS IN THE DARK*

Be not simply good; be good for something.

HENRY DAVID THOREAU

I find it useful that faith is both a noun and a verb. It is a thing, something we can possess, and it is an action, something we do. I believe we are accountable for both the noun and verb forms of the word, but just as stories are more actions than things, so faith, it seems to me, is primarily a verb.

Skeptical Believers, living as they do in their heads, often approach faith more as a noun than as a verb. It is a thing—something to be probed, thought about, studied, evaluated. All of these are legitimate activities, and we are the better for people having done so over the centuries. But this approach also has the ability to kill the thing it is studying. In ninth grade biology I learned about frog hearts by cutting open a frog. Good for my understanding of frog hearts, bad for the frog.

This is not an argument for not thinking or reasoning about faith. Nor for "just believe it." But it does suggest that the very act of analyzing something affects the conclusions one comes to about the thing being analyzed. It affects one's experience of that thing and therefore affects one's conclusions about it. In physics, Heisenberg pointed out that the act of measuring something affects the thing being measured, rendering the results imprecise. In Freudian analysis, one shines a light into the unconscious, and once the light is on, it isn't the unconscious anymore. Looking changes your perception of the thing you are looking at, making it something different than when you weren't looking. (*Too clever by half. Do you have a point?*)

So what's the point? If you treat faith exclusively as a noun—a thing—you will never know what faith is. You can describe it endlessly, list its characteristics, compare it to other things, but you will not know it, much less fathom its depths, even less be able to build a life on it. You will have made an object out of it, likely a dead object, when you need to know it as a living thing. (This is one reason the critiques of atheists so often ring hollow for me. Though they may be very intelligent, for the most part they literally don't know what they're talking about.) (*And do you know what you're talking about when you talk about atheists?*)

Faith in God can be investigated as a noun, but it is known only in the living—as a verb. Rather than saying "I have faith," as though faith is a object, like a toaster, one should perhaps say, "*I* am faith." That would not mean, "I myself am the object of my own faith," nor "My life defines what faith is." It would mean something like, "I know what faith is only to the extent that it flows through and out of me as I act in the world."

In fact, it might be better yet to declare, "I faith," as one does in saying "I sail" (*"I just let the boat do the work"*) or "I fish" or "I love." Faith is everything that flows out of my life—from thoughts to deeds. Faith is the act of being me in all the ways that God has created for me to be me and you to be you. Faith expresses itself in actions, manifested in both the inner life—reflection, contemplation, prayer, desire, compassion, will—and the outer life—service, worship, fellowship, repairing shalom.

Of course, the line between the inner and outer is often artificial or blurred. Compassion, for instance, is an inner feeling that should result in a tangible outward action. Likewise, worship is an inner attitude that often manifests itself with outward actions (singing, raised hands, going to church, reciting creeds). Many inner realities demand an outward expression, and many outer actions originate in some inner state of being.

Many of the great "verb believers" I have known personally do not spend much time thinking about the noun side of faith. They do not analyze their faith a lot, are not well-versed in arguments for and against faith in the modern world, are not skilled debaters (nor are they interested in becoming such). They simply live their faith as a verb. Marsha takes her faith into women's jails and takes ex-offenders into her heart and house. Dottie vibrates with the love of God and channels it into love for whoever comes into her life. The women of the local prayer ministry welcome broken people week after week and pray the healing power of God into those broken lives. (*What? No men in your cult?*)

Love and service (also both nouns and verbs) are not the only forms a living faith takes. John Milton, in responding to his own blindness, wrote, "They also serve who only stand and wait." Some think that line refers to us humans, humbly waiting for God to reveal to us what we should do. Others think it refers to the "angels" in the previous line of the poem and indicates that the highest form of service is the worshipful contemplation of God. (An encouraging word for the more reflective and private among us.) Neither of these is passive. All living of faith, as opposed to analysis of faith, requires all of who we are.

Faith is both noun and verb. There is value in standing back from the everyday living of faith to reflect on it as a thing that is larger and more varied than my own experience of it. I take great comfort, for instance, that my faith is something that stretches back through the centuries and even to before the beginning of time. It helps me to consider its various expressions in different lives and different cultures and, at the same time, to contemplate the core of beliefs that have given it unity even in its variety. So there is this thing—this noun—that we can rightly call "the Faith"—and I am glad to be a part of it.

But I am only a part of faith (and only truly understand it) as a verb, as one whose actions—inner and outer—are a response to this great action of God in time and space and in my particular life. Faith can only be known and judged from the inside, as a lived and living thing. We can be verbs, individually and in community, because God is the first verb.

WHY DO I BELIEVE? THE ANSWER IS NEVER THE SAME

I know what it is until I try to tell you.
SUZANNE PAOLA

The heart has reasons that reason does not know.
BLAISE PASCAL

Some things we believe for a single reason. Other things we believe for a complicated web of reasons. And not a few things we believe for no reason at all.

I believe chocolate tastes better than asparagus because my taste buds tell me so. I believe water freezes at 32 degrees Fahrenheit because the thermometer tells me so. I believe there are things called black holes that suck up everything around them, including light, because the scientists tell me so. I do not believe in God for any one reason. I do not believe in God, as some seem to do, for no reason. Why do I believe in God? I like Wim Wenders's response: "The answer is never the same."

I like that response because it fits my own experience. When I am feeling very intellectual, and the question comes from an intellectual direction, I find myself constructing logical arguments. I consult the probability number crunchers who calculate how unlikely accidental life is. I glance at academic philosophers and apologists who reason very closely upon their presuppositions and arrive, voilà, at the God of the Bible. (*While other philosophers arrive, voilà, at wherever they want to arrive.*) I check in with those who defend the accuracy and historicity of Scripture. I may even consult the Intelligent Design folks for the scientific arguments they offer (trying not to be too bothered by the smear that they are just closet Creationists). I look for weaknesses in the alternate explanations of atheists and agnostics and materialists (not least their lack of any foundation for making moral or ethical claims). I read people who tell me how perfectly logical, even inevitable, the existence of God is. I return to old buddies like Pascal and Kierkegaard and Chesterton and Flannery O'Connor for ways of thinking about the issues that break down simplistic objections to God.

And all along I think hard myself. I devise assertions, consider objections, make rejoinders, ask "what ifs" and throw in "on the other hands," and try to be fair to everyone—including Dame Reason (while still staying on track toward my goal of confirming, of course, what I already believe). I think until the veins pop out on my forehead. And sometimes it seems to me I make progress—at least a bit.

At other times, however, my answer to the question of why I believe is entirely personal and subjective. I will offer you no proofs, only testimony. Here is what I was before I believed, and here is what happened to me after I believed. Life before God. Life after God. It is, you could say, autobiography as apologetics. "My life is my evidence." It is, in fact, the single most common form of evangelism. I simply tell others my own story. And it is very powerful evidence as a person makes the case to themselves for why they believe. If my life is much richer and more meaningful with God than without, why is not that an evidence for God's existence and goodness? We believe it when someone testifies to how a diet caused them to lose thirty pounds, why not when someone testifies that faith in God changed their lives for the better? (*Because we can verify the weight loss.*) We can verify weight loss easier than a changed life, of course, but there are ways of measuring the latter, too.

But I am straying from my own life here. I accepted God's place in my life and my place in the story when I was five years old. I don't have a dramatic before-and-after narrative. I do have some closer and further away times in my life, but they are too ephemeral to coalesce into a particular story. I will simply say that sometimes I answer the question of why I believe God with a subjective appeal to my own very human need. I believe because my needs are legion and nothing so fully meets those needs as the grace of God.

And at still other times I believe because faith so accurately describes my experience of the world around me that I can't help but conclude that its claims are true. The Bible talks of sin and alienation, and distance from God and from the good, and selfishness and doing that which you hate, and emptiness and purposelessness and spiritual sloth, and so many other things that are exactly what I experience in my own life and feel the need to overcome. One of the most compelling evidences of the truth of the Bible, in my estimation, is its accuracy and cogency in depicting human nature and the human condition.

Page after page, story after story, describes me and those around me with relentless realism. It is actually quite unsparing in this description. "The heart is desperately wicked; who can know it?" "There is none that is good, no not one." (Not even Mother Teresa?) And it is not a generic description. It bores into my own heart and life. The Bible knows me, and it knows that, left to myself, I am exactly what the sociobiologists and other materialists say that I am: a power-seeking, self-centered mating machine intent, albeit unconsciously, on leaving as many replications of my DNA around the landscape as possible—which is to say, a jerk. And not a happy jerk at that.

I say this as a person not given to self-flagellation, self-abasement, or an inclination toward feeling guilty. I am much more likely to be too easy on myself than too hard. Try to motivate me by guilt, and I'll take your best punch without a blink. "I was raised fundamentalist," I'll say. "You are going to have to do a lot better than that." I don't think of God as pleased with me, but I am given to taking false comfort in the delusional hope that he must be distracted by and really upset with the sins of some other people we all know.

Guilt-resistant though I am, I feel keenly the unsatisfactoriness of my own purely physical life. Personal failures aside, I simply can't work up a sustaining belief in the meaningfulness of an entirely material cosmos. If collectively we started as an explosion of particles and will end when our sun goes supernova and absorbs the earth—and in between we are slaves of our biology (Darwin), subconscious (Freud), and history (Marx) or are making it all up as we go (name your favorite postmodernist)—then, I, for one, am opting out.

I agree with Camus when he says our longing for clarity and meaning in a world that does not satisfy that longing renders our lives absurd. Take away true transcendence (as opposed to mere psychological self-transcendence) and, for me, life is too short of meaning and significance to sustain the life of the soul, which is the life I care about most. All the happy talk in the world about human beings overcoming meaninglessness through this or that is simply trying to lift ourselves by our bootstraps. We can (and do) distract ourselves until the end, but that kind of life adds up to little more than one long evasion of the truth. (*Boy, are you ever the life of the party! Have a drink and lighten up a bit.*)

So, sometimes I answer to myself, though not often to others, that I believe in God because God is the Alpha and Omega of meaning and purpose, and is the ultimate validator of the human experience. I believe in God because I need God as a ground of meaning, and without God there is none. It couldn't be simpler. I have this need. God fills this need. Therefore I believe in the one who fills it. (*The idea of God is filling your need, not a real God.*)

I resonate with the novelist Ron Hansen when he says, "My faith is based in just that sense of being sustained. I have no proof that my faith in God is not a product of ignorance, superstition, wild hope, or wishful thinking, but I have felt loved by a concerned and caring holy being greater than my imagination." And he adds, "And if my faith in God has more basis in emotion and intuition than in logic or science, I'm frankly untroubled by it."

Need, of course, is not proof. But the meeting of a need is powerful evidence, both in everyday things and in ultimate things. Others claim that they meet these fundamental needs without the God of the Bible. That is fine. If you find these people convincing, follow their example. I am only answering this question for myself.

So ask me why I believe in God, and on some days I will give you all the intellectual arguments I can muster—including a few good ones. But on other days, intellectual approaches to anything, much less God, seem as weak as newborn puppies. On those days I will say I believe in God, as I argued earlier, on aesthetic grounds. It is simply the most beautiful story I have ever heard. God made the world. God loves the world. God died to redeem the world. It is a story of sin and brokenness and suffering, to be sure, but it is finally one of grace and redemption and healing and joy. The Bible tells me I am a jerk and that shalom is in shambles. It also tells me there is a solution to this problem—it's called the Good News.

This story of faith has everything that draws me to any great story (because it is, itself, the original story), and it has it on a cosmic, infinite scale. Romeo and Juliet, Lear and Cordelia can break my heart for a time, but the story of the Crucifixion is a story that includes both time and eternity. The stakes are higher than our ability to conceive; therefore the horror and the beauty are beyond calculation—and beyond the confines of mere orthodoxy. It is a story that would make us weep every time we tell it, had we not tamed it with dull repetition. (The problem is the dull, not the repetition.)

And if the Crucifixion is tragedy (in the very highest sense), then what of the Resurrection? It is pure comedy (also in the highest sense)—that is, a story with a happy ending. (Dante called his understanding of the Christian story a divine comedy.) We laugh deepest and celebrate most ecstatically when a precious victory is sudden and unexpected (think sports or Tolkien's eucatastrophe in fairy tales). When victory comes as a precipitous reversal of fortune after all seemed lost, our joy is compounded of relief and disbelief and pure delight.

The biblical story draws me by these epic moments—of Creation, Incarnation, Crucifixion, Resurrection, and Return—but also by the recurring small moments of grace and forgiveness and friendship and hope. I love the love David and Jonathan have for each other and their willingness to express it. When Jesus comforts and exhorts the woman caught in adultery, I feel the comfort and exhortation myself. When he weeps over Jerusalem, I am softened toward my own fallen city and nation and world.

And I cannot ignore the ugliness, for that too is part of our story. There is shocking violence, and lust, and perversion in this story, and every manner of meanness. And even God seems implicated in some of it in ways that I cannot explain, except to say there is something here I must not be understanding. The ugliness is deeply disturbing, but if it were not there, it would all be unbelievable indeed. And so, at times, I believe the story of God simply because it is the most beautiful and compelling story that I have ever been told. And it does not bother me, at those times, that I cannot prove it.

And let's be honest, there are days when I will respond to the question of why I believe in God with, "I'm not sure that I do." There is a significant element of feeling in any deep conviction, and feelings wax and wane. Sometimes the entire concept of God just seems too abstract and improbable and contrary to what is happening in my life and in the world for me to say with any force that I believe at all, much less that I can offer reasons. It is where the disciple Thomas was after the Crucifixion, and where David was in more than a few of the Psalms, and where many people of faith have been over the ages during dark nights of the soul. And, if you are a Skeptical Believer, it is where you have been more than once. Take heart. You are in good company, and joy comes in the morning.

It's acceptable not to be articulate in defense of your core commitments, including faith. Most people have neither the training, nor inclination, nor innate skills to be apologists. Not everything that is true can be explained. Faith is a story, and it often resists translation into the foreign language of explanation and defense.

This is how it is with anything that we love. We can state our love, and try to live out our love, but we may have a difficult time proving or defending our love. Others may be indifferent or hostile to that which we love, yet we love anyway.

Why do I believe in God? Intellectual answers. Personal answers. Aesthetic answers. No answers. For every reason and for no reason. Sometimes, like Dostoyevsky's Alyosha, I will simply answer with a kiss.

FAITH AS AN ENGAGED EXPERIMENT

Taste and see that the Lord is good.

PSALM 34:8

"Can anything good come out of Nazareth?"
Philip said to him, "Come and see."

JOHN 1:46

The Bible tells us to "test the spirits." We are also told that God tests us, but are warned against testing God. On the other hand, Gideon is allowed to test God with the fleece. And we are told to "taste and see that the Lord is good," tasting being a kind of test. And sometimes God even *invites* people to test him. (*I told you the Bible was self-contradictory!*) Perhaps the key is the attitude with which one conducts the test.

With one eye on God's invitation to test him (Malachi 3:10) and the other on the danger of testing God (Acts 5:9), I am going to propose the legitimacy of responding to the uncertainties of the life of faith by treating it as a kind of experiment. I invoke both my father-in-law and my own experience.

Fred Smith was an Englishman from a family of coal miners from the Midlands (Coalville, no less). His ancestors and his brothers went into the mines. He, alone among them, went to university. He became a world-class scientist and was one of a handful of men sent to America by the British government to work on the atomic bomb during World War II (the later use of which caused him great grief).

Fred placed all his faith (and it is a faith) in science and reason and human efforts to solve our problems. He had neither time nor respect for religion. Almost fifteen years after the war ended, when he was teaching biochemistry at the University of Minnesota, he was invited to attend an evangelistic crusade led by Billy Graham. His curiosity was stronger than his repulsion, though his verbal response to invitation clearly showed his disdain: "Sure, I'll come hear that psychological deviate." He wanted to see for himself the diseased thinking that was influencing so many.

Billy Graham preached that night on the story of Nicodemus, an intellectual who came to Jesus in secret to find out more about what Jesus was teaching. Nicodemus was initially obtuse—despite his education, position, and intelligence—but eventually became a follower of Jesus. Fred Smith, sitting in that crowd, listening to Billy Graham, saw himself in Nicodemus. He became greatly troubled. This was a challenge to Fred's way of explaining the world and his own life. He too was a proud intellectual. He too was being faced with things he had never seriously considered.

The family story is that Fred spent the next few days in his garden (an Englishman, after all), wrestling with this new information and smoking furiously (in part to keep the mosquitoes away, in part a manifestation of the churning of his mind). Could it be there was, in fact, a god—*the* God? Was it possible that sin was real, that estrangement from God was the central tragedy of every human being, that this estrangement could be overcome through simple confession and faith?

In the end Fred decided to conduct an experiment (a scientist, after all). He would accept the claims of the gospel, would live his life as though they were true, and test the claims in the only way they could really be tested—in the particularity of his own life. (Later he would use his own body to test treatments against the cancer that was killing him.) If Billy Graham was right, he would experience it himself. If he was wrong, he would find that out as well. (*Too subjective to be a real experiment.*)

Not scientific at all, you may say. Too subjective. Too many variables. Too open to bias or manipulation or self-delusion. Okay, but I would counter that any experiment has to be constructed so as to genuinely test the hypothesis. There is no way of testing the hypothesis of the gospel except in one's life. So though Fred's experiment was of a different construction than, say, an experiment to test for the presence of a chemical in a given compound, it was the best form of experiment to test the hypothesis under consideration. One has to work with the nature of the thing being tested.

It's an experiment I have conducted (and am conducting) myself. Unlike Fred, I was raised within a community of faith, and I adopted that faith explicitly myself (starting at age five). The doubts of childhood (could I ever be good enough to escape hell?) and adolescence (what use was faith in helping me be acceptable to my friends?) gave way to the doubts of a growing awareness that many intelligent people saw reality differently than this, and there was no way for me to prove, even to myself, the certain truth of what I had always believed. I had a choice but no sure way of deciding what to choose. I was like the donkey between two piles of hay who was starving because it could not decide which pile to eat from first.

While a young man, my reason confessed to me that reason alone was not going to solve this problem for me. Decide I could not, and yet decide I must. And so, having never met Fred Smith, I did the same thing he did. I decided to conduct an experiment with my life. I would act as though the faith I'd had since childhood was true and see if the truth of it was borne out in my life.

The truth of the gospel was, in fact, borne out in Fred Smith's life. He became an even more aggressive spokesman for the things of God than he had been for the things of science. He witnessed to gas station attendants, painters up on ladders, other scientists, and anyone else who would listen, including some who didn't want to. Then he died of pancreatic cancer, caused by the radiation with which he worked while helping to build the atomic bomb, only a few years after first beginning his experiment with God. Many, many people, to this day, are members of the Kingdom of God because of Fred's personal experiment.

Fred's experiment lasted a few years and then he was welcomed into heaven by the God he tested. I say that with confidence, even if without proof, because I am more than forty years into my own experiment and my reason, emotions, desires, and will are all satisfied with the results.

So I have no problem saying to the Skeptical Believer, or to the one just outside belief, if you are like the donkey paralyzed between the haystacks, conduct the same experiment. Do the things that believers do—confess your sins, accept forgiveness, go to church (as defective as it might be), read the Bible, pray as though something is at stake, put yourself among other believers, ask for confirmation if you wish, be wise about what constitutes confirmation.

Unlike with some experiments, you cannot, however, remain detached and neutral. You cannot treat this as simply an intellectual question. If you do, you are not truly experimenting. Your detachment renders the experiment invalid. This must be an engaged experiment in which you risk everything or it is not an experiment at all.

How long should the experiment last? When should you declare it a success or a failure? Six months? A year? A lifetime? Let the importance of the experiment be your guide. Most scientists would devote a lifetime to finding a cure for cancer. How long to decide life's most important question?

Test God. Do it with all your might. "Taste and see... "

WHO HAS THE RIGHT TO SPEAK OF RIGHT AND WRONG?

That was morality; things that made you disgusted afterward. No, that must be immorality. That was a large statement. What a lot of bilge I could think up at night.

ERNEST HEMINGWAY, *THE SUN ALSO RISES*

One consideration in assessing the value and attractiveness of a story for my life is what it allows me to believe and do. As I say so often, such things do not prove anything (*Then why bring it up? If you can't prove it, it isn't real*), but they are evidence for why I should value and choose one story over another. One reason I value and choose the story of faith is that it gives a basis for genuine right and wrong. It lets me say, for instance, that racism is wrong, rather than simply not useful or unpleasant, the latter being the most a materialist can logically say.

I will tell a story that does not reflect well on my father. But, then again, it does. When he was a child on the school playground, a bunch of kids were harassing a particular girl. They had encircled her and were yelling demeaning things at her, and my father was one of them. Suddenly, without thought, he spit on her. He escalated verbal abuse into physical abuse, though the wounds were suffered in her heart and spirit, not on the body.

Did my father do something wrong? Was his act, to use the less fashionable word, evil? (*Evil is just anything you don't happen to like.*) Was it genuinely wrong, in the way that gravity is genuinely a force in the universe, or was it only wrong in the context of a particular culture and its norms? We readily say that is was wrong, but is that intolerant of us, given that another culture might judge it differently? Would it be wrong, for instance, in a culture that taught that strength and dominance are the most important values, and that pity is unjustifiable weakness? (Think Nietzsche or Klingons.)

And am I wrong to say that, in one way, this story reflects well on my father? For when he told me the story, he said he still felt deep shame at his actions, even forty years later. I think his sense of shame and his willingness to tell his son of his failure are to his credit. Am I right to feel that? (*Right is just whatever you feel good after. See Hemingway above.*) And does that reflect a deeply natural moral impulse on my part, or am I simply reacting as I have been conditioned to react? (*Answer B. Conditioned.*)

One reason I value the story of faith is that it allows me to think that my father was genuinely wrong to spit on that girl and that he was genuinely right to feel shame about it. It allows me this because it claims that God built right and wrong into the very fabric of the universe. If this is true, right and wrong are as real and universal as atoms and energy. If it is not true, then we are making it all up.

Which is what I think materialists must say if they are honest about the consequences of their view of the world. Sociobiologists, for one, have tried to answer the charge that Darwinism does not adequately account for morality by showing how concepts of morality have adaptive value. That is, if a person behaves in certain ways (nurturing his or her children, for instance, versus killing them), then the gene pool (the Holy of Holies for sociobiologists) of that person has a better chance of survival and expansion. It is useful then for that person to behave in certain ways (which society will call moral), given that the purpose of life is to perpetuate one's genes.

That link is clear enough if one is deciding whether or not to kill one's children, but what does it tell us about my father's actions on the playground? Did spitting on that girl further or diminish his chances of someday passing on his genetic code? How does racism figure in that calculation? (Wouldn't killing other men, especially those who do not share my gene set, reduce the competition for women with whom I could reproduce myself?) Or how about my selfishly eating all of the pie that was made for everyone? (Does that repel the women in the room, or does it make them want to mate with this strong, alpha, pie-eating male?) (*Answer A. Repel.*)

Let's leave the sociobiologists to their strained, presupposition-soaked speculations. What about the more common, less tortured view that we all know, more or less, what good and bad are, and that people with no belief in God are just as capable of being good as are those who do believe in God? (Nothing creates more hostility toward Christianity, by the way, than the perception—or misperception—that Christians believe they are better than other people.)

I think the common notion that "I am just as good as you are, without all this God stuff" is parasitic on a religious view of life. It wants to retain a notion of good that its own core understanding of the universe does not support. Some people say they can love justice and compassion, for instance, without believing in God. But I think the very concept of justice or compassion is vitiated by the idea that we are making it up, and that they are only adaptive mechanisms. (Sorry, no one will die, or even inconvenience themselves, to promote the further adaption of the species.) I can't even form in my head a compelling notion of why justice or compassion matter if all we are as human beings are complex configurations of atoms. Such a view tells the conscious me that the only reasonable thing to do is to look out for number one, everyone else be damned. (Which may include faking morality so others approve of me. And don't tell me it can't be faked. Humans are expert at it.)

All this abstract argument is laborious. I will put an end to it for both our sakes. Let me cut to the chase. What does any of this have to do with the Skeptical Believer and the concerns of this book?

Most important, I think that the support the story of faith offers to seeing right and wrong, good and evil, justice and injustice (and on and on) as genuine realities built into the nature of things is evidence of its value and attractiveness, even if it is not proof of the story's truth. All these things are directly linked, for me, to meaning and significance. Root them only in the shallow soil of what is merely useful (narrowly conceived) or what we can force each other to do (through laws, prisons, and shunning), and they shrivel up (as I think they are shriveling up in our own time), leaving life more sterile and more hostile to human flourishing.

Let me tell another brief story, one I have told at greater length elsewhere (in *Creating a Spiritual Legacy*). I once took students to Cuba and told them to bring along something useful to give away to a Cuban they might meet. (I was thinking aspirin, perfume, ink pens, and the like, things then in short supply in Cuba.) We were sitting in a public square in a small Cuban town one day, and I saw one of our students engaging a small boy. She pulled out of her purse a baseball, the useful thing she had decided to bring to Cuba. The boy's face lit up like the sun, and he ran to show others his prize.

Social scientists will explain to us how that act of generosity was useful to the young woman because it contributed to creating a social climate in which people cooperate to help each other (and their genes) survive. Psychologists will explain how she did it because it made her feel better. It gave her a little high and raised her image of herself in her own mind. The openly cynical will say she did it to impress others and gain power in her circle of relationships. Such behavior is approved, and approval is power. We can even require such behaviors and forbid others through social pressure, rules, and even physical coercion. (Think rules against drinking and driving or against hate speech.)

A purely secular or materialistic outlook can say that morality is useful and therefore to be approved, even though we are only making it up. And it can force you to follow the culture's morality because it has the power to do so (or to lock you away if you don't). What the materialist logically cannot say to his or her neighbor, in any profound sense, is "What you are doing is wrong." People are not under any moral obligation to be useful, nor to follow your rules—especially in a universe that is only colliding atoms.

I have not done these secular views justice. They can be stated in more persuasive and attractive and subtle ways. (*Straw man! Straw man!*) My own view can be argued against. But I can't help but prefer a story that sees this act on my student's part and my father's shame at spitting on his schoolmate as real, metaphysical, universal goods that are part of the nature of things and not just something we make up. Perhaps my moral oughts are an act of faith, but I think it is an act approved by reason. Science—social or otherwise—cannot determine the (ontological) status of moral acts. It can only describe them. I am free to believe in genuine right and wrong and still be a rational person. (And if I couldn't, I hope I would believe it anyway and acknowledge reason as the leaky thing that it is.)

There is an ancient conundrum that arises in Greek philosophy called Euthyphro's Dilemma. Briefly stated, it is the question, "Is something good because the gods will it, or do the gods will it because it is good?" Thinkers have argued both sides through the centuries. When I once suggested to Salman Rushdie (*Name dropping doesn't improve your argument*), an aggressive atheist as well as a famous novelist, that believers in God had the advantage in believing in genuine good and evil, he replied, "That just bumps the problem up one level—to God—it doesn't answer it." He was, without identifying it, invoking Euthyphro's Dilemma. If something is only good because God wills it, then it appears to be still arbitrary—a display of power—not genuinely *good*.

Actually, I don't feel the need to choose between the horns of the dilemma in this matter. I don't think of it as much of a dilemma at all—not if you can hold two things in tension in your head at the same time. (See Keats on Negative Capability.) Does God will something because it is good? Yes. Is something good simply because God wills it? Yes. The problem resides in the artificial *or*.

Yes and yes. Reason is very adept at creating either/or choices. But many times it strikes me that they are false dichotomies. The truth lies in part in both choices, and beyond both choices. False dichotomies arise when we do not even frame the questions adequately or when we force something complex, even mysterious, to be something simple and reducible to a few possibilities. Our insistence that something must be one thing or the other simply shows our limited ability to get beyond artificial categories that express artificial polarities (as in predestination versus free will). It is another illustration of reason's ability to tie itself in knots and is one of the liabilities of an exaggerated confidence in reason.

Rushdie may well be correct that invoking God as guarantor of the good "just bumps the problem up one level," but the word "just" is misleading. It is not a trivial thing that the status of good gets bumped up a level. Bumping it up brings it to a level appropriate for the deciding of such a weighty matter. (Just as "bumping up" a medical question to the world's leading medical expert in that area is rational, wise, and practical.)

For ultimate questions involving the creation, it is sensible to go to the Creator. (If there is a Creator and if the Creator has spoken on this issue, which my story tells me is the case.) If you don't believe there is a Creator who addresses this question or anything transcendent at all, then you've supported my basic contention: which is that without God we're making up the categories of good and evil, and we have no logical right to tell anyone what they ought or ought not to do. (No moral imperatives.) That may not matter to you (if not, then don't get mad when someone cheats you), but it does to me. It makes me glad for my story, and it makes it more believable.

6. THE FAITHFUL SKEPTIC: LIVING THE STORY

ALLOWING AN ANSWER TO BE AN ANSWER FOR ME

Looking at the man, Jesus felt love for him. "There is still one thing you need to do," he told him. "Go and sell everything you have and give the money to the poor, and you will have treasure in heaven. Then come, follow me." At this the man's face fell, and he went away very sad, for he had many possessions.

MARK 10:21-22

Telling someone the truth does not mean they will accept it. Or, if accept it, live by it. History is replete with examples of people ignoring all kinds of truths. (Hitler, for instance, said openly that if war came, it would be the end of the Jews in Europe. Too many thought it was just hyperbole.) (*Always safe to invoke Hitler. Why not mention the witch burners instead?*)

Skeptics think of themselves as truth seekers. We persistently doubt other people's claims in hopes of not believing something that isn't true. In theory, we want answers to our questions, but only answers we find believable. Which raises, of course, some questions. What does a believable answer look like? What does it take for me, a Skeptical Believer, to judge that an answer is worth acting on?

How do anyone's doubts about anything get resolved? One starts, I think, by matching one's expectations with one's questions, as I argued earlier regarding the range of kinds of answers from definitive to evasive. The manner in which a doubt is addressed differs depending on the nature of the doubt. One does not resolve a doubt about a relationship, for instance, in the same way that one resolves a doubt about a physical fact. (Hammers are good for nailing, but not for sawing.)

I want to discuss further the nature of answers, especially as they relate to the Skeptical Believer and to the things of faith. I am interested not in what makes something an answer in the abstract, but what makes something an answer for me and for my life.

To begin with, if an answer is not an answer to your question, it's not an answer for you. All questions and all answers arise within a context. That context is as large as time and eternity, as moderately-sized as the culture moment in which we live (with all its defining characteristics and reigning orthodoxies), and as small as your own heart. You cannot ask a meaningful question that has not been asked, but by asking it in the specificity of your own life, you are asking the question uniquely, and the answer, to be an answer for you, must also operate uniquely in your life.

For a question that arises not just from the intellect but from your whole life, the answer must also address your whole life. Since many answers will come from people who do not know you (including from the distant past), you will often have to adapt the answer to your life in a way that makes it work as an answer for you. There is an existential quality to both questions and answers, by which I mean they arise from and must address a particular human experience.

My doubts about God are not your doubts about God, even if the words we use to express the doubts are exactly the same (nor is my believing the same as your believing). My doubts and questions are the consequence of my unique combination of personality, character, education, and life experiences. They are not generic doubts even if they are generically stated; therefore they cannot be addressed by generic answers.

This is one reason to talk to God—who made us, knows how we work, knows our life experiences, and knows what answer matches our need. (Questions always arise from need.) This is not to suggest that a question to God will result in the answer by return mail. But it does suggest that the only answers that matter for me are the ones that operate in the context of my particular life.

For an answer to be an answer, certain things have to take place:

- The answer has to be accurate or true to how things really are.
- It has to be relevant to my particular life—and seen by me to be so.
- I have to allow the answer to be an answer, which means I not only accept it with my intellect, but allow it to shape my will, my choices, and my actions.

This last point can make Skeptical Believers a little testy.

"Of course I want answers. That's why I'm asking the questions. Do you think I'd voluntarily remain in this state of turmoil and uncertainty if I could get out of it?"

Well, yes, actually I do.

I agree with C.S. Lewis's depiction of many people—I would include many Skeptical Believers—as carrying their doubts (sins in Lewis's parable) on their shoulder like a pet lizard. They stroke the lizard, they feed the lizard, they show the lizard to others, they talk to the lizard. They are "the lizard guy" (or girl). Take the lizard away, and they wouldn't know who they were. Ultimately, they are quite fond of their lizard and do not wish it taken away.

I have a friend who had someone staying with him who said he wanted to kill himself. He told everyone this. He talked about it all the time. Many people were greatly concerned about him. They tried to comfort him, to talk him out of it, to argue for why he should want to live. After wearing himself out doing the same, my friend tried something new. He told the fellow there was a gun upstairs. If he wanted to kill himself, it could be done in the next few minutes. The fellow moved out instead, still declaring how much he wanted to do himself in.

That seems a risky strategy to me, but I can see what my friend was thinking. This guy doesn't want to kill himself. He wants the attention he gets by saying he does. Skeptical Believers can be like this too, especially when they confess all their doubts and struggles among the faithful. Whereas secular acquaintances may find your struggle merely puzzling, empathetic believers rally around and offer everything from logical arguments to consoling words to prayers. Even if a community of believers offers rejection instead of consolation, that can be a kind of satisfying confirmation as well, something else to talk about.

Part of being skeptical about skepticism, a stance I advocate, is being honest with yourself about what you will accept as an answer to your skeptical questions. If all you will accept is certainty, no possibility of being wrong, then you are not being honest about the human condition. If you refuse to commit to anything until all your questions are answered, then you will commit to nothing of value (and you shouldn't get married or have children) because nothing of value is for sure.

Let me suggest a few (and only a few) additional characteristics of an answer to any question that is central to having significance and meaning in life (beyond the three mentioned above). These are not exhaustive, or even the most essential, but I think they are at least clues to what might be a good answer. They address the question, "How would I recognize a good answer to a skeptical question if it were offered to me?"

One characteristic is that a good answer asks something of me. If it's an important question, the answer probably asks a question back: "Shouldn't you be different than you are?" A good answer will call me to something higher, something better, perhaps something more difficult. It likely will call me to change (one reason that skeptics and cynics prefer to disbelieve certain answers).

The answer, for instance, to the question "What is justice?" will likely call me to be more just. Similarly with "What are my responsibilities to the poor?" or "What is love?" or "How should I treat my spouse or friend?" It's no different with "What does God require of me?" or "How is Jesus, gone these two thousand years, relevant to me?" (Is he gone?) (*The Jesus you promote was never here!*)

Another characteristic of a meaningful answer is that it explains things. Not everything, not in every detail, but enough to help me better understand myself, my life, and my responsibilities. It sheds light, even if I don't like what the light reveals.

God's answers to my questions may reveal my own timidity or self-absorption or rationalization or laziness. Or, perhaps more irritating to a professional question asker, the answer may be the one Jesus gave to Peter when he asked whether John was going to be spared the suffering that was in store for the rest of them: "None of your business." Even that is a kind of light, one that should result in a change of focus.

A third clue to a good answer is that is seems to work in other people's lives. This is not a proof but it *is* an evidence. I remember standing in a long line in the school hallway when I was seven in order to receive a polio shot. The only reason the authorities in my life (parents and teachers and doctors) were requiring this of me was that the shot seemed to prevent other people from getting polio. I could have exercised my individual rights (like a good American) and screamed and kicked, but even a seven-year-old could see they were probably right. It seemed to work for others; it was logical that it would work for me. (*Fine. I'm collecting stories of people for whom religion* doesn't *work. So there!*)

I get the same feeling when I look at the lives of those who have embraced and are trying to live out this Christian story. It has worked well for many people like me for thousands of years. Many others, of course, have rejected it or lived by another story, but that only means that this test is not a proof, only an evidence. If I am drawn to it, the fact that it has worked so well for so many at least is a clue that I am not foolish to take on the risks that any master story entails.

Skeptical Believers need responses to their questions that respect their uniqueness. They also need to be less infatuated with their questions and their self-image as doubters and more in love with the one who loves them. My questions to God are legitimate. So are God's questions to me.

FAITH AS PERFORMANCE

Believing in God... is "work."

PATTY KIRK, *A FIELD GUIDE TO GOD*

The secret of life is to have a task... It must be something you cannot possibly do.

HENRY MOORE

While you are not required to complete [the work], neither are you free to desist from it.

RABBI TARFON, SECOND CENTURY

I remember as a kid feeling sorry for (and superior to) those people who I heard went to early Mass every morning before they did anything else in the day. I felt superior because it just proved what I had been told about Catholics trying to earn their salvation through "works"—not like us Baptists who were all about grace, grace, grace. (*Baptists? Grace?*) (It's true—we talked about it all the time.) And I felt sorry for them because I thought it must be a pain to have to dress for church every day of your life (this being the era when you didn't go to church wearing the same clothes you did going to the grocery store).

Now I understand a bit more the logic of it. Faith in God is not an addition to an already good life to make it better. It is life. Otherwise, don't bother. (*Thank you very much—I won't.*) As a believer, one participates in the life-giving acts of faith. Worshipping early each morning gives life to the day—a day that may otherwise be filled mostly with wood, hay, and stubble.

That's fine for the Robust Believer, chest covered in Sunday school attendance pins, but what about for the Skeptical Believer? How can you be expected to engage in "the acts of faith" when it is exactly the legitimacy of faith that is in doubt? This is a recipe for hypocrisy (one of the few remaining sins, as noted earlier, in our dwindling moral vocabulary). Do you mean to tell me I should pray even if I have huge doubts that there is anyone at the other end? Do you mean I should read the Bible even when I know it has been used, sometimes with the blessing of the church, for racist and sexist and homophobic ends? Do you mean I should fast for anything other than losing weight? (*What, God only pays attention to your petitions when your stomach is growling?*) Do you mean I should go to church when it's church people who are my problem?

That's exactly what I mean. If belief is hard for you, then you need the practices of faith more than anyone. (Compare it to exercise. Some people are naturally thin; others have to work at it.) It's not only that belief should lead one to certain practices; it is also true that certain practices can lead one to belief. Or lead one deeper into belief. Or, for some Skeptical Believers, keep the possibility of belief alive.

I would never have accepted the idea of faith as performance in the past, because I always associated performance with legalism, salvation through works, insincerity, or compulsiveness. (*How about with mental illness?*) But as I have learned to think of faith as a story, and myself as a character in that story, the notion of performing faith has become more acceptable to me. A character in a story performs a role. It is what brings that character into being, gives him or her a body, words to speak, an action to complete. The performance gives the character life.

Similarly, my performance of the role of person of faith gives life to me and my faith. It transforms it from something abstract (propositional) to something lived (storied). Rodney Clapp says, "In worship and through the sacraments, and in other practices of Christian spirituality, we learn the story of Christ. We are, as it were, written into it—body and soul. Participating in this story, hearing and imitating parts of it like a child learning how to read, we learn a vocabulary, a grammar, and a plot line not otherwise available to us."

It is helpful that he includes "body" along with "soul." Performing the acts of faith engages us as whole persons, as story always does. Going to church requires me to put my body somewhere, praying often involves a positioning of the body, fasting includes a disciplining of the body, singing is a physical act, serving and engaging in acts of compassion will take me physically into places I may not often go—and will leave me tired and needing rest. Even thinking, though we seldom acknowledge it, is a physical act (and also leaves us weary). We are not disembodied beings, and neither is our faith. If we are to be resurrected in soul, the Bible teaches us, we must also be resurrected in body.

So if you are an attenuated believer, one just roving around the edges of faith, you are no different from the actor who must play Lear for the hundredth time. He does not feel like it. He hasn't the energy for it. It threatens to become mechanical and rote and meaningless. He would rather stay home and watch television. He is not sure he even likes Shakespeare anymore. Something more contemporary sounds very attractive.

But he is committed to this play, to these performances, to his fellow actors, to performing, one more time, this story. And, what do you know, in saying the lines and in doing the actions he becomes, again, for the hundredth time, Lear. After a scene or two, he is no longer performing Lear, he *is* Lear, and when Lear's heart breaks, so does his. And so does the heart of the audience. He is not a hypocrite; he is a performer of a story.

Who is our audience when we perform, with feeling or otherwise, the acts of faith? It includes each other, of course, but ultimately God is the audience. And strangely, given that many theologians tell us God is complete in himself and does not need us, we are also told that our performance of faith pleases God. Is it possible that what we do, every morning at Mass or otherwise, actually gives God pleasure? Does God have feelings? Has God, perhaps, chosen to need us, or to express who he is through us?

If God is the primary audience of our performance of faith, he is not the only member of the audience. We also perform for our fellow actors, for the community of believers of which we are a part. We are an audience for each other's performance. When I am in the midst of others singing songs of belief and hope, I am blessed by their performance, as I am by those who teach and pray and pass out the Communion bread and wine—even by those who hand out the bulletins at the door. I find my own faith, often tenuous or tired, refreshed by their faith and the actions that arise from it. It is very important that we are performing this together. I do not think I could perform it for long alone.

Yes, my performance of faith is for God and for my fellow believers, but it is also for me. Continuing in the acts of faith, even when faith seems absent, keeps me in a place where faith can return. When I was young, I began throwing a ball toward a circle of steel bolted to a backboard. At first, I could not even reach the rim with the ball. But I kept throwing it up there, visualizing the ball going into the steel circle, as it did for others. In time the ball starting going in, and with more time it went in more often and more easily. At some point I started thinking, "I can play basketball. I am a basketball player. This is something I do."

So with faith. I was introduced into the acts and activities of faith very early. Sunday school, Sunday morning service, evening youth group, Sunday evening service. Monday night Boys Brigade, Wednesday prayer meeting, Friday or Saturday night youth outing. Bible verses on little cards—to be read aloud before breakfast each morning. Prayers before meals and before bed. Bible memorization to earn points in Sunday school. Bringing a friend to church—more points. Visits to the Veterans home, a mission trip to Mexico, being a shepherd in the Christmas play, listening to a thousand sermons (what am I saying? many thousands of sermons). Need I go on? (*Please don't. I'm feeling queasy.*) It did not take me long to say, "I believe in Jesus. I am a Christian. This is what I do."

I am no longer a good basketball player. Too slow, too fat, too winded, too little spring in my legs, too everything. But guess who shows up at noon on Mondays and Wednesdays to play basketball. I do. And so, yes, I am a basketball player still.

And guess who still shows up at church, and prays, and reads the Bible, and sometimes feeds the hungry and clothes the naked. I do. I do it whether I am feeling close to God that day or not. I do it on days when faith seems reasonable and good and on days when it seems wildly irrational and not so good. I keep myself in the game. I keep myself in the story. Some days, God shows up too. If I hadn't been there, I would have missed him.

I DO THIS EVERY DAY: RITUAL AND THE CLOSENESS OF GOD

These are only hints and guesses,
Hints followed by guesses; and the rest
Is prayer, observance, discipline, thought and action.

T.S. ELIOT, "THE DRY SALVAGES"

Eighty percent of success is just showing up.

WOODY ALLEN

Oh Lord, why do you feel so far away? (*Because he ain't there. You may as well ask why Big Bird feels so far away.*")

Every believer has at some point in life cried or sighed this question to God. It is a kind of prayer, actually, because it has within it a longing and a petition. It implicitly asks God to do something about a situation—a condition—that is not right.

If every believer feels this from time to time, the Skeptical Believer feels it with perhaps a sharper point. For the typical believer, this feeling of distance raises the question of one's current relationship with God and what should be done about it. For the Skeptical Believer, it raises the question of whether there is a God at all. Maybe God feels far away because I was making him up in the first place. (*I already said that. You aren't listening to me, are you?*)

You can argue this point with your Inner Atheist if you wish. (*Please do. Things have gotten dull around here.*) Or you can simply smile and go on doing the acts of faith anyway, feelings or no feelings. One of the most effective responses to your nagging Inner Atheist is ritual—the small, recurring acts of faith performed with regularity over time.

I never thought I'd say it. Having spent my most formative years in Southern Baptist churches in small towns on the plains of Texas, I was taught that the word "ritual" was always preceded by the word "empty" (making it effectively one word, "emptyritual") and that it was what the high-church liberals and Catholics did. We worshipped God; they had empty ritual. We prayed as the Spirit moved (*Or was it just off the cuff?*); they read their prayers because they didn't have the Spirit. (But of course you didn't want *too* much of the Spirit, like those Pentecostals. Plainness, we were sure, was pleasing to God.)

Actually, I don't want to mix up these reflections on ritual with high church/low church battles. All human beings are creatures of ritual in the same way that they are creatures of habit, and any expression of religious faith at all will involve ritual. If you take Communion, sing songs before the sermon and one after, take an offering, end a service with a closing prayer or blessing, have a quiet time for Bible reading, celebrate Christmas and Easter, or wear different clothes to church than you do to a ball game (admittedly a dying practice), you engage in religious ritual.

Religious ritual is whatever you do repeatedly for the purpose of positioning yourself before God. Ritual becomes empty when it is done only for the purpose of performing the ritual, with no thought or concern for positioning yourself before God.

So why is ritual helpful when God seems distant? Because its regular performance keeps you within hailing distance. It is not, of course, that God is not always near and always able to meet you, while washing the dishes as much as when taking Communion. It's that performing the rituals, the acts of faith, helps keep you from becoming deaf to the still, small voice of God. God does not stop speaking, but we are able to stop listening. Performing the ritual creates a space in which God can engage you, even when you don't feel like being engaged.

No theologian has expressed this truth for me better than the writer

Andre Dubus in his short fiction "A Father's Story." This is a story of a recovering alcoholic who expresses his love for his adult daughter by helping her escape punishment for accidently killing a man with her car. More profoundly, it is a story of how a man with a shattered past precariously rebuilds his life, hedged in and protected by a series of daily rituals that hold off, for the moment at least, a return to dissolution.

One of those rituals is going each morning to partake in the Mass. And within that ritual, its heart and reason for being, is the Eucharist, the taking of Communion—a ritual within the ritual. The man knows himself to be a spiritual weakling. His hold on faith is, perhaps, as tenuous and threatened as his hold on sobriety. Taking Communion is not a moment of spiritual ecstasy. It is simply what he knows he must do if he is going to make it:

> Do not think of me as a spiritual man whose every thought during those twenty-five minutes is at one with the words of the Mass. Each morning I try, each morning I fail, and know that always I will be a creature who, looking at Father Paul and the altar, and uttering prayers, will be distracted by scrambled eggs, horses, the weather, and memories and daydreams that have nothing to do with the sacrament I am about to receive. I can receive though: the Eucharist, and also at Mass and at other times, moments and even minutes of contemplation. But I cannot achieve contemplation, as some can; and so, having to face and forgive my own failures, I have learned from them both the necessity and wonder of ritual. For ritual allows those who cannot will themselves out of the secular to perform the spiritual, as dancing allows the tongue-tied man a ceremony of love.

I hear myself in these words. Even as I pray to God, my mind is on to other things. Sometimes I feel like Hamlet's stepfather who laments that his prayers just bounce off the ceiling rather than reaching God. I, too, can sustain only "moments" or at best a few "minutes" of spiritual contemplation. I am often one of those "who cannot will themselves out of the secular"—the world of getting and spending and doing that takes no account of God. What is one to do?

The man's answer is ritual—*performing* the spiritual. Not performance as in pretending or faking—as my Texas roots taught me—but performance as *enacting* the spiritual—giving it a bodily form for the nurturing of the spirit. Or at least creating the space where this can happen.

The beauty and insight of the closing metaphor in Dubus's description stuns me. Reread the last line. The tongue-tied man cannot speak the words of love to his beloved. But he can dance. The skeptical or weary or distracted believer sometimes cannot feel the closeness of God, but he or she can take Communion, can pray, can do the acts of faith—"perform the spiritual"—in order to stay within the story.

But don't you have to feel it? If you aren't feeling it when you perform the acts of faiths, aren't you being—here's that word again—a hypocrite? Your Inner Atheist says exactly that. "Hey, why are you going to church? You hate church. What, are you becoming a Republican?" (*Well, well. You've been listening after all.*)

Performing a ritual when you feel nothing is no more hypocritical than dancing with your wife or husband when you are too tired to dance. The wedding went on too long, the reception is even longer, and you want to go home. Your spouse asks you to dance one dance. It's the last thing you want to do. But, given your commitment to this story called marriage (A*nd your sense of what's good for you*), you reluctantly agree to dance.

And, lo and behold, in the dancing you discover pleasure—the pleasure of pleasing your spouse, but also just the pleasure of moving to the music with someone you love. You are performing the music, giving physical form to disembodied rhythms. You are, in fact, enjoying dancing and feeling closer to your spouse.

Or maybe you aren't. Maybe you still wish you could go home rather than finish this dance. Maybe you find it irritating that your spouse insisted on this one dance. It doesn't matter. You are doing the wise thing. You are putting yourself in a place where something good at least has the potential of happening. If it doesn't happen this time, you should still take the next opportunity to dance. This is how it is with rituals—we perform them regularly, apart from our feelings, as a realistic expression of hope.

The common mistake is believing that the feeling should precede the act. Blame the Romantic poets. They taught us the glories of inspiration and left the impression that writers don't start writing until they feel this frenzy of creative emotion. Horse feathers! Consider what Joyce Carol Oates, as prolific a writer as has every walked the planet, says about inspiration:

> One must be pitiless about this matter of "mood." In a sense, the writing will *create* the mood. If art is, as I believe it to be, a genuinely

transcendental function—a means by which we rise out of limited, parochial states of mind—then it should not matter very much what states of mind or emotion we are in. Generally I've found this to be true: I have forced myself to begin writing when I've been utterly exhausted, when I've felt my soul as thin as a playing card, when nothing has seemed worth enduring for another five minutes... and somehow the activity of writing changes everything.

For "writing" and "art" substitute "ritual." Ritual performs a transcendental function, allowing us to transcend the mundane and merely material. Performing ritual does not require us to be in a certain state of mind or emotion before we begin. Our souls too can feel "as thin as a playing card." And then, in the performance of it, the inspiration (filling of the Spirit) comes. And it "changes everything."

Not every attempt at writing produces beautiful prose or poetry. Not every performance of a ritual produces a feeling of spiritual fulfillment and closeness to God. But nothing is written if one is not sitting in the chair trying, and God will rarely feel close if one shuns the acts of faith.

What, exactly, are the acts of faith? What counts as a ritual? As I said before, rituals are anything you do repeatedly for the purpose of positioning yourself before God. Traditionally, these things include prayer, Bible reading, worship, confession, and tithing. Even the most tentative believers should perform these acts to place and ready themselves for the work of the Spirit in their lives.

But there are many other acts of faith that can have the feel of ritual. These include regular acts of charity and compassion (think serving at the soup kitchen or visiting the aged); dispensing blessings, nurture, and encouragement (perhaps while caring for children); offering to God the work of your imagination and craft (an artist sitting prayerfully before the canvas or the musical instrument or the blank piece of paper); and any worker doing any work as unto the Lord (as the Reformers taught).

Some rituals are physical gestures—the raising or folding of hands, the sign of the cross, the bending of knees, the bowing of heads, the wearing of sacred objects. These can be rote, or they can be redeeming, filling the passing moments with small reminders of an awareness of transcendence.

Rituals fit a sacramental view of the spiritual—that Spirit becomes visible in the world in material form—something even this former Texas Baptist can understand. God has shown himself willing to become flesh and dwell among us. He dwells among us still, no matter how close or distant we feel him.

When he feels distant, maybe not even there at all, perform the spiritual. Do the acts of faith. Keep alive the ritual of belief.

Then keep your eyes and ears open.

FAITH IS CHOSEN

This social situation obligates one to choose, but once the choice is made—given the ubiquitous presence of alternatives in a market culture oriented toward consumer choice—one must reaffirm that choice again and again.

JAMES DAVISON HUNTER, *TO CHANGE THE WORLD*

Faith is not compelled—neither by reason, nor by tradition, nor by government, nor, any longer in Western culture, by common practice. This is mostly good news. Faith, like one's love of anything (a writer or a musician or another human being), is chosen. All love, of course, is influenced by many things outside oneself, but faith is, by definition, chosen rather than imposed. This is how it must be for the things we love to truly have value and be valued. I would even say, this is how God wants it. (*Now he speaks for God. I guess somebody has to, since there is no God to speak for itself.*)

Modern secularism actually enhances the chosenness of faith. In this sense, disbelief does belief a favor. It weakens the cultural supports for faith and thereby makes the choosing of it significant and full of meaning. You do not believe because your parents did, or because everyone does, or because there is no reasonable alternative, but because you have chosen it (in response, many would insist, to God having first chosen you).

Aggressive secularism often thinks it is making it impossible to choose faith—for anyone up-to-date and rational. (*Neither of which, alas, describes you.*) But the same skeptical acids that supposedly erode the foundations of belief—in anything—also corrode the foundations of triumphant disbelief. In making all truth claims "just" one point of view among many, postmodernism, for instance, also makes skepticism, rationalism, and materialistic naturalism just points of view as well, thereby freeing us to choose the story to live by that most attracts our hearts and minds.

This way of thinking bothers absolutists of all stripes—religious and secular. It bothers religious absolutists because it seems to play into the hands of relativists who say all truth claims are subjective and beyond verification. My response is that of course they are subjective. I am a subject and therefore can know even absolute truth only in a subjective (and fallible) way. And yes, they are beyond absolute verification—beyond certainty—because such is the nature of the human condition. And, I believe, such is the nature of faith.

If I have certainty, as I have argued earlier, I do not need faith. If I know something without any possibility of being wrong, I do not need to believe it. Belief is, I think, more valuable than mere knowledge because belief operates in the realm of the most important issues in life whereas knowledge deals largely with things of secondary importance. I know that the world is round. I believe that justice is worth suffering for. I know that there is cruelty in the world. I believe that love is stronger than cruelty.

To say that belief in God, like other beliefs, cannot be proven or that it is subjective is not to say anything very shocking. It is also not to say that there is no evidence for such belief. There is an enormous amount of evidence—revealed and experienced and discovered in the human experience—but it is not uncontested or uncontestable. Others take the same evidence and interpret it differently, come to different conclusions. This is unsettling if your expectation is that you must have certainty about such things. It is freeing if you see it as allowing you to commit—in a risky, life-giving way—to the story God is telling the world.

This understanding of commitment is not based on an abandonment of the idea of truth, even absolute truth. It is based on a thoroughly biblical understanding that "in this world you will have trouble"—even trouble believing sometimes—but that "Christ has overcome the world." When you choose to shape your life by that conviction, you are accepting all of the following: the risk that you might have chosen wrongly, the sometimes painful responsibilities that being part of that story entail, and the unearned benefits the story bestows.

The primary way of choosing in the tradition I grew up in was to "go forward" in answer to an "altar call," something I described earlier. I did so more than once as a child and once as a young adult. We were taught that you could only be "saved" once, but it was considered acceptable to go to the front of the church at the preacher's invitation again if you needed a makeover or a freshening up. A first going forward was called "a public confession of faith" and any subsequent public expressions were "recommitment" or "renewal." I sometimes felt the need—not for the public's sake, but for my own.

And each time it felt like a risky choice. Part of the risk was everyone looking at you as you trudged down the aisle (including your friends, to whom you wanted more than anything to seem cool). Part of it was knowing that it was a declaration that you would have to live differently than you were currently living.

Risky, yes, but also immensely rewarding. Each of the three or four times I did it, I recall a great feeling of reluctance as I stood in the pew, singing the songs that we always sang at such times. ("Just as I am, without one plea.") I said to myself, *I'm going to stay where I am at least until the end of this verse.* But there was always another verse. (*Shameless manipulation of the weak.*)

Each time I wanted desperately to stay where I was; each time I felt that everything hinged on my not doing so. We called it being "under conviction," and attributed it to the power of the Holy Spirit working in individual hearts. I don't much go to churches anymore that talk that way, but I still believe in such things. And I remember very clearly the immediate sense of relief and rightness when I made the first step out of the pew in answer to that call. I chose then; I am still choosing now.

Faith must be chosen, not coerced, because the story God is telling the world is a love story. God woos us, sometimes shyly—calling but not coercing. He courts us mysteriously, with strange words that speak of sacrifice and shalom and grace. He often seems to retreat or stay in the shadows. He withholds his power to compel belief and obedience. He speaks in "a still, small voice" more often than in the voice of the thunder. He allows us to ignore him.

I am not describing a weak or gloomy lover whose feelings are easily hurt. (God is not Piglet.) I am trying to understand the God whose essence is love, who made us to love, and who therefore understands what is necessary for love (see, of course, 1 Corinthians 13). One of the things necessary for love is that it must be voluntary. But voluntary is not a strong enough word. A belief in God must be chosen, committed to, embraced, lived out, because I love (value above all things) as best I can the God who is telling the world this story and because I have chosen to be a character in it.

FAITH AS PILGRIMAGE

A pilgrimage is a journey undertaken in the light of a story.

PAUL ELIE, *THE LIFE YOU SAVE MAY BE YOUR OWN*

Life as a pilgrimage. It's one of the world's oldest and most recurring metaphors for the human experience. For people of faith, it's not a metaphor at all; it's a literal description of daily life. We are on a journey, in mind and spirit always, sometimes in body. Each day we progress—or not—toward a goal, a destination. We more or less know what the goal is; we are often unsure how to get there.

The only reason we know the goal is because we have a story. *Pilgrimage* in the most literal sense is *physical travel for a spiritual purpose* (see my book *In Search of Sacred Places*). Pilgrims start on a journey toward a place because of a story that has been told about that place and of others who have been there. Pilgrims have heard a story; the story promises something valuable; they undertake a journey "in the light of" that story. The story illuminates something; it draws people to a place because they have first been drawn to a story. No story, no goal, no pilgrimage.

Faith in God is such a story, and Jesus (as Messiah) is essential to the Christian telling of it. That story begins before time and it has no end, because we have no end. (*We'll see about that.*) At the moment that we choose and are chosen by that story, we begin a pilgrimage. Perhaps it's better to say that we become more aware of the pilgrimage we have always been on.

This sense of both choosing and being chosen is the occasion for a long history of theological wrangling. Which comes first? Are we even able to choose before being chosen? Does God grant us the freedom to choose? What is the relationship of freedom to foreknowledge or Providence or God's sovereignty? I wish the theologians well on this one. I prefer to read Tolkien. (*Make lit, not war?*) He writes in *The Lord of the Rings* that "the Ring wants to be found." In this case, it is an evil wanting, an active force that seeks to impose its will. God's story is the archetypal Good Story, a love story, but it likewise is not passive; it is a story that wants to be found, wants to be chosen (but will not coerce). It is the story that initiates this pilgrimage called faith.

The goal of the pilgrimage is nothing less than union with God, though it sounds a bit bombastic to say so. (*Then why say it?*) We begin moving toward that goal from the moment we enter the story. (More likely God has us moving toward it even before that moment.) The story both provides the goal and guides us in the paths to the goal.

A crucial part of that guidance is stories within the story—creation stories, prophetic stories, apocalyptic stories, history stories, love stories, quest stories, biographies, exemplum, parables, memoirs, and cautionary tales. (*Fairy tales, I say.*) The stories guide us in living out *our* story within our own pilgrimage.

One cannot overstate the significance of having a story to live by. Without it, we are literally making it up as we go. That may sound attractive. "I am creating my own story. Nobody tells me what to do. I'm free."

Free? In a sense, perhaps, but for what end? Free to be clueless? Free to have no direction or purpose to your life? Free to fake it? Free to think you are flying when you are only falling (Wendell Berry)? Free to put in your few years and then disappear like a vapor? (*Free to face the facts!*)

I'm not going to argue that only people of faith can have a story or sense of meaning in their lives. That's just a version of the old line that only Christians are happy. (A longtime friend of mine died last week who was a thorough pagan—in the best sense of the word—and got more simple pleasure out of life than the great majority of believers I know.)

I'm simply going to argue that Skeptical Believers should be eternally grateful that they have been offered a story to live by. And yes, I believe it is not just a story, but *the* Story. The story of faith, I am betting, is the world's master story. (And I do not think it intolerant to say so, because I grant others the right to make their story claims, and because the people who accuse me of intolerance are doing so in light of their own master story, which they believe is superior to mine.)

Having a story does not mean that life is easy, least of all for those whose pilgrimage is guided by the story of faith. Having a story doesn't make life easy; it simply makes life meaningful. In fact it is my story which itself guarantees me that life will be hard ("In this world you will have trouble"), but it also gives me hope ("But take heart—I have overcome the world").

If Skeptical Believers today think they've been given a tough row to hoe when it comes to faith, consider, again, Abraham, the best-known of the many biblical pilgrims. For one thing, we are told he set out "not knowing where he was going" (see Hebrews 11). This was true spiritually and psychologically as well as geographically. He was, literally, starting out and starting over and starting something new—from scratch.

Second, Abraham didn't have what any reasonable person would consider adequate information. He didn't have anything to read that told him about God or what God expected. He didn't have a tradition to work with. He didn't have mentors or the example of others who had gone before. He didn't have a synagogue or church or fellow believers to accompany him. There must have been many, many days and nights during the wandering when his companions and he thought to themselves, *Why are we doing this?*

Third, he was given lots of promises, but the big ones seemed implausible at best. (*So are yours, buddy.*) Prosperity when he was leaving home with only what was portable; a son when his wife was far past fertility; many nations from that son—whom he was later told to kill. What are we promised—love, peace, meaning, forgiveness, shalom, heaven? A bit hard to believe as we look around our world, but no harder than the promises Abraham was given.

Yes, Abraham lacked a lot of things. But he did have one thing. He had a story. Or at least the beginning of a story, dimly understood. He had the personal story of having heard God speak to him, and now it was his job to grow the story, all his uncertainty notwithstanding. Same with us—pilgrims all, moving in light of a story.

FAITH AS TRUST

If I could easily grasp how and why God exists,
if the scope of my mental capacity could account for such a God,
I think this would be cause for some despair.

GINA OCHSNER

If you could figure God out, he wouldn't be God. He'd be closer to Zeus—you but with super powers. Which is what I think we often mistakenly conceive God to be anyway. So who or what is God *really*, and what does it mean to say, "I have faith in God"? It's the "really" part that is problematic. We have no problem coming up with ideas about God, concepts of God, reflections on God, claims about God, but *really*? That's another thing altogether.

At the same time (literally), just because we don't know everything— or even most things—about God, doesn't mean we don't know anything, or that we don't know enough to live on. You don't know or understand everything about your spouse or best friend. Why would you expect to understand everything about God and God's ways?

And what about the claim, "I have faith in God"? What does that mean? (*It means you're still living in the Middle Ages.*) My best shot is that it means "I trust this story." And trust here means nothing less than "I'm betting my life on it." Not that I will die prematurely if I don't believe it, but "This is the story I am counting on to give my life meaning, purpose, and value." And in the case of the Christian story, I am also saying, "I am counting on this story not only for my life but for my eternity."

If that seems like an awfully big wager for one story, consider that you have no choice but to wager on one story or another. Everyone is required to place a bet (apologies to my Sunday school teachers for this metaphor). Everyone is choosing a story, and no story is without risk. Actually, we place our faith in stories all the time. We trust doctors, scientists, economists, financial advisers, therapists, counselors (*Mechanics*)—often without even knowing who they are. All of them are operating within stories—within narrative frameworks—that tell them what is true or good or advisable—and all of them are themselves trusting other experts, many of whom they do not know and are unable to fully evaluate. We live within a complex web of trust and hope and taking people's word for things. If we didn't, we couldn't get through the day.

So we are constantly trusting stories. "Yes, this plane will get off the ground as we barrel down the runway, because the ten planes in front of us all did." "Yes, this pill will help me and not harm me, because the people who told me to take it have studied these things, and they wish me well." (*No, they want your money.*)

Trust is most often based on history. What is the history of this thing or person or institution I am considering trusting? What is my own history with it? What have others reported? In the Bible, people are not asked to trust God blindly. They are asked to trust the God who has proven worthy of trust. The God who has a history, including a history with the people who are expected to do the trusting. That's one reason the Bible tells so many stories about the past. Stories of events in the past are the primary basis for exhortations to act in certain ways in the present and to have hope for the future. "Remember," the Israelites are told over and over, "that this is the God who rescued you (or your ancestors) from slavery in Egypt. This is the God who has proven trustworthy." (*Can't prove it ever happened. Just a story.*)

But of course a skeptic can, and even in the Bible sometimes did, counter with another story. "That was then. *Now* we are surrounded by the armies of Babylon and they are starving us out and they have already carried many of us into exile. Why should we trust God now? God is failing us."

The people who ask these very human and legitimate questions are caught between what they see with their eyes and what the stories tell them, and they are tempted to trust their eyes, as humans usually do. To trust God instead requires the ability to hold in suspension what one is seeing and feeling, to compare it with the past, and to wait for further developments. (*I call that wishing.*) Being suspended is not a comfortable position. But it's not uncommon either.

When someone we love is seriously ill, we wait in suspension for further developments. When our marriage or friendship hits a prolonged rough place, we wait in suspension for further developments. When we work to make a shaky business succeed, we wait in suspension for further developments. In none of these cases ought we to run away because things are uncomfortable or because we are required to wait. In each of these cases we wait because experience—history—has taught us that in the past such waiting has been rewarded. We would rather not wait. We would rather know now. But that is not how life presents itself to us. Nor faith.

So what is one trusting when one says, "I am trusting God"? When I say this, I think I am putting my trust primarily in a mixture of stories, personal experience, reflection, and commitment. The stories include ancient as well as contemporary stories, the stories of others and stories of my own, written stories and oral stories, beautiful stories and terrible stories, stories that appeal to the heart and stories that appeal to the mind and sometimes stories I don't find appealing at all.

Trusting God will depend on what I make of these stories and what I choose to do with them. I will reflect on them, probe them, evaluate them, and then either reject them or make them my own. I may try to keep them at a distance without either accepting or rejecting them, but these are stories that will not tolerate such timidity. They are big stories that make big demands, even when spoken quietly.

But it's not all up to me. As we've seen, the story chooses me as well as I choosing the story. The aspect of God we call the Holy Spirit works on me in and through the stories. I can answer the call because I have first been called. The story comes before I do, and it tells me who I am.

And do not think that by rejecting faith or by keeping it at a distance you can avoid the hazards that come with trusting. If you do not trust the stories of faith, you will trust other stories instead. And these stories are also based on faith in things that cannot be proven, though they may try to conceal that fact. It is not a question of whether you will operate on trust in this life. It is just a matter of what you will choose to trust and with what results.

THE STRANGE, DIFFICULT, BEAUTIFUL CHURCH: DOING THIS TOGETHER

I think that the Church is the only thing that is going to make the terrible
world we are coming to endurable; the only thing that makes the Church
endurable is that it is somehow the body of Christ and that on this we are fed.
FLANNERY O'CONNOR

I open the book
which the strange, difficult, beautiful church
has given me.
MARY OLIVER, "AFTER HER DEATH"

God says to us, "Do this together. You will not do it well, but you will do it
better—together." (*That's not in the Bible. Speaking as God again, are we?*)

The line between being a respectable skeptic and a whiner is often very
fine. One of the things Skeptical Believers like to talk (and whine) about is
"the church." The church is this, the church is that, the church is screwed
up. It's one of the single most common excuses Skeptical Believers give for
their own halfheartedness: "I don't want to be associated with an institution that is this _____" (fill in the blank: judgmental, homophobic, sexist, politically liberal/conservative, outdated, gossipy, intolerant,

hierarchical, unbiblical/biblical, trendy/tradition-bound, ad infinitum).

I accept whining about the church if the whiner accepts that it is whining about himself or herself. There is no particular "church" apart from you and me (though there is always a universal Church that transcends all its individual expressions). *All legitimate criticism of the church is self-criticism, and the only proper response to healthy self-criticism is self-improvement.* If the church is screwed up, then be less screwed up yourself. If it is judgmental, refuse to be judgmental, including about your companion believers. If the church is not doing right, be a model of doing right within your local church. Help it be better, more a bride of Christ and less a mistress of the culture or the subculture. (*I like that. "Bride" versus "Mistress." Now how about that "Whore of Babylon" stuff we grew up with?*)

The specific manifestations of the church are countless. If your particular church is toxic—at least to you—then find another expression of the faith, perhaps only a few blocks away. But be aware that you are not leaving brokenness behind; you are taking your own brokenness to another place. Look for a place more likely to heal you and a place in which you can contribute to the healing of others.

Of the three adjectives Mary Oliver uses to describe the church ("strange, difficult, beautiful"), the Skeptical Believer will most readily identify with the word "difficult." It is a word with many meanings. The main reason the church is difficult, in the sense of "troublesome," is that it is made up of human beings—you and me in particular. Every failing to which we are liable, and they are legion, is also a failing to which the church is liable. Are we hypocrites? Yes, and so, at times, is the church. Are we self-absorbed? Yes, and so is the church. Are we liable to be judgmental, short-sighted, contentious, bored and boring, indifferent, culturally captured, obtuse, ad infinitum? Yes, and so is the church.

The church is also difficult in the sense of "hard to understand"—because the church is trying to live out a mystery. Not an "if we investigate adequately we will solve it" mystery, but a "these are things beyond our ability to encompass" mystery. The church lives at the nexus of the immanent and the transcendent, of time and eternity, of the transient and the permanent, the physical and the spiritual, that which is and that which is to be—and that is a place of mystery. It is a place of glimpses and guesses and "through a glass darkly." Therefore, difficult.

And therefore also "strange." If we have been long in the church we may have lost an awareness of how strange it is. It is a gathering together of people who say they are on a pilgrimage with God. Strange. People who call down God to be amongst them. Strange. People who say they love God more than life—and love life because of God. Strange. People who say we will all live forever. Very strange.

All of the following synonyms for strange also apply, or should apply, to the church: alien, weird, aberrant, abnormal, bizarre, unconventional, foreign, queer. If we are not queer, we are not the church. (*Never heard it put that way before!*)

And because the church is difficult and strange and both human and not, it is also beautiful. We are beautiful to God—we are the bride of Christ. We are good news to the world. We are agents, sometimes secretly, of shalom. We repair the world. We feed the poor, bring sight to the blind, and declare freedom to the prisoner. Sometimes. Often actually. But then we are also difficult.

I disparage the church less than I used to. It is a gift. It gives me the chance to be—with the help of God and those with whom I gather—strange and difficult and beautiful.

HUMILITY AND THE MANY VOICES OF TRUTH

It is quite possible to imagine and postulate a unified truth that requires a plurality of consciousnesses.

MIKHAIL BAKHTIN

For God, truth may be something like a fine wine—a single, excellent, unadulterated thing. For human beings, it is, I believe, something closer to a stew, made up of many things, each contributing its part, simmered for long periods in the crockpot of finite experience.

I resort to metaphor because metaphors at least deal in references to the everyday world in which we live—are tiny stories if you will—and carry more meaning and power than bloodless abstractions. Truth, small t or capital T, is of little value as an abstraction. It is of ultimate value when it simmers within our lives.

Truth is a much battered notion in the modern world. We have people who say they have it—all of it—and will hit you over the head with it if you claim otherwise. We also have people who say they don't have it and neither do you (although they claim that statement is a truth). Such people think truth is just something people make up, individually or collectively, and that all claims to truth are just power grabs.

There are other possibilities. The Russian literary critic Mikhail Bakhtin, for instance, sees truth as real and attainable, but only in a continuous process of dialogue among many voices. He praises writers like Dostoyevsky for allowing characters (such as Ivan in *The Brothers Kara-mazov*) to articulate in persuasive ways views and values that Dostoevsky himself not only doesn't share, but perhaps even fears.

One could say that Dostoyevsky trusts the truth he believes in enough to allow it to be spoken powerfully against. Actually, Bakhtin is saying even more than this. He is arguing that we need Ivan's contrary truth in order to arrive at a fuller truth. We are not required to embrace it, but we are required to allow it to speak, because it is saying something that needs to be said. It is, at best, a partial truth, and therefore it would lead to error if taken as the whole truth, but it would also lead to error if it was ignored altogether. Ivan is Dostoyevsky's Inner Atheist, and he allows him his say. (*I wish I had been Dostoyevsky's Inner Atheist instead of yours. Soooo much classier.*)

Let me offer another metaphor. Truth is a choral symphony. It is composed of many voices and many instruments, all in service of an ultimate goal. (If you prefer similes to metaphors in these contexts—"Truth is *like* a choral symphony"—I ask whether you are bothered by the statement, "Jesus is the Lamb of God.") I have written elsewhere of attending a wonderful performance of *The Messiah* in London. (*Nice music. Nauseating text.*) We sat directly behind the massed choir, and I could hear not only the unified blend of voices and instruments but also the different sections of the choir—basses through sopranos—as each made its own contribution. And, of course, at times I heard the soloists, the one pure voice. The *truth* of the performance was in all the separate elements coming together, but it required the varied contribution of many.

Most of us have had the experience of hearing their neighbor's music coming through the wall. It is usually irritating not because you don't like the music, but because you only hear parts of it, usually the bass thumping, thumping along by itself. You hear only one voice instead of many, and the music is not "true."

It is equally unsatisfactory to hear only one voice when trying to understand how one should live. I need to listen not only to many voices from within the long history of faith but also to listen carefully and respectfully to the voices of those who do not share my faith. What have they experienced that I need to know? What do they believe? What truths to they have to teach me, even if, like Ivan's, they are partial truths? This is an argument, I believe, not for relativism but for humility.

Humility is one of the most attractive and useful of the virtues, but it will get you nowhere in the culture wars and no respect at all from your Inner Atheist (who will take it as weakness). (*Well, I'll grant that you have a lot to be humble about.*) With humility plus four dollars you can get a cup of coffee at Starbucks.

The word ultimately derives from *humus*—the Latin for earth (soil, ground)—and includes the idea of being grounded and down-to-earth. It suggests modesty, respect for others, and a realistic understanding of one's place in the universe (and before God).

I would like to suggest that humility is an indispensable virtue for those who would be wise. It is also necessary for those who would engage helpfully in the contemporary dialogue regarding values, worldviews, politics, remedies to social problems, intellectual and artistic endeavors, and the like. Requiring humility in public (and internal) debate would be like requiring cowboys to check their six-shooters at the barroom door.

One kind of humility appropriate to public debate is epistemological humility. That is, humility about how certain any human being can be about anything, including what we know. Given our limitations (fallenness), the complexity of anything involving human nature, our penchant for being self-serving, our tendency to ignore contrary evidence and balancing truths, and our general desire to "win," humility is not only desirable, it is the only reasonable stance in proclaiming most anything, especially truth.

Humility, then, is simple wisdom, not weakness.

The companion of epistemological humility is humility of expression. It involves how one engages others and the world. It involves related virtues like modesty, kindness, self-deprecation, humor (not to be confused with mockery), openness, flexibility, wise tentativeness (not timidity), and eagerness to listen. It may result in losing some arguments but in the long run will strengthen your cause.

Humility is not a synonym for weakness, wishy-washiness, or lack of commitment. One can and should be both humble and committed. Committed because it is our responsibility as human beings (made in the image of God) to work diligently for truth and shalom in the world. Humble because we are fallen and because others, equally committed and wise, often disagree with us. Kierkegaard wisely prayed that truth would not be overcome in his hands, and we should pray the same.

There are two seemingly opposite offenses to humility. The obvious one is pride—arrogating to yourself more credit than is due you. Less obvious, but perhaps also a form of pride, is so denigrating your (God-given) capabilities as to see yourself as having nothing to contribute to the faith, or the larger human, community.

The Skeptical Believer should avoid both offenses. It is healthy to be humble about how much you know about God, eternity, the Bible, good and evil, salvation, and everything else. But also be humble about your doubts, frustrations, questions, and accusations. Do not let their mere existence keep you from commitment to the story of faith—as best you understand it. Take them with you as you try to live out that story, but do not give them more power than they deserve.

Arrogance is a failure. So is timidity. Listen to many voices, and then speak with your own.

KEEPING FAITH NIMBLE

On subjects of which we know nothing... we both believe and disbelieve a hundred times an Hour, which keeps Believing nimble.
EMILY DICKINSON

Doubts are the ants in the pants of faith. They keep it awake and moving.
FREDERICK BUECHNER, *WISHFUL THINKING*

Faith is a restless form of knowledge.
ANSELM

Sometimes it's as bad as Emily Dickinson says—alternating between belief and disbelief a hundred times an hour—especially on undecided things on which a lot is riding. Go to this school or not, quit this job or not, marry this person or not, buy this house or not. Make the issue something with life-shaping, even eternal, consequences, and the stakes and the anxiety rise proportionately. Believe in God or not, give up on faith or not, become a universalist or not, chuck this whole church thing or not, believe the Bible or not, tell others my doubts or not, rove around on the edges or not.

Many writers and thinkers have explored this maddening mill of the mind—grinding, grinding, grinding, but coming to no conclusion that is not itself grist for more grinding. (*I love the sound of grinding in the night!*) Pascal, Kierkegaard, Dostoyevsky, Gerard Manley Hopkins—and the Teacher of Ecclesiastes—come to mind. A bit closer to home, *I* come to mind. That is, I don't have to have this process described to me; I need only pay attention to that grinding sound in the back of my own head.

At one time that grinding was attended by a fair degree of anxiety (*The good old days!*)—and I didn't understand why. I thought I should be able to figure all these things out—define the issue, collect and evaluate evidence, consider alternatives, apply reason, and come to clear conclusions. Definition, collection, evaluation, consideration, cogitation, and—presto!—unimpeachable conclusion. Sort of like choosing a pair of shoes or deciding how to vote.

It never quite worked out that way on faith issues. Instead of clear conclusions I got consternation, isolation, and, on occasion, desperation. The only thing to do?—more grinding. Or give up altogether and watch television. (*With a little smackerel of something.*)

The grinding has not stopped altogether, but now I have more peace about it. I am living by a different metaphor. It is less grinding and more of a flow. My mind and spirit flow in and around and over issues of great importance with an awareness that I often must come to conclusions (and make commitments) but without an insistence that I know or understand everything before doing so. It is less like choosing the right pair of shoes and more like responding to a great novel or work of music or art. I live with it, think and feel my way through it, probe it, allow it to work on me, and come to some, often tentative, conclusions.

I emphasize coming to conclusions and commitments because I am not advocating always pondering and never deciding. I am advocating deciding—and committing—as part of an *ongoing* process, rather than as the final *conclusion* of a process. I commit even as I explore, with the possibility of revising my commitment. (*Revise it to death, I hope.*)

There is a once and future aspect to the things of faith, as there is, for instance, to the Incarnation. Jesus came once and changed everything ("thrown everything off balance," according to Flannery O'Connor's Misfit), but the consequences of that change are still being worked out and will continue to be throughout time and eternity. Similarly, I understand parts of the story of faith now and commit to it, but there is much that I do not know or understand, and much yet to work out both in my life and in human history. In brief, I commit *in the midst* of uncertainty, not demanding the elimination of uncertainty.

But what about Dickinson's "subjects of which we know nothing"? In the letter, she clarifies the "subjects" she has in mind are actually "Beings" of which we know nothing. She is referring specifically to the recipient of the letter, a close male friend with whom she has exchanged intimate letters but has not met.

But she is also alluding to God, one of many "Beings" and aspects of life of which she claims we know nothing. This is hyperbole. She actually believes she knows quite a few things about the seemingly unknown, including God—and she says so in her poetry. But it is not conclusive knowledge, and the subject is ever so important, so the result is a kind of questing disquiet that in her case results in great poetry. For the rest of us, it may only result in acid in the stomach.

I like Dickinson's smiling assertion that simultaneously believing and questioning (or even disbelieving) "keeps Believing nimble." Notice that she uses a verb form of continuing action, "Believing," not a noun of stasis, "belief." I believe more in believing than I do in belief. Believing is nimble; it is alive; it adjusts and grows (and wanes); it adapts to new thoughts, new evidence, new revelations, new circumstances; it knows itself to be limited and partial and incomplete; and it is not mournful about any of this. Belief, on the other hand, is too often static, unreflective, self-satisfied, and cramped. It often comes to a conclusion once and for all and sees no need for further exploration. It has the answer it wants and expects experience and the world to conform to it.

There may be a bit of whistling past the graveyard in Dickinson's assertion. (Sort of like saying when you are out of money, "Well, at least I don't have to worry about being robbed.") I suppose we would all prefer to "really know" about God and life and eternity. But we don't—and we won't—at least not with any certainty. In that case, I am content with believing—nimbly.

FAITH IS HARD? SUCK IT UP!

I asked myself: "What *art* thou afraid of? Wherefore, like a coward, dost thou forever pip and whimper, and go cowering and trembling? Despicable biped!"... And as I so thought, there rushed like a stream of fire over my whole soul; and I shook base Fear away from me forever.

THOMAS CARLYLE, *SARTOR RESARTUS*

My intention is to make it difficult to become a Christian, and yet not more difficult than it is.

SØREN KIERKEGAARD

If it is disagreeable in your sight to serve the Lord, choose for yourselves today whom you will serve.... But as for me and my house, we will serve the Lord.

JOSHUA 24:15

Because I'm a Skeptical Believer myself, I have a fair amount of sympathy for others trying to stay on the same horse. But my sympathy isn't limitless. And it doesn't extend to long-term whiners.

Life is tough, faith is difficult, the world does not pat you on the head. Get over it! (*And finish those vegetables, buster!*)

Okay, maybe that's a little harsh. (*Think so?*) But it gets at something worth saying. It requires a bit of fortitude to be a thinking, reflective, engaged, honest, committed believer in the twenty-first century. When has it not? Life is not, and never has been, conducive to any faith that requires you to be different than you would instinctively be anyway. There will always be a gap between what you wish you knew and what you do know, between how you would like things to be and how they are, how you would like *yourself* to be and how you are. That gap is where doubt and skepticism—and your Inner Atheist—make their home. (*Actually, I live in the cerebral cortex, frontal lobe—next to the donut shop.*) You can narrow the gap with, among other things, careful thinking and committed living, but you can never eliminate it entirely.

So what are you going to do about it? Are you going to let that gap keep you from the faith that, when healthy, offers you sustenance and meaning and life? Are you going to let "I'm not sure" trump "Lord, I believe. Help my unbelief"? Are you going to trade in the possibility for eternal life for the cold comfort of "no one is going to fool me"? (*A bit melodramatic, don't you think?*)

But, you say, "Is faith, then, merely a roll of the dice or the result of a cost-benefit analysis? How could that either fulfill me or please God?"

It doesn't do either. But it could be enough to keep you in the story until you are stronger. Anything that keeps you, literally, within the community of believers increases the chance that you will experience (holistically) the kind of verification for faith that will move you beyond a minimalist, grudging assent. You will get tastes of God's love and shalom in your life, and that will make you hunger for more.

But you are not likely to get there if you love your protective skepticism more than you love meaning.

Nor if you insist on a level of proof that you do not insist on in other important areas of life.

Nor if you are a slave to intellectual fashion.

Nor if you enjoy feeling sorry for yourself.

Nor if it's important to you to believe the same things as the characters in sitcoms and on talk shows. (*Jerry! Rosie! Ellen! Bill! Chris! Queen Oprah!*)

Nor if you lazily equate faith with its worst expressions in the church.

Nor if you let the failings of other Christians excuse you from being faithful yourself.

Nor if you use other people's pain as an excuse to reject God (even when they usually don't do so themselves).

Nor if you are spiritually lazy.

Nor if, to put the most positive spin on it, you find other ways of living and thinking more truthful and attractive. I have no effective response to "I don't believe it, and I have no desire to believe it." If someone says that to me about faith in Christ, as they have, I have no blockbuster reply. I can only nod, continue to hold them in my prayers, wish blessings on them, and live my own life the best I can.

If I had never been a believer, perhaps I would look at Christianity from the outside and, absent the promptings of God, find no sufficient reason to become one. But as someone within the community of faith who has roamed to its edges, I do not find any of the reasons people give for leaving it convincing.

In fact, it is only within the community of faith that I feel any hope of satisfactorily addressing all those reasons for leaving. The same things that lead some to declare, "I am out of here," lead me to say, "I must stay here." I can only find answers to the problems with my story from within my story. And so I persevere.

Perseverance, in fact, is one of my core reasons for carrying on when the light is dim. *Perseverance is continuing in the same direction in spite of unfavorable conditions.* It is a quality I admire in many of my heroes, and it's one that my faith story commends. I have already cited Abraham's setting out "not knowing where he was going." And Stephen persevered to the end. Even while the stones were breaking him, he commended his spirit to God and asked that his killers be forgiven. Similarly with those throughout history who were burned at the stake, beheaded, sawn in two, and lived in holes in the ground, people of whom we are told "the world is not worthy" (Hebrews 11).

So what about me? Can I only believe under ideal conditions? Must all my questions be answered, all my desires met, all my hurts soothed before I, too, will commit to following the one who made me, loves me, and calls me—accepting the risk that such a commitment entails? We would not think that a reasonable condition upon which to base a marriage or friendship or travel adventure, or even a business investment. So why is it a reasonable condition for faith?

If I cannot commit to faith, I will blame neither faith nor reason. The life of faith is there for the living, as it has always been. Reason will neither completely approve nor reject it. It is left to the will to decide. ("Choose for yourselves today whom you will serve.")

The Bible also says that the prompting of the Holy Spirit is crucial. Certain theologies teach that I do not have it even in my power to will belief. All right. I am not inclined to argue these things, which we not only inadequately understand but cannot even adequately frame. Perhaps the promptings of the Holy Spirit take the *form* of a question for my will. It may well be that something transcendent is doing the work, but that work *presents* itself to me in the form of a question which I must answer: "Do you choose to believe?" "Do you accept this story as your own?" or, in one biblical form, "Who do you say that I am?"

There is much that I do not know, but I know enough to answer these questions. My answers today, which I must renew every day, are "I do," and, with Peter, "You are the Messiah."

GETTING OFF THE TREADMILL OF WEARY CONSIDERATIONS

It's when I'm weary of considerations,
And life is too much like a pathless wood.
ROBERT FROST, "BIRCHES"

Behold, now is the acceptable time. Now is the day of salvation.
2 CORINTHIANS 6:2

It is foolish not to think long and hard when making life-shaping decisions. It is also foolish to think too long. So it is with marriage and investment opportunities, with whether to swing at a two-strike curveball, and with all kinds of other decisions. So it is with the call to faith. You must decide, you can't decide—decide. (*Why so hasty? There's more data to gather.*)

Some of the Athenian Mars Hill philosophers decided not to decide when Paul presented them the beginnings of the gospel in Acts 17. (*Smart. Love those philosopher types.*) That was not unreasonable or recalcitrant on their part. Unlike others who mocked, they said, with good philosopher's caution, "We will hear you again about this." Meaning, "We'll chew on this, see if it has any merit, and get back to you." It's probably what I would have done if some stranger had ridden into town with talk about unknown gods. (No, actually, I would have been one of the scoffers.)

Some who said we'll hear more later were undoubtedly looking for a polite way to end a conversation with a dubious character. But others, including Dionysius and a woman named Damaris, followed Paul from the scene to learn more and became believers. I want to know more about these two, especially Damaris (a woman among the philosophers and civic leaders?), but, as so often, I do not get everything I want, only their names. (Cue the historical novelists.)

But I think Dionysius and Damaris have something to teach us skeptical types. They came that day likely knowing nothing about Jesus (much less Jesus the Christ), heard what Paul had to say, followed him to learn more, and, at some point, became believers. One tradition says Dionysius became the bishop of Athens and that Damaris (perhaps his wife) was instrumental in overseeing the Athens Christian community (she gets a saint's day in the Orthodox church). They were smart, accomplished people (or they wouldn't have been on Mars Hill). They had much less to go on than we do. They risked their comforts and social standing. And the Bible indicates they joined the story.

"We will hear you again" is actually the default response of the human brain whenever confronted with a difficult choice. (This is the yin response. The brain's yang response is to decide instantly without thinking at all. Skeptical types lean toward yin.) The brain (mind, really) always wants more information. (*Mind* is *brain, buddy boy. No ghosts allowed!*) It employs the "procrastinating habit of thought" (Henri Bergson) to say, "Let's wait. Let's gather more evidence. Let's think a while longer. There's always time to decide." (*I'm all about yin!*)

But of course there isn't "always time." Life can end abruptly and isn't overly long at best. If life lasted forever, we could ruminate forever. If not, then not. The carpe diem poets say to their beloved, "Time (and your beauty) flies, kiss me." The carpe diem Messiah says, "Work while it is daylight, for the night is coming" (John 9:4). Even Bob Dylan, who lives on the edge of belief, sings of the shadows falling and says, "It's not dark yet, but it's getting there." Bobbie knows.

The word "shadows" puts me in mind of the nine kings in *The Lord of the Rings*. Stripped of their humanity by their lust for power, they have become wraiths—shadowy, soulless creatures, neither living nor dead, existing between two worlds. That's a little too dramatic to describe those who agonize over whether and how to believe, but there are similarities.

When plagued by a mind boiling continuously about what to believe and what to do, I have felt, at times, a bit wraith-like myself.

Cook a meal in the oven too long, and it turns to burned crusts. Similarly with cooking too long in the mind on the meaning of life. After a season (or lifetime) of simmering, a Skeptical Believer must choose. (Not to choose, again, being itself a choice.) At some point, he or she realizes, "I'm not going to get what I want here. I'm not going to get that piece of clinching evidence that will make a decision about God unassailable, trouble-free, without risk or the possibility of being wrong. I'm going to work while it is daylight—or I am not. Because, for certain, the night is coming."

The word "work" is as important as the word "decide." A *decision* to get off the treadmill of endless reflection and debate should lead to the *work* of being a character in a story with things to do. We are made to work, to do and make things, as God does. A passive protagonist in a novel kills the story. Passive characters in the story of faith are little better. You were not rescued from being a wraith in order to become a pew polisher.

You also were not rescued in order to become a Christian zombie—mindlessly parroting spiritual clichés, killing the inquiring part of your brain, and changing all the "favorites" buttons on your car radio (*Seinfeld*). Commitment to faith is not the end of reflection, struggle, or doubt. It is a declaration in the midst of it. You do not change your personality or many of your values or your core political convictions. You simply understand these things in a new way. You see them in light of the story whose call on your life you have decided to answer.

Skeptical Believers rarely lose all their skepticism when they join more wholeheartedly the story of faith, nor should they. There is a lot in life and in church to rightly be skeptical about. But skepticism can be wedded to commitment, and commitment to action, in a way that gets you off the treadmill and onto the path. Living on the treadmill is a waste of energy. The right path can get you home.

IGNORANCE, MYSTERY, AND MYSTERIUM

Perhaps the first danger of the theologian is being able to write without astonishment.

BELDEN C. LANE, *THE SOLACE OF FIERCE LANDSCAPES*

Not everything has a name.

ALEXANDER SOLZHENITSYN, NOBEL LECTURE

Mystery is as much a part of the human experience as death and taxes. It can be avoided only by not thinking very much or very deeply, and many choose to do so. If you can't live with mystery, then don't even consider the life of faith. Choose a profession such as fixing washing machines or mapping genetic codes, buy a condo, and, preferably, stay single.

Do not—I repeat, do not—think about God, beauty, or the meaning of life. Don't mess with sin and grace, transcendence, eternity, or what women want. Read *People* and *Money Magazine* and the *Diagnostic and Statistical Manual of Mental Disorders*. Do not read Shakespeare, Dostoyevsky, Elie Wiesel, Rudolf Otto, or the Bible. Watch endless hours of sitcoms and sports. Look to politicians and cable news to explain the world to you. Calculate your net worth. (*Just a wee bit condescending, don't you think? Bitter about our net worth, are we?*)

If, on the other hand, you are okay with mystery, maybe even drawn to it, then consider the difference between various types of mystery. One meaning of mystery is that which is not known but which could be known (and may already be known by some other human being). This is not genuinely mystery at all. It is simply ignorance—temporary or otherwise. Something may be a mystery to me that someone else knows perfectly well—for instance, how computers work. (*Or how to sell books?*)

Mystery novels are mysteries of this kind. We call them mysteries, but we expect the mystery to be solved by the last page (which is why we seldom reread them). The mystery associated with distant lands and cultures can be resolved by visiting them. The mystery of AIDS or cancer can be solved, we are confident, by study and experimentation. Such mysteries can be resolved by more knowledge, and they often are. These are the only kind of mysteries that are important for some people and some kinds of minds.

I once heard a sociologist declare that there was no mystery to the Holocaust. "The Holocaust can be explained quite precisely in sociological terms," he said. And he proceeded to sketch out such an explanation in terms of the history of anti-Semitism, the dynamics of German life between the two world wars, the psychology of the Other, and so on—blah, blah, blah.

If he had only claimed that sociology has something to offer in exploring why highly educated and sophisticated people designed gas chambers to kill millions of their fellow human beings with insecticide, I would not have protested. But his confidence that he and his fellow academics could deal adequately with the conundrum of evil left me with the feeling that I was listening to a fool. He took mystery in the most superficial sense and thought he had solved this one. He understood nothing of mystery, and little about the Holocaust beyond the bare facts.

There is ignorance, then there is genuine, irresolvable mystery. This involves things fundamentally beyond human abilities to fully comprehend or even frame. That is, we not only cannot understand such mysteries, we cannot even ask the right questions about them or describe them adequately. The nature of evil or suffering, for instance (don't even pretend that psychology is up to this task), or many other things involving human nature and motivation.

The life of faith abounds in such mysteries: the nature of the Trinity, the relationship between free will and God's foreknowledge, what happens during the Eucharist, the action of grace, the full meanings of the Cross and empty tomb, and on and on. (*The only mystery is why a rational person would bother with any of them.*)

There is so much mystery in faith not because faith is irrational, but because it is suprarational. That is, the things of faith invite and reward rational discourse, but they refuse to be confined to it. (The same can be said for other areas of human experience such as beauty, love, and the imagination.) We ought to think about such things as deeply and as carefully as we can, but we ought not to be either surprised or discouraged when our thinking reaches its limit before our desire to know is fully satisfied.

And we certainly shouldn't use our inability to fully comprehend or explain a mystery as an excuse for dismissing its reality. That would be like a thirteen-year-old dismissing gravity because the physics behind the Newtonian law is beyond him. And this is what secular materialists and Skeptical Believers are often tempted to do: "No one can explain it to me to my satisfaction; therefore it isn't real." Bad logic, but perfectly human. I've done it myself. (*What's the good of claiming something is "real" if you admit you don't understand it?*)

When we think such things, however, it is not usually because we have come to an intellectual impasse. More often it is because we have come to an emotional one, or to a whole-person stop. Life has punched me in the stomach. I feel pain and uncertainty (or boredom and directionlessness). I look for solace and solutions. I expect faith, if I have made it my life story, to provide both. If I'm not feeling it, I wonder if I've been sold a bill of goods. I doubt the story.

In this situation the invocation of "mystery" seems like a cop-out. "Yes, God is good and wants only good for us, but God also allows evil, allows suffering. It's a mystery." Sounds a bit too glib. In such cases, it is often easier to quit believing—or at least to quit acting out of faith—than it is to live with the tension of the mystery.

This is why Kierkegaard says that the command of God to Abraham to sacrifice his long-awaited son, the fulfillment of the promise to bless the nations through him, is a terrifying example of the absurdity of faith. Abraham had to hold two thoughts simultaneously in his head: "God is good" and "God commands me to murder my son." (Call it sacrifice, not murder, if that makes it easier for you. It doesn't for me.) It would have been much easier not to believe in God or not to believe in God's goodness than to believe a good God required this of him. And if you think the terror and the mystery of this disappear because it all turned out okay for Isaac in the end, then you are seriously diluting the story.

Some believers don't even like the concept of mystery. It seems a catch-all strategy for dodging tough questions. Whenever we hit some aspect of faith that is inconvenient (suffering), or unpalatable (the doctrine of hell), or quasi-paradoxical (the Trinity), someone invokes "mystery," and we scurry around the issue, glad to be safely on the other side.

Other believers pretend that mystery is only for the ill-informed or spiritually weak. Their theology has an answer for everything. The heartbreak of human suffering is neatly answered by the doctrine of the Fall, the shocking teaching of eternal separation from God is taken care of with references to God's holiness and justice, the logic-resisting complexity of One God being Three is waved away with an analogy to water, steam, and ice. (*Answers-R-Us: You got questions? We got answers!*)

Personally, I think that if you haven't made room for mystery in your story of faith, then you haven't made room for God.

There is yet another, higher level of mystery. For lack of a better term, I will call this the mysterium. *Mysterium* is the Latin word from which our word *mystery* is derived (itself based on an earlier Greek word that means "an initiate," as with the initiation into secret knowledge of the ancient mystery religions). The term has a long history in Christian theology that involves an experience with the numinous—another word suggesting a spiritual reality beyond human comprehension—that is, with ultimate things, which is to say, with God. Both mystery and mysterium are relevant to the Skeptical Believer.

Mysterium includes those aspects of reality that defy our categories and conceptions and yet which we feel (with all parts of our being) are of ultimate significance. It is that part of the real (a part which suffuses and sustains the whole) which we most successfully explore with the strategies of art, religion, and mystical contemplation. Knowledge of these things is possible, but that knowledge will never be encompassing, and it will not be primarily the knowledge of the intellect.

The main difference between mystery and mysterium is that the former deals primarily with *thinking* about the numinous or the mysterious and the latter with *experiencing* the numinous. This is a huge difference. Both are valuable, but only one is life-changing. (And that is exactly the problem for people like me, and perhaps like you)

Rudolf Otto describes the experience of the numinous as being in the presence of the divine and feeling its overwhelming power, holiness, and otherness, a description found time and again in sacred writings from Moses (the burning bush) to Paul (Damascus road) to the desert fathers to medieval mystics (Teresa of Avila, Julian of Norwich) to modern contemplatives. (*It's in other religions too, you know. Equally bogus of course.*) Common denominators include an overpowering sense of awe and of being in the presence of ultimate reality (expressing itself as both fear and fascination), a strangely liberating sense of one's own insignificance and unworthiness (a death of ego), and a compulsion to praise and worship.

Otto suggests that this experience is more central to true religion than is the more common distillation of religion to moral codes that guide ethical conduct and appeal to reason. To oversimplify, he's on the side of holy rollers (though he thinks many of them are faking it) over against the fundamentalist rule-mongers or liberal do-gooders.

The problem for me is that I have never had a numinous experience in anything like what these others (extremists, if you will) describe. I can't even say that I seek it. It would be too much, too disorienting, and, well, too unmodern. Skeptics are likely never to have had an experience with the numinous, because such an experience banishes skepticism (though not doubt). People like me, who have only glancing (and deniable) experiences with the numinous—the mysterium—usually confine themselves to intellectual questions regarding mystery.

Even if we've had some powerful experience, it was often in the distant past (perhaps in youth) and we have long been unsure what to make of it. Was it a genuine encounter with something real and profound or simply a passing emotional spasm? (*I vote spasm—spasms being very common in the young.*)

Some have argued that one can experience the highest levels of the spiritual without believing in a transcendent spiritual reality at all. They speak of elevated states of being and consciousness that are entirely consistent with a materialist understanding of things. I smell Smoke. Listening to them, it does not seem to me the same thing at all, sort of like comparing infatuation with love. Perhaps the closest a materialist can get is a sense of wonder in the face of complexity, or a delight driven by curiosity satisfied, or an aesthetic experience of marveling at a realization of the connectedness of things. But none of these is a genuine experience with the numinous which the materialist by definition must deny.

But I'm not worried at the moment about materialists; I'm worried about me and you. What should we do with mystery and the mysterium? I have no problem believing there are more things in heaven and earth than are dreamt of in my or anyone else's philosophy (*pace* Hamlet). And there are too many reports from too many healthy people of full-fledged encounters with the numinous for me to dismiss them as psychological aberrations. And yet I do not have the experiences myself (or do I?).

So how should I deal with mystery and the mysterium? Here is the counsel I give myself.

Do not call mystery that which is only ignorance. Ask around. Someone may know something more about it than you do.

Acknowledge the mysterious element in almost all important things. Anything that is genuinely significant in life is likely to have an element that transcends our categories and ability to fully describe and understand it.

Do not use the fact of mystery as an excuse not to probe and wrestle. It's not a "get out of jail free" card. No genuine mystery can be *solved*, but every mystery can be *explored*.

All things related to God, faith, transcendence, eternity, love, grace, and the like are, and should be, mysterious. Personally, I wouldn't expect or want it to be any other way. (I agree with Gina Ochsner that thinking I had figured God out would be more a cause for despair than celebration.) But that is no reason not to look deeply into things.

Do not use unsolved mysteries as an excuse for lack of commitment. I do not fully understand my wife, but that doesn't make me any less committed to my marriage. It is neither reasonable nor wise to say, "I don't understand, no one understands, and therefore I should not be expected to commit to that which I do not fully understand."

Be genuinely open to encounters with mysterium—with the numinous—but do not expect God to perform for you. God is not a dog that comes when you whistle. If he did, you would often be wetting your pants.

Realize that in the Christian understanding, the numinous is intertwined with the material and yet also distinct from it. If you wish to experience God, look in the face of the person across from you, especially if that person is in need (see Matthew 25). The infusion of God with his creation is seen most clearly in the Incarnation, but it started with the Creation. "Christ plays in ten thousand places," says Hopkins. If you have missed him by looking up, try looking around instead.

RETURNING TO THE STORY: BELIEF VERSUS BELIEVING AGAIN

[There is] a great difference between believing something *still* and believing it *again*.

G.C. LICHTENBURG

As an adult, I have occasionally tried to talk myself out of Christianity.

SUZANNE PAOLA

Reality is that which, when you stop believing in it, doesn't go away.

PHILIP K. DICK

Only God knows the precise border between belief and disbelief, though many have their opinions. Those who live in the vicinity of that border—either just inside or just beyond—know that it can be troubled territory—sometimes desolate, often stagnant, many times lonely. It is a poor place to set up permanent residence. I think it better, and more honest, to either fish or cut bait. This book is addressed primarily to those who lean toward fishing.

W.H. Auden said, "Every Christian has to make the transition from the child's 'We believe still' to the adult's 'I believe again.' This cannot have been easy to make at any time, and in our age it is rarely made, it would seem, without a hiatus of unbelief" (see Roger Lundin's extended discussion in *Believing Again*). Poet that he is, Auden's observation is a bit enigmatic, at least to me. But I think he is on to something. He is speaking not just of making the faith of one's parents or childhood one's own, but of the kind of faith one returns to after a period—brief or long—of living at a distance from it.

By living at a distance from belief, I mean living as though the claims of the gospel (which are immense) are not fully relevant to your own life, even if you never actually announce that to yourself. Renewed faith is not the same thing as new faith. Joining the story of faith for the first time is not the same as returning to faith after what Auden calls a "hiatus." The former is often accompanied by wide-eyed wonder, the latter by something more complex—open-eyed caution, perhaps.

Returning to faith—or to a more lived faith—is something like returning to the home of one's youth after long absence. One knows the place, but only as a different person, not as the person you are now. Things are both familiar and unfamiliar. Certain aspects of a home long left behind are haunted, filled with memories, good and bad, of a past life. Some things fill you with appreciation and joy; others remind you why you left. You can live there again, but only in a new way.

To change the metaphor, returning to faith can be like recommitting to a troubled marriage. You never left the marriage in body, but you moved away in spirit. You first imagined and then lived a life apart from the person to whom you were committed. You may or may not have weighed divorce, but you slowly edged away from giving yourself completely. You lived on the border of the marriage, rather than at the center.

A recommitment to faith, like a recommitment to a marriage, will not feel like the first commitment. There will likely be no honeymoon, no giddiness, no flights of rapture. You will come back in your maturity, perhaps wounded, as a veteran returns from war. You will come back changed, not necessarily better for your experiences away, but a different person. You will have fewer illusions and greater awareness (and perhaps caution). You will bring with you more life experience, more reflectiveness. You may even be wiser.

If you are wiser, you will know that you cannot return to living on the border. You can no longer be one of T.S. Eliot's hollow men or women, trapped "Between the conception / And the creation / Between the emotion / and the response." You must work to make this marriage work; you must live this story of faith as though it is what it claims to be—the greatest story ever told.

Which means you must do the things the people in this story have always done. You must pray, you must worship together, you must serve, you must ask for and give forgiveness, you must take chances, you must live as someone who has a hope (see Ephesians 2:12; 1 Thessalonians 4:13). In short, you must accept your place in the story and live accordingly.

You must be something like Jamie.

I had thought to pick someone from the Bible or church history or some contemporary writer or thinker to illustrate what I am talking about. But my wife suggested Jamie, our nephew, and I think that's right. Why not someone from the family? If what I am saying is true, I should be able to see it close by.

Jamie was raised in faith, mostly in a medium-sized Lutheran church in a western suburb of Minneapolis. He spent his boyhood looking out at the world through brown mop hair, and what he saw was adventure. Big Wheels gave way to skateboard ramps and bicycles and then to skis and cars. All went fast. All gave a rush. All made him feel more alive. Especially the skis.

Jamie became a professional skier. Not a racer but a jumper. He jumped off things, over things, down things, through things. He jumped where other people wouldn't jump. And someone started taking pictures. Then filming. And eventually he was perhaps the most famous jumper of his kind in the world. Because he jumped off the biggest cliff of all (255 feet), and if you do anything the biggest, people pay attention. Even if it's just to watch you die.

Jamie was not only an extreme skier, he was an extreme liver. Nothing wrong with living extremely—I admire the ascetic saints more than most—but one must ask, extreme in service of what? Extreme for what purpose? Just for the hell of it? Just to pile up sensations (or perhaps numb them)?

In Jamie's case his extreme living was mostly cliché—lots of drinking, lots of pot and partying, lots of big talk, lots of quarrelsomeness, lots of concussions, lots of aimless wandering. And very little of the faith of his youth. I don't know enough to say how little, but let's just say God was kept a few mountain ranges away.

Jamie was not a Skeptical Believer or an unbeliever. He was sensory not cerebral. As far as I can tell, he did not ski away from faith because of doubts but because of distractions. The physical pulse of what was in front of him was stronger than the spiritual pulse of what lay within him. For a season—a long season.

But God waited—and preserved—while Jamie skied and jumped and partied. God kept him alive through that slow, backward-turning free fall through space—the space beyond that 255-foot cliff edge and the space of his free fall through that part of his life.

You know how this ends, more or less. If Jamie had kept falling, I wouldn't be telling you this story. (I pick stories like I pick friends, favoring the ones that make my life better.) Jamie fell eventually into the deep powder of God's grace. In fact, he was falling into and through it the whole time. But now he began to recognize it. Now he saw it for what it was, the most important thing of all. The thing he had to build his life around.

It helped that he got married and had two children and started going to church again. He had been telling people for quite a while that he did all this crazy stuff for Jesus ("What did he say?" people asked. "Did he just say he did this for *Jesus*?"), but now he began living his everyday life as though it were true. He moved his wife and kids to Montana. His new pastor was thrilled that he had someone in his congregation who could reach the young ski crowd. For the first time ever, Jamie had a steady, long-term job, one that made use of both his skills and his notoriety. Life was good. Life was also soon to be over.

He started the avalanche himself, snowboarding out of the trees and into the top of a rocky chute. It was early in the season (two weeks ago as I write), and the snow was not deep but dangerous. It gave way just above him, washing over his board and taking him down eight hundred feet over rocks and small cliffs. He had skied out of many such slides in the past. He had conquered much steeper and much more dangerous places countless times. Today was just an outing, a chance to hike and snowboard before a long-planned trip to see family. A trip he would never take.

The Jamie who died in faith was not the same Jamie who had wandered away from it. Neither was he the same Jamie who had once believed in his youth. He didn't return to the same faith; he embraced a faith that was fitting for him as a man who had lived the life he had lived. It was more mature, more open-eyed, more aware—and more valued. Same God, same Jesus, same promises, same responsibilities, but now a new understanding. And a new commitment. Not a new story, but living the story in a new and fuller way.

I think of Jamie's story as having a happy ending for him, while at the same time a heartbreaking one for those he left behind, especially Aimee and Clementine and Royal. He didn't die a saint (and may have laughed to hear how we polished up his life in the days after), but Jamie departed as a member of the story, as healthy in many ways as he had ever been. Now he is one among the cloud of witnesses. Those left behind to grieve and find their way have the realistic hope that the God who preserved Jamie until the time of blessing in his life will also preserve and bless them.

You may see very little of your own life in my nephew's. But you may share this with him. You may have believed once in a way you do not believe now. You may now be living in the borderlands, believing some things, not believing other things, unsure about many additional things, living on a spiritual diet of roots and tubers.

The life of faith you once lived may seem unreal to you, impossible, perhaps undesirable. But that is not the faith you are called back to. That is the faith of a previous you in a previous life. God wills your good now, as you are now, in your present. If the old faith strikes you as not having "worked," then now is the time to discover and create a faith that does. It will, in one sense, not be a faith of your making, having existed from before the cosmos, but it will be a faith you have a role in creating, for the story is different because you choose—again—to be part of it.

7. MY STORY WITHIN GOD'S STORY

MEANDERING TOWARD GOD

I am not one
Of the public; I have come a long way
To realise it.

R.S. THOMAS, "A WELSHMAN AT ST JAMES' PARK"

No array of terms can say how much I am at peace about God and about death.

WALT WHITMAN, "SONG OF MYSELF"

Speaking of two icons of twentieth-century Christianity, Dorothy Day and Thomas Merton, Paul Elie writes of "their different approaches to religious experience. Day meanders toward God; Merton throws himself at God headlong." I am a meanderer (married to a thrower).

I am more inclined to see Jesus in the distance, beckoning to me with an inviting wave of the hand, than to see him as walking beside me in intimate conversation. I answer his wave with a returning wave of my own and continue in his direction. But I am not in a hurry to get there, and part of me doesn't want to catch up at all. I would not be unhappy for him to keep moving ahead of me, showing me the way, but also keeping a bit of distance between us.

This is contrary to how I was raised and to what I am told should be the case. "What a friend we have in Jesus," declared the hymn of my childhood, "all our pains and griefs to bear." Who wouldn't prefer to feel God close, attentive, speaking and listening, involved in each detail of everyday life?

Well, me for one. I would prefer God not be quite so close. I want him nearby but not necessarily in the room all the time. I know God has a lot to do, and it's okay with me if he's away doing it for stretches. (*Oh, he's away all right. He's visiting his friend Santa Claus.*) I've got stuff to do as well, and having to attend to God right next to me each moment seems more than a little nerve-racking.

I do not think this is the best attitude on my part. I'm sure it's a product of my own weaknesses and woundedness ("Fear of intimacy," I hear a familiar voice saying). Okay, but I also want to defend myself. Dorothy Day, the meanderer, was a warrior for the Kingdom, and I am confident God welcomed her into eternity as a "good and faithful servant." And one of our family's favorite films is Bill Murray's *What About Bob?* Bob is an absolute basket case—emotionally and in everyday living—and yet he declares plaintively regarding his comic-heroic attempts to straighten himself out, "I'm doing the work!"

Me too, Bob. I feel like I'm doing the work. I do the things that my faith story tells me to do. I go to church, worshipping as sincerely as I can. I read the Bible (translate it even, for goodness' sake), searching out its wisdom and trying to live it out in my life. I pray, briefly for the most part, and haltingly, but I pray. I try to bless others as I have been blessed. I write books like this one. Not widely read, but I write them nonetheless. I am a meanderer but, like Dorothy and Bob, I'm doing the work.

And in my sixth decade of life, I'm not likely to change. "That's because you don't want to change," says the familiar voice. And it's true. I'm not unhappy enough with my life with God to want to have a different life with God. (Is that Screwtape I hear, chuckling contentedly?) (*No, it's me.*)

I am glad there are many believers, like Thomas Merton, who throw themselves headlong after God. I live with one. Flannery O'Connor's Misfit was right when he declared of Jesus, "If He did what He said, then it's nothing for you to do but throw away everything and follow Him"—right before shooting the grandmother. The throwers have the best of the logical argument against the meanderers. If there is a God, how can we want anything less than the closest possible relationship?

We can't. And I will honestly try to do better. But we Skeptical

Believers have to play the hand that's dealt us. (*Blame the genes. "It's just the way I am, judge."*) To change the metaphor, I may be meandering and dawdling, but I'm on the path. I see Jesus ahead, leading the way. I take comfort that this is a path that many whom I admire and love have chosen as well. I'm keenly aware of the cloud of witnesses (that now include my father and great friends and mentors). We're doing the work together. I hope to meet up with Jesus fully—face-to-face, as Paul says—at heaven's gate, if not before. I'm trusting that God loves meanderers, too.

A BIG STORY—THE MORE UNBELIEVABLE, THE BETTER

In the beginning, God created the heavens and the earth.
GENESIS 1:1

The one who testifies to these things says, "Yes, I am coming soon."
Amen. Come, Lord Jesus.
REVELATION 22:20

The problem today is that there are no deserts, only dude ranches.
THOMAS MERTON

I like the audacity of the Christian story. A personal Creator-God, counting the hairs on our heads, injecting himself into human history, parting seas and bringing back the dead, becoming one of us, chatting us up whenever we ask, forgiving our sins, bringing time to an end, welcoming us back. The very "unbelievability" of the story is one reason I believe it. (*How can you argue with a guy who makes a virtue out of unbelievability? It's maddening!*)

If you find it totally and absolutely "unbelievable," then of course you will find something else to believe (likely just as far-fetched, only with much diminished returns). But if you only find it mind-boggling and improbable, then, if you are reasonable, you should put it in the same category as other mind-boggling and improbable things—such as that polio can be prevented by swallowing a pill; that if you travel the speed of light, then time slows to a stop; that holes exist in the universe that can suck in whole stars and keep light from escaping. Or in the category of other kinds of improbability, such as that someone else in the world finds you lovable and worth spending a life on.

"But," you protest, "I only believe polio can be prevented with a pill because it has been proven." Ah, yes, proven. But someone had to envision that possibility before it could be "proven." Until someone did, the idea would have seemed a fantasy to most.

I would say the same about my faith in God. It has been proven—in the only way it could be: within people's lives, including mine. The greatest proof of any life story is that it works—that is, provides meaning and significance and a reason for being. (*Other stories work too. How many times am I going to have to say that?*) And one must include eternity as well as time in the calculation. If it only works for your four score and ten, it doesn't work well enough or long enough.

If I'm going to give the only life I have to a story, I want it to be a big one. (Like the big Russian novels I love.) I want it to be risky and adventurous and have the possibility for a big payoff. That it also has the possibility of being a big disappointment—no God, no genuine morality, no lasting significance to human life—does not concern me much, certainly less than it used to. No risk, no reward, they say. Give me a challenging, mysterious desert, not a dude ranch.

As I said before, if I'm wrong about this story, I'll never know it (Pascal). I will pass into nonbeing with the expectation that eternal life awaits me. I will have taken a chance on a story that tells me that goodness and grace and love are at the foundations of the cosmos. That conviction will give me the best life I can imagine. The only proof that the story is mistaken, if it is, will come when the earth is eventually consumed by an expanding sun—and even then only if we haven't moved elsewhere in the meantime. That doesn't seem an unreasonable wager.

There are safer stories. Little, safe stories. Believe only what you can prove. Believe only in material things—only in what you can touch and see. Live by the ruling (and transient) ideas of your particular age. Follow John Lennon and limit your imagination to conceiving only sky above us and only earth below.

But what is the danger that this kind of safety protects you from? The danger of believing too much? The danger of being thought stupid or backward or unmodern? The danger of being out of step with your time (knowing that the ruling ideas of this time, as always, will be judged shortsighted, even laughable, by a future age)? Sorry, that doesn't seem much of a danger to me.

Give me a big story, one big enough for all time and beyond time.

MY OWN STORY OF FAITH—
THE CONDENSED VERSION

Truly, truly, I say to you, we speak of what we know and testify of what we have seen.

JOHN 3:11

Every story has within it the strands of many other stories. My story of faith is itself a weaving together of many stories—stories from the Bible, stories from history, stories from the world around us, stories from my ancestors, stories from my own life. I have told many of those stories in other books, and I am telling some more in this one. (No one runs out of stories, because every day of living spawns new ones.)

Some stories are close-ups, taking a small slice of a life and telling it in fine detail. Other stories are panoramas, giving a sweeping view from the side of a mountain. What follows is a panorama, maybe even a plot summary, of the long arc of the story of faith in my life.

I was born, as were you, into stories. One of those, a master story, was the story of faith. This story, which I experienced before I even understood words, was undergirded by the three foundational, story-based claims that I identified earlier as the master plot of the Bible: God made me, God loves me, God calls me.

It is a story that has no known beginning and has no end. It is a story that entered time with the creation of the universe and entered known human history with a man named Abraham (or Adam if you prefer). It expressed itself centuries later in the freeing of a group of slaves from four hundred years of bondage, and in the announcement to them that God would be their God and they would be his people.

This story required of the people of God that they believe certain things, but more important that they live in a certain way. From the very beginning with Abraham, God made clear that his grace was not limited to these chosen people, but was intended for "many nations"—that is, for the whole world.

That promise was fulfilled at the story's climatic moment, the moment when God chose to identify completely with his creation and become Emmanuel—God with us. At that point, and more particularly at the moment of Christ's death and resurrection, it became possible for you and me to join the story in a way that was less possible before.

This is the story that each of the named disciples, who had every reason not only to doubt the story but to reject it if the resurrection were a lie, chose instead to give their lives to telling. It is a story that many have continued to tell and to die for over two thousand years of bloody history —a history that, alas, has too often reflected poorly on those who call themselves Christians.

And so that story came to me, through my parents, and their parents before them, and theirs before them, and it was offered to me as a story by which to shape my life.

In my early years, my trust in the story was total and unquestioning. I knew the Bible was true because this story was told to me by the people who loved me and wished me well.

And because I saw paper cutouts of Goliath and Jesus on the flannel board.

And because we had these great potluck dinners after church.

And because even as a five-year-old, I knew that something about me wasn't right and that I could never make it right on my own.

I assumed everyone lived in this story—just as everyone breathed air and ate hot dogs. Eventually I learned otherwise. I learned not only that not everyone was part of my story, but that many people thought my story was only for stupid and ignorant people. Of course, this was surprising to me and sort of hurt my feelings.

And so as I got older, I developed an appetite for proof. Because what I found out was not only did other people question my story, but I began to question it myself. In fact, I found that the doubts about my story from outside couldn't hold a candle to the doubts about my story that came from inside my own heart and mind.

And the doubts only got stronger when I tried to shush them and tell them to go away. And so I decided to actually read the Bible from start to finish, like my Sunday school teachers said. And that made it much, much worse.

I didn't like the idea of hell, which I also heard a lot about in church.

I didn't like David acting like a terrorist when he slaughtered every third prisoner he had taken on raids.

I didn't like young boys getting killed by a bear because they made fun of a bald prophet. (Now I do like that story, even though I've since discovered it has nothing to do with baldness.)

I didn't like the idea that God chose only a few and everyone else is doomed.

It even offended my environmental sensibilities that Jesus cursed a fig tree for not bearing fruit out of season. (What, it's the tree's fault?)

All these stories added to my doubt, and at the time, doubt was described to me as the implacable enemy of faith. And so I became a proof-monger. I searched for evidence of any kind—rational or experiential—that my story was true and not merely a bunch of wishing. I read books of apologetics with quiet desperation. The more confidently they announced that they would answer every objection to my story, the more eagerly I ingested them, trying to keep their arguments arranged in my head.

And if someone came by in person—a Francis Schaeffer in his Swiss knickers, or an impressively scholarly Clark Pinnock, or anyone with a colored chart—I would eagerly drink in every word, hoping against hope that the goblin Doubt would be cast down, and the all-knowing, all-believing Daniel would rise up in its place.

And, of course, it never quite happened. Some questions did get answered, if not definitively, at least persuasively. And helpful directions were pointed on others. But for every question that was answered, two took its place. And eventually I wearied of the whole pursuit.

By the time I was in graduate school, I was everything Kierkegaard said a person would be who was depending on reason alone to answer any of life's hard questions. Because reason, he said, is a machine designed for the manufacturing of mutually exclusive possibilities. With any difficult life issue requiring a choice—and faith now certainly struck me as a choice, not a given—the reason can and will produce just as many "reasons" to choose one way as another, in this case reasons to believe and reasons not to believe.

Even more, reason will always tell you to wait. Wait for more evidence, wait until you know more, wait until things are clear. Explore even more alternate possibilities, do not commit, do not risk being wrong, do not risk looking foolish, give it more time.

Fortunately, God gave me a wife who was only mildly sympathetic to a paralyzed bookworm committed to a long-term, low-grade existential crisis. She said, with her actions more than with words, "Life is short and eternity is long, and I can't wait forever for you before following the God who made me and has things for me to do." Which I thought was just a touch unfeeling of her.

In short, with my wife, Jayne, as a model, I decided that I would not be like that donkey who stands between two haystacks and starves because it cannot decide which stack to eat from first. I decided I had been born into this story, that either I needed to be a character in the story who takes the responsibility to choose and act, or I was required to find a better story.

I had looked for a better story—and I have kept my eyes peeled since— but I haven't found it. All of them have proven just as doubtable as the story I was born into, and with much less to offer. So I decided to live this one the best I can and ask God to bless me in it.

I did not abandon my reason or my questions, but I decided that doubt and uncertainty would be something I accepted as part of my life but not the thing I would allow to dictate the essential contours of my life. My Inner Atheist was still a long-term boarder, but he didn't own the house.

I would live as if the essence of what I had been taught about God was true—as if he did in fact make me, love me, and call me. I would cast aside as best I could those things I had been taught that I now believed were not true (for instance that smoking, drinking, dancing, and movies were all Satan's bait to lure me to hell). I would embrace my part as a character in this story—keeping my eyes and ears open and giving my questions their due—and see if, experientially, in my own life, the truth of the claims of God would bear themselves out.

And, of course, I wouldn't be writing this book today if I did not think the story had proved itself true in my own life.

But my story is not over. And I am not through with my questions. Today, as yesterday, I am a believer. But in my life faith is not something that is settled once and for all. It must be renewed every day. I live with the possibility that someday, for some reason—intellectual or because of some great pain in my life or something else unforeseen—I will again find myself paralyzed, perhaps even unable to believe at all.

If that happens—as it happened to the disciple Thomas in the hours after the Crucifixion—I hope for two things. I hope the community of faith does not kick me out because I am unable to believe. And I hope I choose to stay within the community even if my faith has dried up—to see if my dry bones can live again.

That's what happened to Thomas, and eventually he got back into the story. And tradition tells us he headed east when others of the disciples and apostles headed west. And Thomas is said to have spread the Good News of the story of the Kingdom of Christ all the way to India, where, like the others, he died a martyr's death.

If the man we unfairly label "doubting Thomas" can make it to the end of his part of the story in such a way, I think perhaps I can too. I would hope, like Thomas, not only to believe, but to make a contribution to the story.

Every good thing, in my estimation, involves risk: painting a painting, giving birth to a child, loving someone, working for justice, and on and on.

Why should it be any different in the realm of faith? Why should I expect faith in God to entail no risk, to insist that every question be answered before I will act?

I know that everything I explain in terms of God, someone else will explain in other terms. (This is one of the facts of life that Kierkegaard prepared me for: the existence of alternate explanations.) I realize that many, perhaps even most, will find those alternate explanations more persuasive than my explanation. I am happy to talk with those people—to hear what they have to say.

But until I decide that their story is better than mine, I am not likely to exchange my story for theirs. I am still willing to take the chance that the universe is founded not on randomness and entropy but on love and grace. I will give my doubts their due, but I will not allow them to tell me who I am or how I should live.

WHICH JESUS?

He had no majesty or beauty to attract us; and nothing about his appearance that we should desire him.

ISAIAH 53:2

In His right hand He held seven stars, and out of His mouth came a sharp two-edged sword; and His face was like the sun shining in its brilliance. When I saw Him, I fell at His feet like a dead man.

REVELATION 1:16-17

Even if one decides, as the people in my childhood would say, to "believe in Jesus," that raises the question, "Which Jesus?" (And also the question, "What do you mean by *believe*?") (*And don't forget the "in" in "in Jesus." What's that about?*) There are a lot of different Jesuses out there. (*Yes, the mental wards are filled with people who think they're Jesus. Even the real Jesus didn't think he was Jesus.*) By "different Jesuses" I'm not talking about the variety of divine figures in world religions, or even about the varieties of Christianity. I'm talking about the way each individual—and whole cultures—create from the biblical account a Jesus they find useful.

Jeroslav Pelikan has discussed the various Jesuses and Christs that dominated theological, cultural, and pictorial imaginations at different times in history (*Jesus through the Centuries*). There was Jesus the Teacher, Jesus the Ruler, Jesus the Ascetic, Jesus the Son of God, Jesus the Revolutionary, and so on. None of these was wrong, but each of them was partial. (And the human tendency is to embrace partial truths at the expense of balancing and complicating truths.)

For the Skeptical Believer, the varying views of Jesus over the centuries play into the notion that human beings make up all this religion stuff to meet their needs and in a reflection of the current views of the world. There is some truth to that: faith does tend to take on the flavor of the dominant worldviews of the time, and it certainly must meet our needs. But this argument cuts both ways. One can as easily say that people *disbelieve* today in order to meet their perceived needs and in response to today's dominant worldviews. Furthermore, something meeting a need is not proof that it is fabricated. (I need oxygen to live—does that mean oxygen is imaginary?)

I am enough a man of my time to acknowledge that we do, in some senses, construct our truths from the materials of life rather than finding them like gold nuggets on the ground. But I am also enough a man of every time to believe that when something is true, it's true apart from me and it's true forever. Otherwise it doesn't deserve the name. (And I think I would argue that God supplies the materials from which we construct.)

Your perception of Jesus will not be exactly my perception of Jesus, just as your perception of your father or mother is not identical to your brother's or sister's. Jesus will make himself known to different people in different ways. This is not radical or hard to comprehend. But we need a true and eternal *core* to our understanding of who Jesus is, no matter how differently we dress him. If that core does not include a reality-changing cross and an empty tomb (*I'm sick of your referring to the empty tomb. Get a new line*), then we are indeed left with little aside from the winds of our culture and the flittings of our imaginations.

I've believed in various Jesuses during my life. One of the first was the Jesus who is sad when I do something wrong, undoubtedly a Jesus encouraged by my mother and my Sunday school teachers. I didn't go around as a little kid thinking I was making God angry when I did wrong; I thought I was making Jesus sad. I had the sense that I was sticking another thorn in him. It made me want to be good so that Jesus didn't suffer as much. A bit of a burden for a little kid.

When I was around ten, I started believing in the Jesus who could influence baseball games. As I've written about elsewhere (*Letters to My Children*), I then wanted to be good less to keep Jesus from suffering than from wanting to bribe him into helping the newly arrived Los Angeles Dodgers. I saw a direct and entirely logical connection between my behavior and Sandy Koufax's curveball—a correlation that was mightily reinforced when Koufax refused to pitch a World Series game on Yom Kippur and the Dodgers still won the series. (That he was a Jew and I a Christian was irrelevant—God rewards obedience!)

I don't think I ever went through the Jesus as buddy phase. I am keenly aware that, as part of the Trinity, Jesus is God, and I have never been able to feel or conceive of God as pal. I am using slightly dismissive language here, which I should not. The intimate Jesus is very real and very important to many believers, and my inability to feel that, or even to desire it, is, I am sure, a symptom of something lacking in me.

At some point, Jesus became less a person to be in relationship with than an idea to contemplate. I spent little time talking to him (though I enjoyed listening to Willie Nelson singing, "Let us have a little talk with Jesus"), but I spent a lot of time trying to work out in my head where Jesus fit in to the whole scheme of things and how I, an increasingly educated young man, could find a way to keep believing in him as the incarnated Son of God (as Pelikan says the Renaissance artists did). I was trying with all my might to believe in the Jesus of Propositions.

I may have unconsciously thought I was doing God a favor. I was working it out so that he could still have a logically defensible place in my own head, and therefore in the world. Lucky God.

At the same time that I was constructing Jesuses I could believe in, I was discarding Jesuses I couldn't believe in. I couldn't believe, for instance, in the Santa Claus Jesus, bringing lots of presents to the good little children and lumps of coal to the bad little children. I couldn't believe the childish version of that, nor the adult, cargo-cult version (the Mall Jesus). The materialism of the church—west and east, north and south—is one of the greatest reasons for its temporal success, and also one of its greatest failures.

I also couldn't believe in Jesus as good man, ethical teacher, or sage. If this is all Jesus is, then he is one of tens of thousands, make that millions.

As the rabbi said to me, "For everything that Jesus teaches in the New Testament, I can show you the same in the Hebrew Bible." To which I replied, "Of course you can. I wouldn't expect God to change between testaments."

This is a fundamental mistake of a popular form of religious pluralism: the belief that the purpose of religion to is to make you a good person. Build my life around some guy from twenty centuries ago who had good advice on how to be nice? I don't think so, especially when that same advice can be found elsewhere (including on children's television).

Besides, the same people who are telling me that the important thing about Jesus is his ethical teaching are also telling me that you can't trust the record of that teaching. They sit around with colored beads and vote on what parts of the Lord's Prayer they think Jesus actually said (God, no doubt, waiting breathlessly to find out). The verdict (drum roll, please): he maybe said, "Our Father." The rest, they claim, was boilerplate. And this unknowable Jesus is the one you want me to believe in as an ethical guide? No thank you.

I have believed in Jesus longer than I have believed in the seasons (having been born in California). During that time, I have believed and disbelieved in a variety of Jesuses. Which Jesus do I believe in now?

I know what Jesus I *want* to believe in. I want to believe in the Isaiah Messiah. I want to believe in the Jesus of Isaiah chapter 9, who is a great light to people who walk in darkness, and who will break the yoke of slavery and oppression. I want to believe in the Jesus who will be called by the titles Wonderful Counselor, Mighty God, Everlasting Father, Prince of Peace, whose governing will be marked by peace, fairness, and justice and will never end. I want to believe in the Jesus who identified himself by reading in his hometown synagogue from Isaiah 61, proclaiming himself the one anointed to bring Good News to the poor, comfort to the brokenhearted, release for the captive, and joyous blessing for those who mourn.

I also want to believe in the Jesus of Isaiah 53, the Jesus who is not handsome, who was despised and rejected, a man of sorrows, deeply acquainted with pain and grief. And I want to believe that, nevertheless, he carried all our sorrows and sins to the cross, where he was whipped, pierced, and crushed in our place so that we could be healed. (Never mind that some find all this violence distasteful and the story insufficiently uplifting.)

And I want to believe in the Jesus of the Resurrection, the event toward which Isaiah looked. I want to believe in the crucified and risen

Jesus who is, thereby, the Christ—Isaiah's Messiah, and now mine. This is the only Jesus substantial enough, in my view, to build a life on. This is not the Santa Claus Jesus, nor the Jesus of Propositions, nor the Mall Jesus, nor Jesus the Good Man. It is the Jesus of the Story—the greatest story ever told.

Why then do I say this is the Jesus in whom I *want* to believe? Do I believe this describes the historical Jesus of the Gospels or don't I? Doesn't the Bible, as explored earlier, warn me against being lukewarm and therefore spewed out of God's mouth (a verse that haunts many a Skeptical Believer—and should)?

I say I *want* to believe this because I am committed to faith as story rather than faith as proposition. If you ask me, "Do you believe that Jesus as the Messiah is all these things," then I will readily, except in my darker moments, say, "Yes, I believe that." And for most of my life, I would have thought that enough. I would have offered to God that yes at the gates of heaven as proof that I should be allowed in (okay, I don't believe heaven actually has gates). But because I now understand faith to be a story in which I must be a certain kind of character, then when I say I believe these things about Jesus, it means I am committed to living a certain way. And because I know I do not fully live it, I am inclined to hedge my declaration of belief, recognizing that the claim of believing doesn't mean a lot if it doesn't guide the living. If I don't live it, how can I claim to believe it?

Does this mean I am seeing faith as works and salvation as something I earn by how I live, contrary to the admonitions of my teachers and the Reformers (the Deformers, according to my Catholic friend)? No, I think it means something closer to "I am living the story as best I can. Jesus help me when I fail to live it."

I am, of course, echoing the man in the Gospel who brought his son to Jesus for healing in Mark 9. This is a man much like me. He believes enough to bring his son—an act of faith. He disbelieves enough to add to his request for help, "If you can." Jesus has just expressed exasperation at the weak faith of this "unbelieving generation," and is in no mood for "ifs." All things are possible with faith, he says.

Surely this is one of the most convicting stories in the Bible for a Skeptical Believer. Fish or cut bait! Quit whining about your doubts and make way for the Kingdom! Ask with confidence that God will do what he says he will do, or don't ask at all!

But even here there is grace for people like me. The man famously replies, "I do believe: help my unbelief." What kind of response is that? How would someone you love respond if you said, "I do love you; please forgive me that I don't love you"?

What kind of response is it? It is a human response, given by a man who, like me, does acts of faith even when his mind and will are unsettled. It is also the response of a man who so much wants his son to be healed that he cannot shake the fear that he may not be. The healing of his son is almost too much to hope for. The request is based so much on hope, in a world where hope is so often unrewarded, that he cannot extinguish from his mind the possibility that his hope will not be realized.

He is, in effect, saying to Jesus, "I am doing, in this moment, what I can. Please do for me what I cannot do myself." So there is actually faith in both parts of his response. There is partial faith in the "I do believe," and there is a completion of faith in his request that Jesus will supply the rest of the faith necessary for his son to be healed. If anything, there is more faith in the second part of his response than in the first, because it has to leap a bigger chasm of doubt (the doubt that Jesus will choose to supply the faith that the man's request requires). The man generates what faith he can and depends on God for the rest. That's something I can do as well, and I do it every day.

I do not think this is lukewarm faith. I am lukewarm about my *certainty*, which I sometimes desire but never really have. I am not lukewarm about my *commitment* to the story. If I were, I wouldn't be sitting here, with a beautiful Irish day outside, writing this book.

Others can disparage this kind of faith if they wish. I do not recommend it as a model. But I do not belittle it either. It is the kind of faith many had in the Bible, and have had over the centuries since. Like Thomas, I have my doubts. But also like Thomas, I am willing to say, as he said when Jesus risked his life to go raise Lazarus, "Let us go, too, that we may die with him."

Faith for the Skeptical Believer will always be risky, but it does not have to be weak. It does not call me to believe, with an unwavering certainty, a certain set of propositions or that Jesus will always do what I hope. It calls me to live in a story. And that's a call I can answer.

GOD WILL NEVER BE PLAIN

"Am I only a God nearby," declares the Lord, "and not a God far away?"
JEREMIAH 23:23

What do you do when your saviour brings you back,
only to leave himself?
NICHOLAS SAMARAS, "THE SECOND DEATH OF LAZARUS"

Generally speaking, I find the poets more help in thinking about God than the theologians. (I suspect some theologians would say the same.) For one thing, poets are content to leave some things unsaid, or half said, or nodded toward, or hinted at, or otherwise approached obliquely ("sidled up to," I wanted to write). "Tell all the Truth but tell it slant," advises Emily Dickinson, adding "Success in Circuit lies." And God is nothing if not oblique and slant. He briefly allows Moses to see his back (or only the afterglow of his now-departed presence according to some) as Moses sits in the cleft of the rock (Exodus 33).

Poets often wrap up truth in metaphors—trying to convey to you something you don't know by comparing it to something you do. (My beloved has things in common with a rose. God has some of the qualities of a thunderstorm.) They don't do so to be clever or pretty. They do so because the metaphor contains the most truth—emotional, intellectual, spiritual, observational. An explanation, by comparison, is a much lesser thing. (*If metaphors were truth, the Irish would all be sages. I'll take a test tube any day.*)

And poets care tremendously about precision of expression. When they speak of ambiguous things, they do so clearly and precisely. They seek out just the right word to say the thing that perhaps can't quite be said. Their ambiguity, where truth requires ambiguity, is stated as concisely and powerfully as language will allow. I don't know that you can say the same for theologians—or for most of the rest of us.

I quote a large hunk of a poem by the Welsh poet R.S. Thomas as an opening epigraph to this book (please see). He talks about a "fast God" who always seems to be moving on just when we arrive, a God who "will never be plain." I find myself saying, "Yes, exactly. I know that thought. I know that feeling."

Thomas says there's no way of getting to this island, on which he is looking for God, except by a small boat. I've been to more than one such island, on more than one pilgrimage, though not to the one this poem is most likely referring to. It doesn't matter. The island of the poem is every island. The place is every place. And the speaker of the poem is every pilgrim, every seeker, everyone who has wondered about—well—anything. But especially wondered about God and time and life and how ultimate things relate to small things (my life this moment), and about what they should do with the one brief streak of a life they have been given.

No way to get to this place—this physical and spiritual destination—but in a small boat. Leave technology and modernity and independence and smugness behind. You can't get there any faster or better than the pilgrims of old, some of whom—the drowned ones—didn't get there at all. And what does he find after the struggle of getting there? An empty church, a stone altar (where suffering and sacrifice are reenacted), extinguished candles, and the fierce face of a stone owl.

Have we come too late, arriving in an age that finds such pilgrimages a sentimental waste of time (as do some of the people now living on the supposedly sacred island)? But then, did not the ancient pilgrims feel the same way—too late, God not here, though clues of recent departure are all around? What can we do with such a "fast/ God, always before us, and/ leaving as we arrive"? What to do about this God who both reveals and conceals—both a "God nearby" (Emmanuel) and, to use Jeremiah's words, "a God far away" (*Deus Absconditus*). What to do about a God "who will never be plain," never "out there" to be displayed and tested and verified, but only "dark" and "inexplicable" and "in here" (the speaker twisting the knife one more time with that last "as though," suggesting that even the few crumbs he—and God—have thrown us might be illusory).

Yes, if you don't bring God with you on your pilgrimage, you won't find him at your destination. (*Like packing a lunch?*) He's not sitting around waiting to be tripped over by camera-toting tourists (or pilgrims either, for that matter). He's on the move (as Lewis says of Aslan). It's comforting to know he's already been in the distant place before we get there. It's a bit disconcerting to feel he's just left as we arrive. (Another poet, above, imagines Lazarus complaining that Jesus brought him back from the dead, only to leave himself shortly after.)

We are always ready, like Peter on the mountain, to build three booths—one for Moses, one for Elijah, one for Jesus—only to find that no place, no church, no movement, no theology is adequate to house God. God will not be housed, except, perhaps, in my heart and yours.

That last sentence comes directly out of the spiritual legacy of my own upbringing. It's a comforting word—"I stand at the door and knock" (Rev. 3:20)—to be heard along with a more difficult one—"Truly you are a God who hides himself" (Isaiah 45:15). God is not plain. God is on the move—including within me if I choose to move with him. After long thought and increasingly long life, I am at peace with a God who is not plain. If God leaves just as I arrive, then I had better keep moving myself. There may not be time for second breakfasts or elevenses (an allusion to another pilgrimage). I will keep moving down the chosen path, even as it dips into the darkened woods, taking the poets with me.

MODELS, MENTORS, AND EVERYDAY HEROES

Let us now praise famous men, and our fathers that begat us.

SIRACH 44:1

The sign of faith is not only the happiness of the passions but the degree of *imitation* that characterizes one's life.

PAUL HOLMER

Therefore, since we are surrounded by so great a cloud of witnesses…

HEBREWS 12:1A

Witnesses, yes, but also models, mentors, and everyday heroes. We Skeptical Believers are good at talking ourselves out of risky commitments; we need examples of people who have talked themselves into them. I couldn't last in this story without them.

One of the raw materials for belief is community. If I am the only person in the world who finds something true, that should give me pause. It suggests I have missed something. But the fact that many others believe this as well, while proving nothing, is nonetheless a kind of evidence that supports the belief. (*In that case, there's overwhelming evidence that chocolate is the world's healthiest food.*)

You wouldn't want to press this too hard. Every sick idea in the world has its followers. And even among the people who share my own beliefs about faith there are lots of unsavory characters. If shared belief was proof of the validity of a belief, then all beliefs would be valid and the highest truths would be reduced to a majority vote.

But I'm not looking for proof; I'm looking for kindred spirits. *Faith is held individually but is lived out collectively.* I don't even know what it means to say, "I believe in God," except in the context of others who have taught me what that means and what the consequences are of affirming it.

When I look at the community of believers, I see kooks, crooks, bigots, charlatans, passive pew sitters, and Smoke Blowers. (*And dupes, such as yourself.*) But I also see countless others who try to feed the hungry, clothe the naked, and visit the prisoner. I see many who seek and give forgiveness and grace. I see people with a hunger for God that coincides with their hunger for truth and justice and shalom. I see people who are honest and imaginative and laugh easily and are curious and compassionate and willing to take chances to find meaning.

I don't think it is misguided to take the company of such people as evidence for the things we believe in common. We are on a quest, and I find that I love my fellow questers. This is not evidence I can use to argue with someone who is committed to a different belief and story, but it is, legitimately, evidence in my internal debate with my Inner Atheist about whether I should continue to believe what I do. (*You want to do battle over evidence? Finally, something to argue about! How about we start with where the dinosaurs fit into the opening chapters of Genesis?*)

It is helpful to name your models and mentors. (Hebrews 13:7—"Remember your leaders who spoke to you the word of God. Reflect on the results of their way of life, and imitate their faith.") Let them guide you in what you believe and how you act concerning politics, social action, living a devout and holy life. (*Talk about outdated ideas—"a devout and holy life"? Really? In the twenty-first century?*) Let them be important characters in your story. Identify *why* you include them among your pilgrimage companions.

My own short list includes minor biblical characters such as Jonathan (who teaches me about friendship and loyalty) and Dorcas (who used her tailoring skills to make clothes for the needy and never tired in doing good). It also includes St. Aidan (who stood outside his church and offered counsel and wisdom to whoever asked), and Thomas More (who valued his soul more than his head), and Pascal and Kierkegaard (whose fiery minds burned broad paths through pretense and convention). It includes people in my own time like Martin Luther King Jr. (whose sacrifices for freedom were rooted in his understanding of the Christian story), and Flannery O'Connor (who used the distorted to testify to the true), and Dietrich Bonhoeffer and Alexander Solzhenitsyn (who both demonstrated that moral courage in service of eternal truths is not just a thing of the distant past). And, crucially, it includes people in my own life, some known only to me, such as Ed, and Arthur, and Phyllis, and Carie.

I call people like this *everyday* heroes because they do not live on pedestals. They live and lived in the same day-by-day world that I do, with the same limitations and distractions. It is helpful that they sometimes failed—Thomas More, for instance, zealously burning others at the stake; King often fearful and—like David—an adulterer; Bonhoeffer (to his lifelong regret) once refusing to officiate at the wedding of his sister to a Jew. Cardboard saints are of little use to me. Those who persevere in the story despite their weakness make it more possible for me to do the same.

There's a healthy expression of the story of faith for anyone who wants to find it. The verse that so famously begins with "Therefore, since we are surrounded by so great a cloud of witnesses... " concludes, as every church veteran knows, "Let us also lay aside every weight and the sin that clings so closely, and let us run with perseverance the race that is set before us." Name those who live the story best, learn from them, be encouraged, run the race.

HISTORY AS A LONG DEFEAT—
WITH GLIMPSES

I am a Christian, and indeed a Roman Catholic, so that I do not expect "history" to be anything but a "long defeat"—though it contains… some samples or glimpses of final victory.

J.R.R. TOLKIEN

I find myself resonating with Tolkien's grim optimism, though I am not entirely sure whether it's because of my temperament, my theology, or my experience in the world. Or all three.

A few observations about Tolkien's assertion. First, he refers to "history," not to the life of individuals. He is not characterizing his life, or your life, or any particular life as a "long defeat"; he is talking about the collective human experience. (So he's not Eeyore grousing in his Gloomy Place—which I have visited, by the way.)

Second, his view is in keeping with a biblically tragic sense of life and with the Christian notion of the Fall. Shalom is ruptured, and things are "not the way they're supposed to be" (see Cornelius Plantiga's book of that title). One of the more profoundly naive assertions in recent years (and I thought so at the time) was the senior George Bush pronouncing at the time of the collapse of the Soviet Union that we were looking at "a generation of peace." What? Seven billion samplings of human nature running around the planet, and you think there could *ever* be such a thing as a generation of peace? (*Maybe he was saying, "Let's start generating peas!" You know, biofuels and all that.*)

Third, the phrase "long defeat" comes from *The Lord of the Rings*, in which the elf queen Galadriel says, "Through the ages of the world we have fought the long defeat." It is spoken elegiacally as the elves understand their time in Middle Earth is coming to an end. These words suggest a number of things to which I am drawn: nobility, honor, courage, perseverance, virtue, realism, tragedy.

But, of course, one must balance this with the "glimpses" and the hope (a stronger word than most realize) of "final victory." Tolkien speaks of the often unexpected turn at the end of fairy stories that we inadequately refer to as a "happy ending" (and which he calls "eucatastrophe"). It arises in stories despite pain and calamity, and he sees in this a foreshadowing of God's ultimate redemption of his creation. Such redemption is true and our great hope, but it doesn't negate the pain and the struggle.

This reminds me of a story—a number of interwoven stories actually.

Karl Bonhoeffer lost his eldest son in World War I. He lost two others—Dietrich and Klaus—in World War II, both for their participation in a plot to kill Hitler. He also lost the husbands of two daughters, plus many friends. Writing soon after hearing of the deaths of Dietrich and Klaus, he described his and his wife's feelings: "We are sad, but also proud."

Such a view can only come from a tragic sense of life. I use the word "tragic" in the high, literary sense that combines nobility with loss and failure, not in the popular sense of "sad." The tragic sense is compatible with a Christian understanding of the human experience—made in God's image for the purpose of shalom, yet broken. One expression of this is Reinhold Niebuhr's well-known "Christian realism," which says that any credible worldview must take into account the twist in human nature (sin and fallenness in Christian terms). The historian Arthur Schlesinger summed up Niebuhr's influence this way: "[His] emphasis on sin startled my generation, brought up on optimistic convictions of human innocence and perfectibility. But nothing had prepared us for Hitler and Stalin, the Holocaust, concentration camps and gulags. Human nature was evidently as capable of depravity as of virtue."

I feel both the emotional and intellectual impact of Dietrich

Bonhoeffer's father's assertion, "We are sad, but also proud." Sad at life's heavy blows, proud about how his sons responded to evil.

At the risk of sounding insufficiently buoyant, I think even the work of Christ and the empty tomb are only "glimpses" of the final victory. They change everything, but even the victory of the cross, while (ontologically) complete, is also still being worked out, often amidst pain and suffering and uncertainty and doubt.

There is, I believe, a kind of permanent longing in faith for that which once was (Eden) and will one day be again (heaven)—but is not now. Or at least is not now in a way that fully satisfies the longing (which, ultimately, is a longing for home). We have not ourselves experienced either Eden or heaven, but we have heard the stories and they call to us. I am willing to admit that this longing and this call may exist only for some kinds of people. Perhaps it is more temperament and personality than anything else. Perhaps it comes from reading too many books.

I hear in my ears the rebuttals to what I am expressing here—everything from Christian happy talk to sober theological pronouncements with phrases like "once and for all." Many will find Tolkien's and Niebuhr's views too Eeyore-ish after all. In some people's lives, the glimpses are much more than that—they are an unending Hallelujah Chorus. (That's the balancing truth.) I love the Hallelujah Chorus, but *The Messiah* also speaks of Jesus as the Man of Sorrows, acquainted with grief. Long defeat, glimpses of victory—we need to feel the weight of both.

JAPANESE FISHERMEN AND THE NARRATIVE OF DECLINE

For he will be like a tree planted by the water,
That extends its roots by a stream
And will not fear when the heat comes;
But its leaves will be green,
And it will not be anxious in a year of drought
Nor cease to yield fruit.

JEREMIAH 17:8

There is a famous early nineteenth-century Japanese woodcut depicting a huge ocean wave towering over small fishing boats, with a dwarfed Mount Fuji in the background (Katsushika Hokusai, *The Great Wave*). Neil MacGregor (in *A History of the World in 100 Objects*) points out that most Westerners see in the image danger and fear. But Japanese art critics, in contrast, see in the image brave and serene fishermen working at one with nature to reap what the provider sea has to offer for the needs of the people, dangers notwithstanding. I would like to apply this to how Christians view the world in which we live.

The prevailing view in my circles (now and perhaps for centuries) has been to see the world as evil, threatening, morally bankrupt, and antagonistic to all that we value most. Christians "fight" against this world, often with a kind of angry fatalism. (*And they wonder why people aren't flocking to them? What a shock!*) I think a lot of Skeptical Believers share this view as well.

I prefer the Japanese view of this woodcut. The sea and the world *is* a dangerous place, but it is also a gift, given as a blessing by a good God, and it has in it all we need to flourish (including God, who inhabits his world). We work *with* the creation, not against it.

There is plenty of biblical imagery to support both views. I would not ignore the imagery of decay and struggle, but I would also not give it precedence over images of blessing and flourishing and shalom. There is more good news than bad even in a fallen world, and we can be serene rather than combative as we explore it.

Why, then, are we so mournful? (*Who are you to talk, going on about tragedy and uncertainty and angst? You're no great drum major yourself.*)

I came of age when academics were officially pronouncing (again) the death of God—as a viable and energizing concept in the modern world— and people in the churches I went to knew that was hogwash. But I have since come to believe that many in those churches actually, in their own way, believed the same thing. They don't believe God is dead, but they want him housebroken. They want him to know his place and to avoid unpleasant surprises. They want him to *act* dead. Or at least be polite.

The Welsh poet R.S. Thomas (*Him again?*) has God say the following in a poem titled "Ann Griffith":

> These people know me
> only in the thin hymns of
> the mind, in the arid sermons
> and prayers. I am the live God...

How much easier to follow a safely dead, dormant, or domesticated God. Most everything that God is going to do, according to this view, has already happened. He has made everything, published the operating instructions, set down the rules, separated (given his foreknowledge) the sheep from the goats, and now, at most, monitors the creation—answering a prayer here and there, counting the days until the buzzer goes off and it's all over. (*Two thousand years and counting. Quite the alarm clock! Do you think maybe he's overslept?*)

A "live God," on the other hand, is quite disconcerting, even frightening. We never know what a live God is going to do. He may even change (at least in our perception)—in ways wildly unpredictable, and yet consistent, in our hindsight, with his nature. (*Maybe even answering to different pronouns?*) It is not possible to be an expert in this kind of God, to sing the "thin hymns of / the mind," nor to rest placidly in our presumed salvation. The Israelites begged Moses to have God not speak to them lest they die. And we are mostly good Israelites ourselves.

When we aren't telling God to mind his own rules (as we understand them), we are complaining to God about how messed up his world is. We don't directly blame God for this, of course, but we do sometimes wonder why he doesn't run a little tighter ship (as in slapping our enemies up the side of the head now and then). And we tell ourselves (historical ignoramuses that we are) that believers have rarely had to live in times as dark as ours.

In the eighteenth century there was an ongoing debate, referred to as "The Ancients-Moderns Controversy," in which one side argued that the present was clearly inferior to the past, especially in terms of art, virtue, wisdom, and the state of civilization in general. The other side trumpeted the superiority of the present and future over the comparatively ignorant past, with rising science as the star witness. That debate is still going on.

My instinct is to favor the "ancients" in this debate, but I am increasingly prone to say, with Mercutio (*Romeo and Juliet*), "a plague on both your houses." It has always been, to the people in them, the best of times and the worst of times (Dickens)—and always will be. (*One more literary allusion, and I'm leaving to watch television.*) That said, I am increasingly tired of the "narrative of decline" among people of faith. We are inundated with moaning about how bad things are in light of how good things supposedly once were.

Once more I invoke R.S. Thomas (*I warned you! Good-bye.*), this time in his poem "Postcript":

> As life improved, their poems
> Grew sadder and sadder.

Thomas does not say in the poem who "their" refers to, but the poem seems a subtle indictment of the emptiness of modern, consumerist society. I would like to use this poem for another purpose. Why, given the hope we Christians claim in God, grace, creation, and love, are we so consistently mournful and pissed off?

I made the case earlier for the tragic element in the Christian vision. I want to balance that here with a call for an end to complaining, whether the whining of moral conservatives and liberal do-gooders (both of whom are obsessed with other people's sin), or the often self-indulgent complaining of the Skeptical Believer (who bemoans his or her own hard epistemological state). The tragic vision does not justify whining; it requires fortitude, a good ancient pagan virtue related to the more Christian notion of perseverance.

God is alive, the ocean is full of fish—so dodge the waves and fish.

8. CONCLUSION: JOY, RISK, ADVENTURE, AND LOVE— JUST THE RIGHT KIND OF STORY

WHAT DO YOU LOVE? FAITH AS RISKY LOVE

[God] cannot ravish. He can only woo.

SCREWTAPE, IN C.S. LEWIS, *THE SCREWTAPE LETTERS*

We can doubt, we must doubt. But we must have something to love, don't you think?

ALEXANDER SOLZHENITSYN, *IN THE FIRST CIRCLE*

The aim of an artist is not to solve a problem irrefutably, but to make people love life in all its countless, inexhaustible manifestations.

TOLSTOY

There is, as every lover knows, a direct link between love and risk. The more we love, the more we are willing to risk. If we love someone, we will sacrifice for that person. We will accept conditions, including painful ones, that we would not accept for someone we do not love. The same is true if we love something rather than someone. People will sacrifice time and money for a political cause or a favorite hobby. Some people have so loved freedom that they have died for it (loving freedom being, actually, another form of loving people—those who want to be free).

I think this unexceptional truth is relevant to questions of faith and doubt. In the case of Christianity, we have both someone and something to love—or not. The more I love God, the more I am willing to accept the risks that such a love entails—including the risk of God's not existing. The more I love the extended life of faith—as worked out over time with other risk takers, primarily within the church—the more I am willing to accept the inevitable foolishnesses and shortcomings of that same church.

When someone loves and defends freedom, they do not love only the abstract idea of freedom. They love the tangible things that freedom brings—the right to say what one thinks, live where one wishes, make choices of all kinds. When one loves God and the Christian story, one loves a long list of quite tangible things—grace and justice at work in lives and communities; life-directing rituals leading from birth through death; fellowship with kindred spirits; a sense of hope, purpose, and meaning; and so on.

So I think it's fair to join the question "What do you believe?" with the question "What do you love?" The greater my love for anything unprovable (which is most significant things), the greater my willingness to risk believing in it. Loving an idea or a story does not make it true or false, but it does affect how much certainty I require before I commit myself to it.

So do I, personally, love God and the Christian story enough to take the chance of being wrong about it? Do I love it enough to continue in it when I am not sure, when I have my doubts? Do I love it enough to stay in it when God seems to have allowed great pain in my life? Do I love it enough to stay in a story that my culture increasingly dislikes?

If by "love" we mean feelings of affection, then I must answer, "Sometimes I love it enough, but not always." The feelings of love in matters of faith come and go, as they do in human relationships. (God feels close, God feels distant, God feels not there at all, God feels close again.) But if one means by "love" valuing and committing to someone or something that is so strong that I organize my life around it, then my answer is "Yes, I love God and the Christian story enough to take all the chances and put up with all the things that such love requires."

Allowing love this role in deciding what we believe and how we are to live strikes me as entirely rational. And it is compatible with what Augustine called "ordinate love"—loving the things one should love, to the degree one should love each thing (and not loving the things one ought not to love), with God, in his role as maker of all things, being the arbiter.

Another word for this is wisdom—rightly valuing things and rightly choosing in light of that valuing.

Linking belief to love is a proper recognition of the role of desire in human calculations. Why do I work hard for anything? Because attaining it is desirable. Why do I sacrifice for anything? Because I judge the goal worthy of the sacrifice. Why would I take risks for anything? Because the desired end justifies the risks needed for achieving it.

The desire for something worth desiring is itself part of the rational argument for acting on that desire. Maybe justice, as I noted earlier, is impossible in this world, but its desirability is so strong that I feel compelled to risk things to bring it into being. Logic does not even require me to succeed. It only requires that the reward justify the risk.

All risk for something desirable takes seriously the possibility of failure. If taking risks always resulted in victory, as in most Hollywood movies, then they would not be risks. That is why faith is not a synonym for certainty. There is no risk in certainty. There is risk in faith. I would argue it is a reasonable risk, though (just between you and me) I hope I would take it even if it weren't.

Including love as a significant component of faith is hard for skeptics because by nature skeptics have difficulty with love. Love entails risks, and skepticism is a methodology designed to limit risk taking. Skeptics fear being suckers. Love can make a sucker out of you.

"Losing one's faith," as the expression goes, is most often a case, then, of falling out of love. When Tolstoy says art aims not to solve a problem but to make people love life, he is saying something relevant to God and the Christian story. That story's aim is not to prove its claims irrefutably but to offer you something and someone to love. You have to decide whether you love it and whether you continue to love it. Many more people abandon faith because they've lost their love for it than because they've been convinced that it's intellectually insupportable.

It's hard to argue against a declaration of lost love. If you are in a formerly loving relationship and someone says, "I don't love you anymore," what is there to say in response? One could reasonably say, "So what? You made a commitment... jerk," but that doesn't fly in our "I have to be happy" culture. In a marriage, one might say, "Stay for the kids."

But what about in a relationship with God? You could stay for the long-term benefits (the promise of heaven), but if you've fallen out of love with the Christian story, you've probably also fallen out of love with the idea of heaven. Just too fairy-taleish and far off and pie-in-the-sky-by-and-by.

When I have found myself falling out of love with faith, I have asked myself some form of the following: Do these promises deserve my love? What is the better story that I will embrace instead? Will I have any fewer doubts about that story than this one? What other story loves me back? And a number of others.

If you have a strained relationship with God or the Christian story or other Christians, my counsel is to stay in the relationship, do the things the story asks you to do, and see if the love comes back (a valuing and commitment kind of love at least, and perhaps affective love eventually). It usually does, if one sticks out the tough parts. Love as commitment can survive for a long time after love as tender feelings has dissipated. It might be enough.

But if it doesn't come back, if faith feels like an albatross around your neck, if you think there's a better story for you out there, then I say move on. I don't think there is a better story for you, especially once you've tasted the real thing, but I wouldn't have anyone pretend to stay in the Christian story who no longer values it. Try the other gods—of which there are many.

But make sure they will love you back.

FAITH AS A RENEWABLE VOW

Every morning you should wake up in your bed and ask yourself: "Can I
believe it all again today?" No, better still, don't ask it till after you've read *The
New York Times*...

FREDERICK BUECHNER

In this, my seventh decade, faith seems to me not certainty but commitment,
a renewable vow.

DORIS BETTS

People—whole cultures—used to take promises seriously. Certainly the
biblical cultures did. Promise, in fact, isn't a strong enough word anymore
to convey how binding and solemn the sense of commitment was when one
voluntarily entered into a covenant. You were offering your honor, your
place in the community, your sense of yourself, and, often literally, your
life as the guarantee that you would perform as you pledged to perform.

My favorite visual confirmation of this seriousness is the strikingly
odd, even macabre, Old Testament ritual (see Genesis 15; Jeremiah 34)
in which vow makers are required to walk between the divided parts of a
slaughtered animal as a guarantee of their oath. The idea was, "May what

has happened to this animal happen to me if I do not keep my vow." That would make you think twice about breaking a promise.

Contrast this with our attitude toward promises today. A promise for us is often just an expression of an intention, an inclination toward something—if it "works out," which is to say remains convenient or continues to fit in with what seems good for me. This dilution of the idea of promise shows itself from lawn mowing to marriage. "I promise" really means, "I'm so inclined at this moment, but, in truth, we'll have to see." We've changed our marriage vows and doctors' oaths to reflect this lower standard.

The same modern sensibility often applies to faith as well. "Yes, I believe in God—or am inclined to believe in God. Yes, I am a Christian, the form of belief in God I am most familiar with. Yes, I acknowledge that I have some responsibilities, but I think trying to be a good person satisfies most of them. Yes, I should take this more seriously. I intend to... at some point... maybe. But, you know, there are some things about this faith and church business that I have a hard time with. Like, for instance... "

Really? You are having "a hard time" with some things? So until those things are answered to your satisfaction, you are going to hang out on the edges—maybe in, maybe out, maybe both in and out at the same time? Poor kid. Lots of doubts, lots of questions, perhaps been dissed by a church lady or offended by a TV evangelist or had your faith shaken by a book you read? So God will just have to wait until you "heal," as therapy-speak has it.

Don't let this sarcastic tone hurt your feelings. I'm talking to myself. As I said before, I have often operated in life as though my believing in God was doing God a favor. Like I'm keeping him on the edge of his heavenly throne, wondering to himself whether he exists or not. The traditional view has been that the Good News of reconciliation with the Creator is an unfathomable gift. To me. Not just good news, the best news. I was the beneficiary of God's gift, not God the beneficiary of my belief. But I find myself, as mentioned earlier, looking this gift horse in the mouth, checking to see if all its teeth are in place. "Yes, I'm a believer," I say. But do I really mean, "As long as it's not too hard and God performs up to my expectations"?

All this is why I find intriguing Doris Betts's understanding of her faith as "a renewable vow." On the face of it, that phrase seems a contradiction. A vow should be unbreakable. It should last until the point of fulfillment— meaning, with vows of faith, throughout eternity. That seems at odds with the word "renewable." Faith is not a magazine subscription, something you take into your life for a while, then either renew or let lapse as you like.

Or is it? Betts and Buechner are on to something. Buechner counsels us to ask each day whether we are still committed to this story. Ask after reading the morning newspaper, with all its own stories—of woe and evil and selfishness and petty bickering. Stories of things gone wrong, of shalom in decay. In other words, ask the question fully aware of the conditions. Make it a real question, with the sense that something is at stake (because everything, in truth, *is* at stake), not the fake inquiry of the smug (believer or unbeliever).

More than half the time, Buechner suggests, an honest answer to "Can I believe it all again today?" should be "no." (Writerly hyperbole?) He goes further: "If your answer's always Yes, then you probably don't know what believing means." The Good News in a bad news world will sometimes just seem unbelievable. Just too much a stretch. Just wishful thinking. When it feels that way to you, be glad that a fellow believer is finding it entirely believable and true today. When that person's faith gets battered a bit tomorrow, it will be your turn to believe for him or her. This is what we do for each other.

So I think Doris Betts is right. It is a vow—so solemn and central that we should walk between the parts of a slaughtered bull (or consume the body and blood of Christ) when making it. We are in this come hell or high water. This is our story. This is our promise. This is our hope.

But it is, strangely enough, a renewable vow. We are given the option to accept or reject it each day. And the acceptance or rejection will not be shown in our minds, or perhaps even in our hearts, but in our actions. Do we do the things today that people do who have promised themselves to this story?

To see the vow as renewable is, I think, a sign of both realism and respect. Realism because human nature and the human condition work constantly against promise keeping. And respect because renewing a vow is a declaration that this matter is still of ultimate importance, still something I keep at the center, still the story that tells me who I am and why I exist. Get up each morning. Read the paper. Renew the vow.

WHAT KIND OF STORY IS THIS?

It takes a story to make a story.

FLANNERY O'CONNOR

This tale grew in the telling, until it became a history...

J.R.R. TOLKIEN, *THE LORD OF THE RINGS*

If I am going to commit myself to a story, and to playing my part as a character in it, I want to know what kind of story it is. When I am living within the Christian story, what kind of story am I in? Knowing the kind of story can help me better know my lines.

I am in a story which participates in most all the different kinds of stories human beings tell and at the same time transcends all categories. My story is an epic story, for epics tell the foundational tales and explain origins (think Homer and Milton). Epics people their story with great characters (Achilles, Odysseus, King Arthur, Abraham, Moses, Satan, Christ) operating on a grand scale, with everything hanging in the balance (life and death, time and eternity, the fate of humanity).

My story is also a quest story. Something lost or distant must be found (reunion with God), and perils must be overcome (sin and Satan) in order to reach a priceless goal (shalom). The quest takes place with companions (the church, fellow believers, kindred spirits), some of whom are lost (in this life) along the way.

My story is that special kind of quest story called a pilgrimage. Pilgrimage, I have claimed, is physical travel for a spiritual purpose. The act of traveling is as much a part of the pilgrimage as the moment of arrival. In our pilgrimage of faith we are both always traveling and always arriving. Each arrival—at some place of insight or communion with God—signals the need for more traveling. We are both at rest and striving, secure and at risk, satisfied and restless.

My story is a mystery story. Faith is not a puzzle to be solved, but rather a mystery to be plumbed and lived. In a mystery story we have enough information to fully engage us, but not so much as to fully satisfy us. We want very much to know more, and we spend whatever time the story takes to uncover that information. In a fictional mystery story, that information comes after a few hundred pages, in a mystery film after a couple of hours. In the story of faith, it comes only through and after a lifetime. We see now as in a glass darkly (the mystery), but then face-to-face (the denouement). We often wish it were not so. We want the complete answers now. Not getting them, we even wonder whether there *are* any answers. But this mystery story, the ultimate mystery, tells us what we need to know only when we need to know it, revealing all only when all is fulfilled.

My story is a love story. A love story above all. It is the story of God's love for his creation. This is, as I suggested earlier, the master plot of all things—God made us, God loves us, God calls us. One could rightfully substitute the words "the cosmos" for "us" in that declaration, but love stories are intimate stories, and so I will say not only "us" but "me." God made, loves, and calls *me*.

I like that the story of faith in which I am a character is a great story composed of many small stories. I like that it is told by people from a wide range of cultures and times and understandings. I like that it includes the fifteen hundred years of stories in the Bible, but also includes two thousand years of stories since, and countless stories from throughout time and eternity known only to God. Such a vast range of smaller stories makes the master story all the more believable to me. God inhabits his creation and his creatures—from before time to after, throughout the world and the cosmos—and wherever he appears, he is telling a story.

If I am to live fully in such a story, I must be willing to let go of some things—the desire for certainty, universal approval, superficial safety and security, perhaps life itself—in exchange for other things—meaning, significance, adventure, hope, grace. Fundamental questions arise: What are the qualities of a story for which I am willing to give everything? What am I willing to give up? What am I willing to risk? Are there enough problems with this story that I must exchange it for another, lesser one?

Although I have sometimes spoken disrespectfully of propositions in this book, I will offer one here at its end. *You should not commit yourself to any story for your life that is not itself worth the spending of the only life you have.* You are spending your life on some story, whether you have identified it or not. You only get one life. Is the story you are spending it on worth the value of your only life? If not, change your story.

I believe the only kind of story worth spending a life on is a love story. I will admit that the reality of God personally and individually calling me by name is not altogether comforting to me. I would actually rather be one among many in the "us" than think of God as looking directly at me—and extending his hand. I am, Lord, a Skeptical Believer. I have had to work hard just to get beyond lukewarm and thereby avoid getting spewed. I prefer, if you don't mind, being in the back rows, watching gratefully from afar.

But this is a love story, and God will have none of that. As the Christ, God came among us. He emptied himself, became Emmanuel—one of us. Not after we had cleaned ourselves up for a royal visit, but while we were still playing in the muck. He lived with us, healed us, forgave us, came into our homes, ate our food, wept when we wept and laughed when we laughed. Then he died for us and rose again—to make things right.

See—there I go again with the plural pronouns—us, we. I want this to be a "God loves *us*" story, and it is. But it is, even more important, a "God loves *me*" story. And so I must put my own name in there—God loves Dan—or it isn't really a love story. When Shakespeare wrote a love story, it wasn't the Montagues love the Capulets (they didn't), it was Romeo loves Juliet. And so it is with the greatest love story of all. It isn't, ultimately, God loves humanity. It is God loves Dan. God made Dan. God died for Dan. God defeated death for Dan. God desires to be known by Dan.

That I use this kind of intimate language to describe a relationship with God reveals the version of the story of faith I know best. I was raised in it. It put its stamp on me. I am not always at ease with it myself, but it is the way I know to tell the story. And therefore it is the way I tell the story to you. For all good stories are particular, rooted in a specific time and place and way of seeing and speaking, even if they also partake of eternity.

So this is how I understand the story—it is, among many other things, an epic story, a quest, a pilgrimage, a mystery. But most of all it is a love story, one in which God calls me by name. Your story will, of necessity, be uniquely your own. But I hope you still hear someone calling your name too.

ALSO BY DANIEL TAYLOR

The Myth of Certainty
    The Reflective Christian and the Risk of Commitment

Letters to My Children
    A Father Passes On His Values

Tell Me a Story
    The Life-Shaping Power of Our Stories

Before Their Time
    Lessons in Living from Those Born Too Soon

Is God Intolerant?
    Christian Thinking about the Call for Tolerance

In Search of Sacred Places
    Looking for Wisdom on Celtic Holy Islands

Creating a Spiritual Legacy
    How to Share Your Stories, Values, and Wisdom

The Expanded Bible
    (with Tremper Longman and Mark Strauss)

Daniel Taylor can be found online at www.WordTaylor.com

9 780970 651150